12/95

D0097654

An Introduction to

Existentialism

by Robert G. Olson

Dover Publications, Inc.
New York

Published in Canada by General Publishing Company, Ltd., 30 Lesmill Road, Don Mills, Toronto, Ontario.
Published in the United Kingdom by Constable and Company, Ltd.

An Introduction to Existentialism is a new work, first published in 1962 by Dover Publications, Inc.

Standard Book Number: 486-20055-8
Library of Congress Catalog Card Number: 62-5794

Manufactured in the United States of America
Dover Publications, Inc.
180 Varick Street
New York, N.Y. 10014

DEDICATED TO

Anne-Elizabeth Leroy

Preface

The purpose of this book is to state the existentialist position, to sketch the arguments by which the existentialists support their stand, to locate the movement within the history of philosophy, and to indicate the critical reaction of other contemporary philosophical movements.

The reader who already has some competence in general philosophy and some acquaintance with existentialist literature will find that the book reads easily, provided that he starts with Chapter I and takes each chapter in order. The reader who knows nothing about general philosophy or existentialism will find that some passages, especially in Chapter III, require close reading; and it is doubly important that he read each chapter consecutively.

Existentialism is the most exciting movement in contemporary philosophy, and almost everybody has at one time or another reflected on the major existentialist themes. As philosophers, however, the existentialists do not merely take a position; they argue for it. Moreover, to avoid misleading connotations of words in ordinary discourse, they normally use a technical vocabulary. An introduction to existentialism cannot, therefore, serve its purpose without reproducing the arguments and introducing the terminology actually employed by members of the movement. Technical terminology is introduced gradually, and each technical term introduced is carefully defined in nontechnical language. At the same time arguments are stripped of all inessentials and presented in two or three different versions wherever necessary to insure understanding. None the less, this book is not recommended to the person who has an insuperable aversion to argument and to the drawing of distinctions. A book on existentialism which merely entertains with amusing anecdotes, titillates with rhetorical paradoxes, or evokes a mood of despair with dramatic metaphor and poetic imagery could no doubt be written. But it would not be an introduction to existentialism, and it would not even catch the true flavor of the movement. The existentialists *are* often obscure, and they *do* frequently have recourse to the tricks of the poet's trade. Contrary to popular belief, however, they are primarily thinkers, and they do not think with the belly or the heart; the three great existentialist classics—Kierkegaard's *Concluding Unscientific Postscript*, Heidegger's *Being and Time*, and Sartre's *Being and Nothingness*— are eloquent testimony to the fact.

The major existentialists are Søren Kierkegaard (Danish, 1813–1855), Friedrich Nietzsche (German, 1844–1900), Martin Heidegger (German, 1899–   ), and Jean-Paul Sartre (French, 1905–   ). Heidegger's major works are still untranslated into English; and of the other three major thinkers Sartre is the clearest and most systematic. Consequently, detailed illustrations of existentialist themes are more often drawn from the works of Sartre than would be justified simply on the basis of his relative importance within the movement.

Of the four major figures Kierkegaard was a Christian of Protestant persuasion; the others are all classified as atheists. Among secondary figures religious existentialists predominate. Miguel de Unamuno (Spanish, 1864–1936) and Gabriel Marcel (French, 1889–   ) are Roman Catholic. Léon Shestov (Russian, 1868–1938) and Nicholas Berdyaev (Russian, 1874–1948) are Eastern or Orthodox Catholic. Judaism is represented by Martin Buber (1878–   ), who was born in Germany and later moved to Israel. Atheistic existentialists of secondary importance are Simone de Beauvoir (French, 1911–   ), Albert Camus (French, 1913–1960), and Maurice Merleau-Ponty (French, 1908–1961). Camus, however, moved away from existentialism in the years immediately preceding his death; and Merleau-Ponty, who was never an altogether typical representative of the movement, drifted away even earlier. Karl Jaspers (German, 1883–   ), whom a large number of persons would rank as a major existentialist thinker, is difficult to classify; he has no formal religious affiliations, but it would be somewhat misleading to call him an atheist. Dostoyevsky, of course, is not a philosopher; but his thinking was so close to that of the existentialists and he has stated so many of their themes so well in his own fashion that his name ought not to go unmentioned. His religion was that of his compatriots and fellow existentialists Berdyaev and Shestov.

Edmund Husserl (German, 1859–1938), founder of the movement known as phenomenology, also deserves mention here. Although not himself an existentialist, Husserl was for a long time mentor to Heidegger, and both Sartre and Merleau-Ponty have professed to be in his debt, especially as regards matters of method. In view of the fact that Husserl is susceptible to diverse interpretations, however, it is not possible to assess with confidence either the precise nature or the extent of his influence upon existentialism. Suffice it to say that the so-called phenomenological method, a term which has been studiously avoided in the present work, is nonscientific and intuitionist. Whether the phenomenological method as practiced by the existentialists is the same as that practiced by Husserl is a matter of more importance to the historian of philosophy than to the student of existentialism.

Most of the existentialists have had interesting lives, and each of them has a distinctive personal philosophy worthy of detailed and separate study. The present book, however, is a topical analysis of major existentialist themes, focusing upon elements common to all or most of the members within the movement. For biographical information about the existentialists and for a systematic treatment of their individual philosophies it will be necessary to look elsewhere.

ROBERT G. OLSON

New York, New York
January, 1961

Acknowledgments

I should like to thank my former colleague Robert D. Cumming, chairman of the department of philosophy at Columbia University, and my friend Lionel Abel, the playwright, for having read an earlier manuscript of the present study. I consider myself most fortunate to have had the benefit of their extensive and detailed knowledge of existentialist literature while preparing the final draft. I should also like to thank the editors of *Philosophy*, *Ethics*, and the *Antioch Review* for permission to use material from articles originally published in those journals. Finally, thanks are due to the publishers of the following works for allowing me to quote from the listed sources:

Bernanos, Georges. *Présence de Bernanos.* Paris: Librairie Plon, 1947.

Dostoyevsky, Fyodor. *White Nights and Other Stories.* London: The Macmillan Company, 1925.

Faulkner, William. *Light in August.* New York: Random House, Inc., 1950.

Freud, Sigmund. *The Standard Edition of the Complete Psychological Works of Sigmund Freud.* Vol. XIV. London: Hogarth Press, Ltd., 1957.

Jaspers, Karl. *Man in the Modern Age.* Revised translation by Eden and Cedar Paul. London: Routledge & Kegan Paul, Ltd., 1951.

Kaufmann, Walter, ed. *Existentialism from Dostoyevsky to Sartre.* New York: Meridian Books, Inc., 1956.

Kierkegaard, Søren. *Concluding Unscientific Postscript.* Translated by David Swenson. Princeton: Princeton University Press, 1944.

────── *Journals.* Translated by Alexander Dru. London: Oxford University Press, 1938.

────── *The Sickness unto Death.* Translated by Walter Lowrie. Princeton: Princeton University Press, 1941.

Sartre, Jean-Paul. *Being and Nothingness.* Translated by Hazel E. Barnes. New York: Philosophical Library, 1956.

────── *Critique de la raison dialectique.* Paris: Librairie Gallimard, 1960.

────── *The Reprieve.* Translated by Eric Sutton. New York: Alfred A. Knopf, Inc., 1947.

────── *Saint Genet.* Paris: Librairie Gallimard, 1952.

Tolstoy, Leo. *Iván Ilých and Hadji Murád and Other Stories*. Translated by Aylmer Maude. London: Oxford University Press, 1957.

Vivas, Eliseo. *The Moral Life and the Ethical Life*. Chicago: University of Chicago Press, 1950.

Whitehead, Alfred North. *Science and the Modern World*. New York: The Macmillan Company, 1925.

Wittgenstein, Ludwig. *Tractatus Logico-Philosophicus*. London: Routledge & Kegan Paul, Ltd., 1922.

For all quotations from Sartre's *Being and Nothingness* the reader is referred to the English translation by Hazel E. Barnes (New York: Philosophical Library, 1956). Many of these quotations, however, have been translated directly from the French by the present writer, who assumes full responsibility for any errors or inadequacies.

Contents

An Introduction to

Existentialism

I. Value Orientation

The Ordinary Man's Values

In the fourth century before Christ, Aristotle declared that the ordinary man regarded the good life as a life of physical pleasure, wealth, or honor. In the seventeenth century Spinoza re-affirmed the validity of the Aristotelian formula for his own time, substituting only the word "fame" for the word "honor." Nor is there any dearth of contemporary philosophers who would be willing to accept Spinoza's generalization as valid for the twentieth century, provided only that a term such as "social approval" be substituted for the word "fame."

Although the adequacy of such classifications of the ordinary man's goals might be debated, there can be no question that philosophers who have seen fit to express themselves on this issue have almost unanimously endorsed such classifications. At the same time they have almost unanimously denounced the ordinary man's pursuits in favor of some mode of life by which the frustrations and disillusionment which they believe inevitably to accompany these pursuits may be mitigated or overcome.

The existentialists are no exception to the general rule. In this respect they fall into a tradition almost as old as philosophy itself, and it is as the chief modern-day heirs of this tradition that they may be best understood. Their originality consists primarily in their sensitivity to certain human values which not only the ordinary man but also the classical philosophical and religious tradition tended to overlook.

The reader who has dipped only casually into existentialist literature or who knows the existentialists only at second hand may be surprised to hear the existentialists represented as advocates of a class of human values. Are they not rather nihilists? He may also be surprised to hear that the existentialists are

1

seeking to mitigate or overcome frustration and disillusionment. Is it not rather their belief that frustration and disillusionment are integral features of the human condition?

The subtlety of the existentialist position makes it difficult to cope adequately with these questions at this point. It should, however, be borne in mind that mankind has clung so long and so tenaciously to the ordinary man's values that the negative side of any doctrine which denounces these values in favor of others will almost inevitably strike the uninitiated more forcefully than its positive side. Christ, for instance, was no nihilist; but the publican urged to abandon the flesh, the rich man asked to renounce his wealth, and the ostentatiously pious man enjoined to pray in privacy no doubt tended to think he was.

Moreover, from the fact that one denounces the ordinary ambitions of mankind as vain and preaches another way of life it does not necessarily follow that one will regard the abandonment of ordinary ambitions as a matter of little moment. Kierkegaard refused a parsonage which would have brought him a steady income, abandoned his fiancée together with the hope of a comfortable family life, and deliberately used his talent to bring ridicule upon himself—all in the conviction that comfort, money, and public approval are inferior values. Nowhere, however, did he suggest that such sacrifices come easily. On the contrary, he would certainly agree with Spinoza, who said: "If salvation lay ready to hand and could be discovered without great labor, how is it possible that it should be neglected by almost everybody? All noble things are as difficult as they are rare."

The point here is that salvation, however dearly purchased, is still salvation. The tragic sense of life which gives impetus to movements of salvation is far from being nihilistic. If the existentialists' pronouncements on the bitterness of the human condition are to be regarded as evidence of nihilism, then logic requires that the same charge be leveled at Aeschylus and Shakespeare. Like the great tragic authors of the Western world, the existentialists have mastered the technique of reaffirming the value of life while boldly depicting its horrors. Two of the most popular pieces of existentialist literature are *The Philosophy of Tragedy* by Léon Shestov and *The Tragic Sense of Life* by Unamuno; but there are few works by existentialist authors which could not appropriately have borne these titles.

There is still a third consideration which may profitably be urged at this point to help dispel the popular prejudice according to which existentialism is a nihilistic philosophy of despair. The focal aims of the ordinary man of today may be the same as those of the ordinary man in Aristotle's day—but they are not his only aims. Though inconsistently and imperfectly, the ordinary man of today has imbibed the values of the Western philosophical and religious tradition. These values figure less prominently in the actual conduct of his life than wealth, pleasure, and prestige; but he clings to them hardly less tenaciously. When, therefore, the existentialist proclaims that the messages of salvation and consolation sanctioned by tradition are no less vain than the hope of fulfillment through wordly pursuits, the ordinary man is doubly offended. Not only his first, but his second, line of defense has been breached. He is in despair. With a logic which is wholly indefensible, though understandable enough, he cries: I am in despair, you have reduced me to despair, therefore you are in despair. But no! the existentialist answers. You were in despair in the first place. It is for that reason you have heard and understood me when I stripped you of your illusions. All that I have done is to make you fully conscious of your despair, and now if you will listen further I will help you master your despair.

If, of course, the existentialists' uncompromising rejection of the so-called worldly values and of traditional messages of salvation is unwarranted or if their own message of salvation rests upon illusions peculiar to themselves, then the movement may properly be regarded as nihilistic in effect. But the movement is not nihilistic in intent.

Values in Traditional Philosophy

In view of the richness and variety of the Western heritage, traditional philosophers' criticisms of the ordinary man's way of life are remarkably uniform, and the basic strategies by which they hoped to free themselves from the evils they believe to characterize that way of life, surprisingly few.

A life dedicated to the pursuit of pleasure, wealth, and fame has been condemned on three grounds. First, the attainment of such goals depends only in small part upon the efforts of the individual himself. External circumstances almost too numerous to catalogue and almost wholly beyond the individual's control may thwart him at any moment. Second, no matter how successful the individual has been, he cannot be secure in his possessions. The caprice of a king, the cunning of an enemy, a natural catastrophe such as flood or earthquake may cause him to lose everything in a single day. Third, even if the individual attained and secured the goals he originally set for himself, the satisfaction he experienced would be short-lived and he would soon revert to a life of painful striving. There is no natural limit to the amount of wealth, fame, or pleasure which a man may covet, and the brief satisfaction he experiences upon the attainment of some degree of these goods only whets his appetite for more. The desire for these worldly or material goods is like an itch. There is a momentary satisfaction when the desire is apparently fulfilled, as there is when one scratches an itch. But it would be better to be without the desire altogether, as it would be better to be without the itch. A life dedicated to the pursuit of pleasure, wealth, or fame is thus by its nature a life of frustration, insecurity, and painful striving—illuminated perhaps by moments of brief satisfaction but without lasting value.

Of the various techniques philosophers have recommended to emancipate oneself from the ordinary man's round of desire, the simplest and most radical is that of the Stoics. Since the common source of frustration, insecurity, and painful striving is desire, one need only root it out. Suppress one's desires and accept willingly whatever the external circumstances of one's life may be. "Seek not," says the Stoic slave philosopher Epictetus, "that the things which happen should happen as you wish; but wish the things which happen to be as they are, and you will have a tranquil flow of life." We cannot command goods such as wealth, pleasure, or fame; these depend upon accident or good fortune rather than voluntary individual effort. But we can command our hopes and fears, our desires and aversions, since these have their source within us.

The signs of resignation and world-weariness in the Stoic counsel are evident, and the great popularity of Stoicism during the Hellenistic period must be attributed in large part to the political disorders and economic uncertainties of that era in ancient history. It would be a mistake, however, to dismiss Stoicism as nothing more than a philosophy of resignation. There was nothing flabby or self-indulgent in the Stoics' renunciation of worldly ambitions, as the common phrase "stoic heroism" rightly indicates. If the Stoics were pessimistic in their estimate of what man could achieve in the world, they were by no means pessimistic about what man could achieve within himself. Their goal was not merely quiescence or absence of desire, but also a sense of individual dignity to be achieved by rigorous self-discipline. Indifference or apathy with respect to the natural and social environment is only one side of their doctrine. The other side is the energetic pursuit of independence through a proud exercise of the human will; and it is this latter half of the doctrine which sets Stoicism apart from the more radical philosophies of resignation which until recent times prevailed in the Orient.

The second basic type of philosophy by which men have hoped to overcome the ills of ordinary life is in one sense directly opposed to that of the Stoics. For want of a more generic title, it will be referred to as the philosophy of the Enlightenment. This philosophy, like that of the Stoics, reflects the social conditions of the era in which it thrived and is utterly unthinkable in a society unacquainted with a well-advanced technology. Let it be granted, say thinkers of this school, that the individual cannot by his own efforts hope to attain and enjoy in security the goods of this world. It does not necessarily follow that the individual must adjust to this fact as an ultimate necessity. To be sure, an unfavorable physical environment may impede the achievement of the human desire for worldly goods, but by a *concerted* and *rational* effort men may and should reshape their physical environment so as to promote rather than impede the achievement of these desires. To be sure, political, economic, and social institutions may stand as obstacles in the way of individual fulfillment, but again concerted and rational efforts may and should be undertaken to devise institutions which will promote individual fulfillment. The part of wisdom is to act upon and to modify the world rather than to act upon and modify original human desires.

The Enlightenment outlook may seem very close to that of the ordinary man. In fact, however, the two outlooks are poles apart. More often than not the ordinary man's political sentiments are avowedly conservative. And even in those cases where he formally favors political or social reform, his primary concern is happiness for himself during his lifetime and his field of action a narrow one. He takes his physical and social environment more or less for granted as a stable framework within which he seeks personal well-being. The Enlightenment philosophers, on the contrary, took it more or less for granted that individual well-being within the existing physical and social environment is impossible; and even the most optimistic of them were aware that the creation of a favorable environment would require the co-operative endeavors of many men over many generations.

Although, therefore, Enlightenment philosophers sanction the goal of worldly happiness and to this extent belong in the camp of the ordinary man, they are in reality much closer to the Stoics. For them it is mankind, not the existing individual, who can achieve worldly happiness. The existing individual lives in a world which must inevitably thwart his primary desires, and he must adjust to this fact, as did the Stoics, by a change of mind and heart. That change of mind and heart will produce a zeal for social reform and lead him to act upon the world, but it will not lead to the fulfillment of his personal desire for worldly goods. The happiness available to the existing individual is that of the generous idealist who can identify in imagination with the whole of mankind, thus vicariously enjoying the happiness of future generations. As these implications of the Enlightenment attitude became more evident, especially with the failure of the French Revolution, the movement itself was gradually transformed into a humanism, of which Auguste Comte's religious cult of humanity in the nineteenth century was an extreme expression.

The third basic method by which philosophers have hoped to escape the frustration, insecurity, and painful striving which they believe to be part and parcel of the ordinary man's life is by far the most common. The values of the ordinary man, it will be recalled, were rejected on the grounds that they are ephemeral and impossible of achievement without external aid.   Why not, then, seek out an object of allegiance which is not ephemeral and to which man may relate with a minimum of outside help? In this case it is not a question, as with the Stoics, of suppressing all desire, nor, as with the philosophers of the Enlightenment, of creating an environment which permits the realization of worldly desires.   The aim is rather to redirect desire toward some eternal object, it alone being considered worthy of deep human concern.

The first of the great philosophers to take this path were Socrates and Plato, but their fellow travelers include almost all the major figures in philosophy up to and including Hegel. They are, in fact, so numerous and their quarrels among themselves occupy so important a place in the history of philosophy that it is only from the vantage point of the present day that the essential similarity begins to come into view, and even from the vantage point of the present day their differences remain as important as their points in common.

In the *Symposium*, one of Plato's most remarkable dialogues, a group of Athenians have gathered together in order to celebrate a dramatic success of the host.   At a certain point in the celebration the entertainers are sent away, and it is proposed that each of the guests, Socrates among them, make a speech in praise of love.   The last of the speeches is by the wealthy, pleasure-loving, and popular Alcibiades.   Unwilling to compete with Socrates on the theme of love, he decides instead to deliver a eulogy of Socrates.   Ironically, he praises Socrates for his total indifference to pleasure, wealth, and honor, illustrating his theme with numerous examples from the life of the subject.   The chief interest of the dialogue, however, is the speech of Socrates, in which indifference to the ordinary man's values is explained and justified.

Socrates begins his speech by remarking that those who spoke before him were too extravagant in their praise of love.   Love, he says, is a symbol of want or need, not of completion or fulfillment.   To love is to desire, and to desire is to seek; but nobody seeks that which he already possesses.   We seek only that which we lack.   The lover may, of course, enter into possession of the body of the beloved, but even then he is inflamed by the desire to perpetuate his good fortune and continues to seek a future happiness, which as future is beyond his grasp.

Moreover, so long as the object of the lover is the beauty of another's body, the lover is doomed to disappointment; for the beauty of the body soon fades. Even if the object of the lover is the beauty of another's soul, he still faces inevitable disappointment. A beautiful soul may survive the decay of the body; but it, too, in its own way is a fragile and finite object. The lover can be secure only if the object of his search is the pure, simple, and eternal Idea of beauty itself—a transcendent object of which finite things are but perishable and imperfect copies.

A fuller understanding of these remarks on love is possible only within the framework of Platonic metaphysics. For Plato all things may be placed within one of two categories. On the one hand, there are things such as the Idea of beauty itself which are immutable, self-sufficient, and eternal. On the other hand, there are things such as the human body which exist in time and which are not sufficient unto themselves. The former alone belong to the realm of Being in the true sense of the word "Being." The latter belong to the domain of Becoming. They come into existence and pass out of existence; and so long as they are in existence, they are subject to change through the impact of other objects. Although for Plato the principal items in the realm of Being are Ideas, the gods also people this realm. For this reason Socrates in his speech on love chastises the other speakers for referring to love as a god. It is ridiculous, says Socrates, that the gods should love; for to love is to lack, and a god lacks nothing.

Generalizations about Christian philosophy are always precarious, since Christianity has come to mean many different things to different people. It would none the less be substantially correct to regard Christian philosophy as a form of Platonism. Although the dualism of creator and creature replaces the dualism of Being and Becoming, the creator retains all the properties of Platonic Ideas (immutability, self-sufficiency, and eternity), while his creatures are invested with all the properties of objects in Plato's world of Becoming (mutability, dependency, and finitude). And, as in Plato, salvation from the ills to which all flesh is heir can come only through a relationship to a reality which transcends the world.

It is true that in the philosophy of St. Thomas Aquinas, which has become the official philosophy of the Roman Catholic

Church, the dualism is less stark than in Plato and the legitimacy of worldly interests partially restored. Similar remarks apply to Aristotle, Plato's greatest disciple and St. Thomas's principal source of philosophic inspiration. But for both St. Thomas and Aristotle wealth, honor, and pleasure are relatively insignificant values, and both of them regarded self-sufficiency, immutability, and eternity as the marks by which an object most genuinely worthy of human concern must be identified.

Aristotle insistently and expressly declared that the best of all possible types of life is the contemplative life, and for precisely the same reasons as Plato. The man who finds his happiness in contemplation is of all men the least dependent upon external circumstances, and he alone has access to the eternal. The fact that the proper objects of contemplation for Plato are transcendent Ideas of which individual things are but imperfect copies whereas for Aristotle the objects of contemplation are essences whose proper locus is in the world must not be allowed to obscure the like-mindedness of the two philosophers with regard to the proper conduct of life. In locating Plato's Ideas in the world and rebaptizing them "essences," Aristotle took every precaution to preserve their eternity and immutability. Individual things as individuals are hopelessly implicated in the flux of the world or the domain of Becoming, and consequently cannot be known. But the essences of individuals, i.e., the properties which they share with other members of their species, are immutable and eternal, and they alone are intelligible objects of contemplation. The individual dies, but the species is fixed and lives on forever.

For St. Thomas the chief human good is rest in God. God alone is self-sufficient. He alone is the cause of himself: in scholastic terminology, God is the *ens causa sui.* Man, as a dependent creature who owes his very existence to God, can find fulfillment only by relating himself to the source of his being. Pleasure, wealth, and honor may come to us in the course of our lives as by-products of a life devoted to the worship of God, and if so, we may be grateful to God for the satisfaction they bring. But these satisfactions rank low in the hierarchy of human values, and they ought in no case to be the object of voluntary search. If taken as objects of deliberate pursuit, they distract us from our true vocation.

For the student of existentialism the most significant forms

this third basic method for overcoming the evils of the ordinary
man's life have taken are those of Spinoza and Hegel, since it is
most often with respect to these later thinkers that the existentialists define their own position. Having convinced himself
that all the evils which accompany the life of the man who lives
for pleasure, wealth, and fame derive from the fact that the
objects of his pursuits are finite, Spinoza tells us that he sought
for a remedy like "a sick man struggling with a deadly disease,
when he sees that death will surely be upon him unless a remedy
be found." Since, however, Spinoza believed neither in God
as the Jews and Christians conceived him nor in Platonic Ideas,
the remedies ready at hand were rejected as quackery.

One object and only one object, Spinoza declared, could be
truly immutable and eternal. One object and only one was
unquestionably the cause of itself. To that object Spinoza
gave the names "Nature" and "God," words which remain in
his system strictly synonymous. But whichever term is used,
the object designated is perfectly clear, viz., the totality of all
that exists. Since by definition there is nothing outside the
totality of what exists, there is nothing but itself from which it
can draw its being. Inevitably it is an *ens causa sui*. Since
there is nothing outside the totality of what is, there is nothing
which can act upon it or induce it to change. By rigorous
logical necessity, it is immutable. Finally, there being nothing
outside the totality of what is which could be its cause, it must
either have existed eternally or not exist at all. Since, however,
it obviously does exist, it must have existed eternally.

From the fact that God or Nature, i.e., the totality of what is,
has the characteristic of immutability, it follows that whatever
happens happens according to strict necessity. Events which
appear to be the product of accident are in fact rigidly determined. The wise man will, therefore, accept the counsel of the
Stoics and, rather than seek that the things which happen should
happen as he wishes, will instead wish the things which happen
to be as they are.

Fear, envy, regret, anger—all the disturbances of the mind—
have their source in the desire that things be other than they
are no less than in the finitude of their object. But once man
recognizes that things cannot be other than they are, disturbing
passions will no longer agitate him. We do not, says Spinoza,
regret that we are born as infants rather than as adults, because

we firmly believe that it could not be otherwise. If, however, most men were born as adults and only a few as infants, then the latter would no longer believe in the inevitability of their fate and would regret being subjected to the painful process of growing up. But all things are equally inevitable. If therefore you are angry and indignant because someone has robbed you, try to remember that this theft is a part of the divine or natural scheme of things and try to understand the infinite chain of causes which has made it happen. In doing so, your anger and your indignation will disappear. You, the theft, and the robber are all necessary parts of God or Nature.

The secret of happiness consists in enlarging our perspective, in viewing all things from the standpoint of God or Nature. In the terminology of Spinoza, all things should be seen *sub specie aeternitatis*, under the aspect of eternity. The mind of man is ultimately one with God or Nature. It can therefore rise to the level of God or Nature and intimately participate in its eternity. By so doing it emancipates itself from attachment to finite objects and from the passions which such attachment entails.

Spinoza and Hegel are separated in time by almost the whole of the eighteenth century, which was marked by the beginning of the Industrial Revolution, the rise of the Enlightenment, and a growing preoccupation with the idea of historical progress. Darwin's theory of evolution had yet to be propounded, but the idea of historical progress had already inspired a number of thinkers to espouse the idea of a cosmic or natural evolutionary process. These eighteenth-century developments provide the clue to the differences between the two philosophers. For Hegel, as for Spinoza, the aim of the philosopher is "to free man from the endless crowd of finite aims and intentions" by making him conscious of his place within a unified and necessary scheme of things. Whereas, however, Spinoza speaks of God or Nature, Hegel speaks of the Absolute Spirit; and whereas Spinoza conceived of Nature statically, Hegel conceives of the Absolute Spirit as engaged in an eternal process of self-realization. The individual person participates in eternity as a moment in the unfolding of the Absolute Spirit.

The spirit of his times, which was one of revolutionary upheaval and continual warfare, also led Hegel to represent the Absolute Spirit as unfolding according to a pattern which he called "dialectical." A given moment of historical development, called the thesis, would in time generate its opposite, called the antithesis. At a later moment, called the synthesis, both earlier moments would emerge in a new configuration which surpasses them while preserving what is valuable in each. In time the synthesis which has emerged becomes the thesis of another antithesis, and the process goes on indefinitely. The Absolute Spirit is not only the sum of all these evolutionary moments, but also the principle which "mediates" or reconciles the conflicts of life as expressed in theses and antitheses.

Surprisingly enough, the attribution of process and change to the Absolute Spirit did not involve much of a departure from the Spinozistic tradition. The Absolute Spirit, though mutable in the sense that it is a process, remains immutable in the sense that nothing outside itself can act upon it or determine its direction. It is wholly self-generating and wholly *ens causa sui*. It also, of course, remains eternal, for it has no limits in time.

Notwithstanding Hegel's importance in his own right, it is largely through Marx and Engels that his influence has been felt in the world of everyday affairs. Through his conception of an inevitable process of historical development of which individuals are but moments, Hegel provided the Marxists with a rationale by means of which the sacrifice of oneself and others for the sake of the community at large or future generations could be justified. Since the achievement of the historically determined goal was guaranteed, the sacrifice could not be useless; and by viewing the sacrifice *sub specie aeternitatis*, much of its horror could be mitigated. This wedding of Enlightenment ideas with Hegelian philosophy had the further advantage of securing Marx against the charge of superficiality, so often leveled at the early Enlightenment, and against the charge of sentimentality, so often leveled at nineteenth-century humanists and latter-day liberals.

Existentialist Values

It was observed earlier that existentialism has often been understood as a philosophy of complete nihilism and utter despair. This misinterpretation was partially explained as a consequence of the fact that the reader of existentialist literature is often so overwhelmed by the existentialists' rejection of traditional values, be they those of the ordinary man or those implicit in the philosophical positions just sketched, that he fails to hear the triumphant and positive note which runs through that literature like a Wagnerian motif. There is, however, another source of misunderstanding which was briefly indicated earlier and which must now be made more explicit.

Almost without exception the biographies of the great philosophers of the past reveal poignant personal tragedies. At an early age Plato was forced to abandon the political career for which he was by birth and social status destined, to sustain the loss through execution of his master and friend Socrates, and to go into exile from his beloved Athens. Later, his one practical political adventure, an effort to establish a sound and stable government in Syracuse, was a dismal failure. Epictetus was not only a slave by birth but was also lame. Spinoza was excommunicated from the Jewish community in Amsterdam where he had passed his early life, was obliged to earn his living in the tedious occupation of lens grinder, and died relatively young of consumption. Hegel was slow to mature as a philosopher, and although he finally achieved great popularity, his climb up the academic ladder was extremely laborious and frustrating. In his student days he was even subjected to the indignity of being told that he had no aptitude for philosophy.

Each of these men had strong personal reasons for doubting the possibility of self-fulfillment through wealth, fame, and pleasure; and behind an often cold and impersonal mask traces of disappointment and bitterness are clearly discernible. If the die-hard ordinary man so chose, he could perhaps make out a plausible interpretation of the traditional philosophers' value orientations as so many instances of sour grapes. The fact remains, however, that in the official expression of their ideas traditional philosophers tended to regard the values which they substituted for those of the ordinary man as sufficient to a complete and fully satisfying life. The sense of tragedy haunts their systems, but it does not ordinarily enter into them.

The existentialists by contrast mock the notion of a complete and fully satisfying life. The life of every man, whether he explicitly recognizes it or not, is marked by irreparable losses. Man cannot help aspiring toward the goods of this world, nor can he help aspiring toward the serene detachment from the things of this world which the traditional philosopher sought; but it is not within his power to achieve either of these ambitions, or having achieved them to find therein the satisfaction he had anticipated. Frustration, insecurity, and painful striving are the inescapable lot of humankind, and the only life worth living is one in which this fact is squarely faced; for, if the existentialists are right, a life of frustration, insecurity, and painful striving itself generates values, and the values so generated are the only ones actually realizable and genuinely worthy of human pursuit.

Total immersion in the quest after wordly goods betokens a misunderstanding of the human situation and succeeds only in turning what could be the noble tragedy of human existence into a petty game of hide and seek. Similarly, a single-minded dedication to the ivory-tower detachment of the traditional philosopher impoverishes the human personality by causing us to lose all that is distinctively human. The ordinary man's way is inhuman, because the person who takes it loses himself in the welter of material things after which he quests. But the way of the traditional philosopher is also inhuman, since the man who takes it loses himself in the ethereal never-never land of philosophic fictions. The history of mankind is a desperate adventure which began we know not why and will end we know not where. And although the same remark might be made with equal justice of the race of elephants, man alone among the animals is capable of knowing that the remark is true. Why should he refuse his birthright by trying to forget what he knows is the case?

It is not surprising that the existentialists should subject both the ordinary man and the traditional philosopher to the same charge of inhumanity. According to the existentialists the underlying motive is in both cases the same: the desire for some state of happiness or well-being which is not only impossible of achievement but which if achieved would reduce us to the status of unconscious brutes.

With the sublime contempt of a man who sees in England nothing but a nation of small shopkeepers Nietzsche once remarked: "Man does not seek happiness; only the Englishman does." As if in anticipation of such an attack, the English utilitarian philosopher John Stuart Mill had remarked that it is far better to be Socrates unhappy than to be a contented pig. Unfortunately for the English and for the utilitarians, Mill's remark passed unnoticed. "Englishman" and "utilitarianism" are still dirty words in the existentialists' vocabulary. Even had Mill's remark been noticed, it would have failed to satisfy the existentialists. It is one thing to say that the life of an unhappy Socrates is better than the life of a contented pig: it is something else again to claim that man never has had, does not now have, and never will have any other choice. And it is only this latter position which is truly existentialist. Mill's concession that nine-tenths of mankind lives in abject misery would not be enough for any of the existentialists, and his assertion that the misery of nine-tenths of mankind is due simply to "wretched social arrangements" would either infuriate or amuse them. For the existentialists it is neither external political circumstances, nor a lack of technological knowledge, nor a want of wisdom, nor an imperfect moral development of the race which prevents the attainment of human happiness. It is the human condition itself which does so. Man could not become happy without ceasing to be man.

The existentialist denial that man desires happiness or well-being has outraged many unfriendly critics, who see in it an obvious untruth and a flat contradiction. What could be more obvious than that man does seek happiness? And have not the existentialists themselves claimed that human happiness lies in certain values to be realized in the very heart of despair? Properly understood, the denial that man seeks happiness is neither an obvious untruth nor a contradiction of other existentialist doctrines. In the first place, terms such as "happiness" and "well-being" are ambiguous. They are sometimes used

in a very general or abstract sense to denote that state of being
which is most desirable for mankind, whatever the speaker may
believe that state of being to be like. At other times these terms
are used somewhat more specifically to denote a state of peace,
harmony, proportion, calm, serenity, or contentment achieved
through wealth, pleasure, and prestige or through detachment
from worldly concerns. Now it should be clear that when an
existentialist denies that man seeks happiness he is not denying
that there is some state of being which is most desirable for
mankind or that in fact all men do in some sense seek this state
of being. What he is denying is that men seek happiness as
specifically conceived by the vast majority of common men and
traditional philosophers. He is not, therefore, in any way
prejudicing his claim that the most worthy and only realizable
human values are those generated by a life of frustration,
insecurity, and painful striving.

In the second place, the term "want" is ambiguous. On the
one hand, in saying that a man wants something we may mean
simply that he deliberately seeks after it in the conscious belief
that it is worth pursuing. This is, of course, the most common
meaning of the term. We may, however, mean that the object
wanted is a legitimate object of pursuit whether the person
involved is clearly aware of it or not, as when we say of someone that he thinks he wants A but in reality wants B. A man
may, for instance, through stubbornness or fear of the unknown
persevere in a chosen career and attempt to persuade himself
that his original choice was for the best despite evidence to the
contrary which only a madman could totally ignore. When,
therefore, the existentialist says that man does not want happiness, it would be most uncharitable to interpret the statement
as meaning that men do not deliberately seek happiness conceived as harmony, proportion, contentment, and so on, in the
belief that it is worth pursuing. The existentialists spend a
great deal of time complaining about this fact. Their intention
is simply to deny that happiness so conceived is worthy of pursuit and to suggest that men who deliberately pursue this kind
of "happiness" are obscurely aware of the futility of their
quest. In this they may be mistaken, but they are not obviously
mistaken.

The existentialists were not, of course, the first philosophers
to make something out of the tragic sense of life or to discover

value in suffering and struggle. In one very important branch of Christian philosophy, whose most notable representatives are Augustine and Pascal, the tragic sense of life appears clearly in the doctrine of man's utter helplessness without the grace of God. For the German romantics of the movement known as Storm and Stress the positive value of strife was a basic credo. And Hegel, who was contemporary to these romantics, made of what he called "the unhappy consciousness" a necessary and valuable stage in the odyssey of the human spirit.

These precursors of existentialist thinking have not gone unrecognized. Christian existentialists rarely have a kind word for St. Thomas, but their praise of Augustine and Pascal is fulsome. Kierkegaard was fond of quoting the romantic Lessing, who claimed that if God were to offer him a life of complete fulfillment and well-being in the right hand and a life of eternal striving in the left, he would unhesitatingly accept the gift in the left hand. As for Hegel, his subtle analyses of various moments in the development of the human spirit have become the inspiration for many of the most brilliant pages in Sartre's *Being and Nothingness*. None of these precursors of existentialism, however, insisted so urgently as the existentialists upon the impossibility of attaining happiness or developed with anything like the completeness of the existentialists a picture of the values which follow upon a clear-sighted appreciation of the human tragedy. Moreover, in one way or another the mainstream of traditional philosophizing invariably pulled them along with it. By a judicious selection of texts a Catholic has little difficulty in reconciling St. Thomas and St. Augustine. And although Hegel's dialectical method permitted him to include just about everything within his system, it is generally agreed that the major outlines of his thinking are far more Spinozistic than existentialist.

The existentialists do not always agree among themselves either as to the precise nature or as to the relative ranking of the values which they say accompany a deliberate espousal of anguish and suffering. Jean-Paul Sartre, for instance, emphasizes freedom of choice and a certain type of individual dignity (although the term "dignity" is not used by Sartre), whereas Nicholas Berdyaev stresses personal love and creative endeavor. Generally speaking, however, freedom of choice, individual dignity, personal love, and creative effort are the existentialist values, and, generally speaking, the most important among these are freedom of choice and individual dignity. Furthermore, all existentialists without exception agree on three points with respect to the values for which they have opted, however different these values may be in other respects or however they may be ranked.

First, a resolute acceptance of anguish and suffering is a necessary condition of their being experienced at all. A man may pretend to have made a free choice without anguish, but if so it is only because the stakes are petty and in the true sense of the word he has not chosen at all. Without having known suffering a man may write a clever or a pretty poem, but not a great one. Similarly, a man may be in love without having known suffering, if to be in love is to be infatuated or simply to be a faithful husband and father. But in the former case what passes by the name of love is simply a nervous itch; in the latter case, a routine or habit. In its essence love is an attitude of care and concern for a being whose death or desertion is always possible and would be an irreparable personal loss.

Second, in the experience of the ordinary man and the traditional philosopher who fail to face up to its inevitability, anguish takes the form of tedium or petty anxiety, apathy or craven fear. The function of existentialist values is to liberate man from these degenerate and unwholesome forms of anguish.

Third, existentialist values intensify consciousness, arouse the passions, and commit the individual to a course of action which will engage his total energies. As Kierkegaard put it, he wants a value by which he is prepared to live and for which, if necessary, he is willing to die. "Let others complain that the age is wicked," he cried, "my complaint is that it is wretched, for it lacks passion." Or, in the words of Nietzsche: "The secret of the greatest fruitfulness and the greatest enjoyment of existence is to live dangerously." It is not blindness to danger, but the intense awareness of danger which makes the blood mount.

In sum, existentialist values have a common source, a common function, and a common identifying characteristic. Their common source is an acute awareness of the tragedy inherent in the human condition. Their common function is to liberate us from the fears and frustrations of everyday life or the tedium of philosophical daydreaming. Their common identifying characteristic is intensity.

Defense of Existentialist Values

The existentialists' critique both of the ordinary man's way of life and of the traditional philosophical orientations is implicit in the preceding sketch of their position. For the ordinary man and the Enlightenment philosopher the supreme value of life lies in the secure and tranquil enjoyment of worldly goods. For the Stoics the supreme value consists in a state of calm and independence produced by the suppression of desire. For the philosopher of the Platonic tradition it consists in release from concern about the things of this world and immersion in the eternal. But in every case the goal is "happiness," i.e., a state of security, peace of mind, calm, or tranquility from which anguish, suffering, and strife are wholly absent. For the existentialist, on the other hand, the commanding value in life is intensity, as manifested in acts of free choice, individual self-assertion, personal love, or creative work. And according to him these various forms of intensely lived experience are impossible without anguish, suffering, and risk.

To make good his case the existentialist has recourse to two major types of arguments. The first is that the values of the ordinary man and the traditional philosopher are, contrary to their belief, impossible of achievement. The second is that even if those values could be achieved, their achievement would involve an unjustifiable sacrifice of superior values. The second type of argument is the more important in the sense that existentialists usually lay more stress upon it, but also in the sense that if this type of argument is sound the other is for all practical purposes superfluous. It is only on condition that one believes in the desirability of achieving a certain goal that the question of its feasibility becomes a matter of urgent personal interest.

In so far as existentialism is a philosophy of tragedy, however, the two types of arguments are not usually independent.

The inability to achieve happiness is an important part of what is meant by the tragedy of the human condition and also an important reason for asserting that intensely lived experience without happiness is the supreme value in life. Most of the existentialists grant that men do in some sense actually desire complete fulfillment or well-being and that, abstractly considered, a life of happiness plus the existentialist values is the highest of goods. Their sense of tragedy arises in great part out of their conviction that happiness is a purely abstract, i.e., concretely unrealizable, value. If, however, they should be proved wrong about this, they would have to reconsider their entire value orientation.

These points may be illustrated by considering existentialist attitudes toward the philosophy of the Enlightenment and its later modifications such as humanism and Marxism. The existentialists often attack one or another feature of this general movement by alleging the impossibility of achieving Enlightenment goals. Karl Jaspers, for instance, has done this in *Man in the Modern Age*:

> Suppose that all the matter and all the energy in the world would be continually utilized without reserve. Population would be regulated by birth control. The sciences of eugenics and hygiene would see to it that the best possible human beings were being bred. Diseases would have been abolished. There would be a purposive economy wherein . . . the needs of all would be supplied. . . . Without struggle . . . the joys of life would be provided for all in unalterable allotments, with the expenditure of little labor and with ample scope for pastime.
>
> In truth, however, such a condition of affairs is impossible. It is prevented by the working of incalculable natural forces. . . . There may be the specific misfortune of a failure of technique. Perhaps the persistence of the campaign against diseases, temporarily to all appearances overwhelming in its success, will rob human beings of their immunity, will deprive them of it so completely that an unanticipated pestilence will sweep away the whole race. . . . Eugenics will prove unable to hinder the survival of the weakly, and will fail to prevent . . . racial deterioration.[1]

Neither Jaspers nor other existentialists, however, are prepared to rest their case against the Enlightenment upon the mere impossibility of establishing the kind of society that Enlightenment thinkers apparently wanted. A few do not use this argument at all; and at least one, Berdyaev, explicitly affirms that the attainment of Enlightenment goals is a genuine possibility. The core of their argument is that the achievement of universal prosperity and general well-being for all would require the sacrifice of more important values. Berdyaev, for instance, appends to his declaration of faith in the possibility of achieving general well-being the remark that this is precisely what is to be feared. Aldous Huxley quotes him to this effect in the epigraph to *Brave New World*, and significantly the brave new world therein depicted is one in which planners have been forced to stifle passionate love and creative endeavor.

Since, however, most existentialists do believe in the impossibility as well as the undesirability of establishing universal well-being and since moreover freedom of choice is usually a greater existentialist value than love or creative endeavor, the following attack upon the Enlightenment by Dostoyevsky in *Notes from Underground* is more typical:

> You see, you gentlemen have, to the best of my knowledge, taken your whole register of human advantages from the averages of statistical figures and politico-economical formulas. Your advantages are prosperity, wealth, freedom, peace—and so on, and so on. So that the man who should, for instance, go openly and knowingly in opposition to all that list would . . . be an obscurantist or an absolute madman. . . . But, you know, that is what is surprising; why does it so happen that all these statisticians, sages and lovers of humanity, when they reckon up human advantages invariably leave one out? . . . The fact is, gentlemen, it seems there must really exist something that is dearer to almost every man than his greatest advantages, or (not to be illogical) there is a most advantageous advantage (the very one omitted of which we spoke just now) which is more important and more advantageous than all other advantages. . . . This advantage is remarkable from the very fact that it breaks down all our classifications and continually shatters every system constructed by lovers of mankind for the benefit of mankind. . . . One's own free unfettered choice, one's own caprice, however wild it may be, one's own fancy worked up at times to frenzy—is that very "most advantageous advantage" which we have overlooked, which comes under no classification and against which all systems and theories are continually being shattered to atoms. . . . What man wants is simply *independent* choice, whatever that independence may cost and wherever it may lead. And choice, of course, the devil only knows what choice.[2]

The dual line of attack in Dostoyevsky's criticism of the Enlightenment is readily apparent. If men are free, the efforts of the social reformer will necessarily be thwarted by the unpredictability of human behavior. And if freedom of choice is supreme among human values, its sacrifice would be totally unjustified—even though its sacrifice would insure universal well-being. As noted above, the second of these arguments is the more important. An argument of this type, purporting to show that the achievement of Enlightenment goals would involve the loss of superior values, is common to practically all the existentialists; and if the man of the Enlightenment were convinced by an argument of this type, the truth or falsity of an argument designed to show the impossibility of achieving his goals would cease to be a matter of practical concern. As also noted above, when the two types of argument go together, as they normally do, they are not altogether independent. It is in part because Dostoyevsky does not believe in the possibility of achieving Enlightenment goals that he ranks freedom of choice so high in the scale of human values. A value which cannot be achieved is by that very fact not a value, at least in so far as values are conceived as objects of deliberate and voluntary pursuit. The man who knowingly pursues an unrealizable value makes himself even more ridiculous than Dostoyevsky represents the gentlemen of the Enlightenment to be.

The same points could be illustrated by detailing existentialist arguments against the ordinary man's values, against Stoicism, and against the Platonic tradition. For the most part, however, these arguments presuppose an analysis of the human condition which will be the subject matter of the following chapter and from which they follow so naturally that it will hardly be necessary to spell them out.

The important problem at this point has to do with the manner in which the existentialists hope to establish their dual claim that happiness is impossible and that intensity is the chief of human values. Most modern Anglo-American philosophers would tend to regard the first of the existentialist claims, to the effect that happiness is impossible, as a judgment of empirical fact which can in principle be decided but can only be decided by the method employed in behavioral sciences such as psychology and sociology. Ignoring refinements, this method consists in observing the reactions of human beings to various types of environmental situation. Once a regular pattern has been discovered to obtain over a certain stretch of time, a rule known technically as the principle of induction is invoked, whereby the observed regularity is postulated as a law of nature and used for the purpose of predicting human behavior in the as yet unobserved future. Basically this method is the one used by all men in the ordinary conduct of life. If, for instance, one wishes to know whether an acquaintance is trustworthy one attempts to discover how he normally behaves in situations where he might profit by betraying others. If it is observed that he has regularly desisted from betraying others, one decides that he is trustworthy and bases one's behavior toward him upon the belief that he will continue to be trustworthy in the future.

To some extent this method is also used by the existentialists when they argue against the impossibility of achieving happiness. Jaspers' contention that medical science will probably not wipe out disease is a case in point. It has often been observed, so he argues in effect, that drugs which give us immunity against one disease kill bacteria which give us a natural immunity to other diseases, thus paving the way for an epidemic of these other diseases. Why should this not continue to happen in the future? Similarly, Dostoyevsky is using this method when he tells us that the plans of social reformers and lovers of humanity have always failed in the past and will therefore fail in the future.

In general, however, the existentialists disdain this method. None of them pretends to be a behavioral scientist or an ordinary man, and almost without exception they are contemptuous or condescending whenever they have occasion to refer to the behavioral sciences or to the common sense of the ordinary man. The reason is not far to seek. The existentialist arguments against the possibility of achieving happiness are usually of such a nature that the method of the behavioral sciences could not even in principle be helpful in determining their soundness.

The argument against the Enlightenment based on human freedom is typical in this respect. Behavioral scientists operate on the assumption that human behavior is predictable, that men will behave in the future much as they have behaved in the past. But, say the existentialists, if man is free, then human behavior is not predictable; for to say that man is free is just another way of saying that men always can and frequently do act in such a way as to render many important facets of their behavior unpredictable. If, therefore, we wish to determine whether man is free, we cannot have recourse to the behavioral sciences; the validity of their conclusions depends upon the validity of their basic assumptions, among which is the premise that man is not free.

It might be countered that past successes in predicting human behavior show the validity of the behavioral scientists' method and consequently of their basic assumption that man is not free. The existentialist would retort in roughly the following way: What behavioral scientist could successfully have predicted an event such as Abelard's falling in love with Héloïse or Shakespeare's writing *Hamlet*? And what behavioral scientist can predict with certainty that there will be a third world war or how it would start? Past successes in predicting human behaviour have rarely touched on matters of great moment either to the individual or to mankind, and when they have, the coefficient of probability has been so low as to render them hardly more than a guess. Most of the successes have been in inconsequential areas of human behavior. And these successes must be explained as a result of the fact that individuals have not bothered to exercise their freedom in these areas. Should, of course, the behavioral scientists succeed in predicting important aspects of individual and group behavior, their position would rest on more solid foundations. But as yet they have not done so. If, therefore, the question of human freedom is to be decided at all in the present, it must be decided on nonscientific grounds. And until it has been decided, the validity of the procedures used by the behavioral sciences remains itself in question.

What, then, is the principal method by which the existentialists hope to establish that man is doomed to unhappiness? Roughly the answer is: by a direct intuition, induced by some intense emotional experience such as anguish, of various features of the human condition. The reliability of this method is sharply contested by most Anglo-American philosophers, and it will be necessary at a later stage to examine it more closely. The point of interest here is that even the obviously factual claim of the existentialists to the effect that man is doomed to unhappiness is based upon an alleged intuition of other facts about man and his relation to the world.

One of these facts about man which the existentialists say they intuit and which contributes to their argument is, of course, human freedom. There is, however, another directly intuited feature of the human condition which is more central to their argument. In fact, if it can be shown that the human condition is genuinely characterized by this feature, a detailed criticism of the various traditional routes to happiness becomes unnecessary. It will be recalled that Hegel spoke of "the unhappy consciousness" as a necessary stage in the unfolding of the human spirit; but for him it was only a stage. At a later moment the unhappy consciousness is surpassed. The existentialists, however, declare that consciousness is inevitably unhappy consciousness. Sartre, for instance, cites as a "self-evident truth" that the "human reality . . . is by nature an unhappy consciousness with no possibility of surpassing its unhappy state."[3] In their own idiom Dostoyevsky and Unamuno have said the same thing. "Man will never renounce real suffering," declared Dostoyevsky. "Why, suffering is the sole origin of consciousness."[4] "Suffering," avers Unamuno, "tells us that we exist."[5] For those who do not themselves have a direct intuition of an inevitable liaison between suffering and consciousness, such statements will probably appear to be wholly dogmatic and unjustifiable. Be that as it may, the existentialists offer no scientific evidence in their support.

The second principal contention of the existentialists, that according to which intensely lived experiences such as free choice, love, and creative endeavor are the chief of human values, is a value judgment. Unlike the statement that man is doomed to unhappiness, which purports to assert simply that something is the case, this second statement asserts that something ought to be preferred. According to most Anglo-American philosophers, judgments of this sort have no scientific status at all, since the procedures of the behavioral sciences could not conceivably either confirm or invalidate them. By observation of human behavior one can tell what men do in fact desire or prefer, but never what men ought to desire or prefer. Such statements are therefore nothing more than an expression of individual preference or an exhortation to others to adopt one's own preference.

This last point would be somewhat qualified by observing that when two persons or groups happen to share the same basic preferences, secondary value judgments may also express a factual claim about the means by which basic preferences or desires may be satisfied. To take a prosaic example, if two persons are known to have much the same taste in music, then when one says that the other ought to attend a certain concert he would normally be expressing the belief that the other would in fact enjoy the concert. And to this extent his judgment could be objectively valid. Since, however, most Anglo-American philosophers believe that basic preferences are a product either of individual temperament or of social conditioning, they do not believe that value judgments relating to basic preferences could conceivably have universal validity.

The existentialists for their part have very little to say about the methods whereby value judgments may properly be established, and at times one has the impression that they, too, are dubious about the possibility of establishing value judgments as objective or universal truths. Heidegger and Sartre have gone so far as to say that they make no value judgments, even though terms such as "authenticity" and "inauthenticity" constantly recur in their writings. These terms, they say, are being used descriptively, not evaluatively. No one, however, has been deceived. Almost to a man, interpreters of Sartre and Heidegger have pointed to these declarations as instances of bad faith. A similar difficulty arises so far as Nietzsche and Kierkegaard are concerned. Both of these men often said that they were writing only for persons who shared their basic preferences, that is to say for their own kind. At the same time, however, they made it clear that they and their own kind were superior beings since they alone had an adequate understanding of the human condition.

Despite the silence of the existentialists on questions of method as related to value theory and despite passages which could be taken as indicating skepticism about the possibility of establishing universal and objectively valid value judgments, the existentialists' actual practice permits us to define their position. According to them value judgments may have universal and objective validity, insofar as the essential features of the human condition, including the basic desires or aspirations of humankind, are themselves universal and objective facts. The person who has a thorough knowledge of the human condition and of basic human aspirations is in much the same position vis-à-vis mankind as is, vis-à-vis his friend, the person who knows that his friend likes the same kind of music he does and what kind of music to expect at the concert.

Individual temperament and social conditioning might influence the manner in which an individual executes his basic desires, but, the fundamental aspects of the human condition being everywhere the same, neither individual temperament nor social conditioning threatens the universal validity of basic value judgments. The position of the existentialists on this score is very nearly the opposite of that developed by Anglo-American philosophers. The latter argue that basic value judgments are conditioned by individual temperament and social conditioning and that only secondary value judgments made within particular groups bound by temperamental affinities or social custom can have any kind of objective validity. The existentialists, on the other hand, argue that preferences determined by temperament or social custom are always secondary and that it is only basic value judgments having their source in a sound appreciation of the universal features of the human condition which have any claim to objective validity.

It must be carefully noted that the existentialist position is acceptable only if the existentialists are right in asserting that the human condition is fundamentally the same for all individuals. It must also be pointed out that this latter assertion is made to rest almost entirely upon intuition. None the less if the validity of intuition as a method of knowledge is granted and if it is further granted that there is a fundamental identity of human aspirations and of means whereby these aspirations may be realized, there remains no good reason for denying the existentialists the right to claim universal and objective validity for their own value orientation.

It follows from what has just been said that the second existentialist contention, that according to which the intense life is preferable to a life of moderation, is not radically different in kind from their first claim, that according to which happiness is an impossible ideal. The first assertion was a factual one to

the effect that a state of security or contentment would involve
a loss of consciousness and could therefore never be experienced.
The second assertion, however, is also a factual one. In rough
outline it could be formulated as follows: All men desire to
live in the full light of consciousness, as evidenced by the fact
that they prefer the life of Socrates unhappy to the life of a
contented pig. Unamuno asks rhetorically: "Which would
you find more appalling, to feel such a pain as would deprive
you of your faculties on being pierced through with a white-hot
iron, or to see yourself thus pierced through without feeling
any pain?"[6] But the desire to live in the full light of consciousness can be fulfilled only through intense experiences of the
kind existentialists value, with all the risk, pain, and suffering
that go with them. Consciousness is a function of suffering
and intensely lived experience, and presumably it varies in
direct ratio with the degree of suffering and intensely lived
experience. It is this which explains what Unamuno calls "the
horrible terror of feeling yourself incapable of suffering and
tears." It is this also which explains the following text from
Berdyaev:

> The ethics of the ancients . . . considered man a being who
> seeks happiness, good, and harmony, and who is capable of
> achieving this goal. Such is also the point of view of St.
> Thomas Aquinas and the official Catholic theology. But in
> fact Christianity has shaken this view. . . . Not the worst but
> the best of mankind suffer the most. The intensity with which
> suffering is felt may be considered an index of a man's depth.
> The more the intellect is developed and the soul refined . . . ,
> the more sensitive does one become to pain, not only the pains
> of the soul but physical pains as well. . . . But for pain and
> suffering the animal in man would be victorious.[7]

To be incapable of suffering and tears is to be swallowed up in
the dread nothingness of unconsciousness. In Camus' play
Caligula the hero's mistress asks him: "Is this dreadful freedom
still happiness?" His answer is that of a typical existentialist
hero: "Be sure, Caesonia, that without it I would be a contented man. Thanks to it, I have conquered the divine clear-
sightedness of the solitary man."[8]

The position of the existentialist as it is represented in this
rough sketch is, of course, debatable. Consider, for instance,
their second contention. If our purview is limited to the
Western tradition it is probably true that men have wanted to

live in the clear light of consciousness. This generalization applies even to the Stoics, as is shown by the fact that their indifference to worldly happiness was maintained through an effort of will which heightened consciousness of self and also by the ease with which Stoic doctrine has been incorporated into existentialist thinking. Sartre, speaking of Jean Genet, says: "It is in suffering alone that he can *feel* himself to be free, because it is the only feeling which can come from within himself. Unless one is a god, one cannot become happy without the cooperation of the universe; but to be unhappy, one needs only oneself. . . . He does not seek the motive of his . . . actions in an appetite for suffering: he wishes that his actions be the effects of an absolute will which draws its motive from itself alone and not from the world."[9]

It is very doubtful, however, whether oriental philosophers have wanted to live in the full light of consciousness. Moreover, even within the Western tradition terms such as "consciousness" and "degrees of consciousness" have been variously conceived, and there is a wide variety of opinion with regard to the relationship between consciousness and other forms of human experience. According to traditional philosophers in the Platonic tradition, for example, consciousness means mind or understanding, and in their opinion intensely lived experience, passion, and suffering cloud the mind or obscure the understanding. An American philosopher once quipped that *sub specie aeternitatis* is Latin for sleeping. But for classical philosophers like Plato and Spinoza the degree of consciousness is equivalent to the range of one's perspective as a knowing being, and true wakefulness is possible only for the person who frees himself from the passions to view the whole of being from the standpoint of eternity. Not they, but the passionate men, are the ones who live in the murky twilight zone between waking and sleeping.

It may finally be necessary to conclude that the "insights" of the existentialists are nothing more than a set of prejudices reflecting their own temperamental bias or the social conditions of our time. But it would be a mistake to conclude that this is so on the basis of a brief introductory outline. The purpose of the preceding sketch of the existentialist position has been very limited, and the full story is yet to be told.

II. The Human Condition

The clue to the analysis of the human condition lies in the experience of anguish, through which the existentialists believe themselves to have acquired direct and intuitive insights which totally escaped traditional philosophers. As might be expected of a movement so diverse, the experience of anguish is variously conceived.

Subjectively considered, anguish is an extremely intense experience with a wholly distinctive emotional tone. On the one hand, there is a sense of dread, terror, and revulsion. On the other hand, there is a sense of awe, exhilaration, and sublimity. Sometimes the sense of terror and the sense of exhilaration blend, sometimes they merely succeed one another; but both affective poles must be present if one is to speak of a genuine case of existential anguish. In this respect the experience of Job before God, in which indignation over the arbitrary exercise of divine power is transmuted into a sense of awe and respect for divine majesty, approximates fairly well to the contemporary experience of existential anguish.

It is only with regard to the alleged object of the experience that the existentialists part company with Job and to some extent with one another. For some existentialists the primary object of anguish is the brute fact of being; for others, human particularity or individuality; for still others, human freedom. It will, therefore, be convenient for expository purposes to speak of three forms of anguish, each distinguished by its object. It must, however, be borne in mind that the features of the human condition which these three forms of anguish are said to reveal have been acknowledged by almost all existentialists and that in most cases their individual experience of anguish has more than one of these features as its object.

The Anguish of Being

The anguish of being could just as well be called the anguish of nothingness were it not for the fact that the existentialists use the term "nothingness" in so many different senses that one would be courting serious confusion by so doing. The anguish of being is the feeling we have whenever the thought comes to us that nothingness was and still is just as possible as being, whenever we ask ourselves how it is that there is something rather than nothing. It is a curious fact that one cannot experience the full wonder and mystery of being without thinking of absolute nothingness. Speaking metaphorically, it could be said that only from the vantage point of nothingness can we get a good look at being.

The anguish of being should not be confused with the anguish of death, although the thought of death can and often does evoke it. The anguish of being is properly the anguish one experiences at the thought that nothing and nobody might ever have come into existence or that everything and everybody might go out of existence in an instant. When we try to conceive the world being created out of nothing or being reduced to cosmic dust we are brought nearer to it. The Italian poet Leopardi expressed the anguish of being with great skill in a text quoted by Unamuno:

A time will come when this Universe and Nature itself will be extinguished. And just as of the grandest kingdoms and empires of mankind and the marvellous things achieved therein, very famous in their own times, no vestige or memory remains today, so, in like manner, of the entire world and of the vicissitudes and calamities of all created things there will not remain a single trace, but a naked silence and a most profound stillness will fill the immensity of space. And so before ever it has been uttered or understood, this admirable and fearful secret of universal existence will be obliterated and lost.[1]

The peculiar liability of twentieth-century man to the anguish of being is in part a legacy of the traditional Christian-Hebraic belief in creation *ex nihilo* and the Christian eschatological doctrine of the Last Judgment. There can be no doubt that meditation upon the Christian mysteries was what produced this form of anguish in Unamuno, who of all the existentialists stresses it in its purest form. "For myself," he writes, "I can say that as a youth and even as a child, I remained unmoved when shown the most moving pictures of hell, for even then nothing appeared to me quite so horrible as nothingness itself."[2]

The ancients and most traditional non-Christian philosophers regarded being as eternal and necessary: eternal, because it had no beginning or end in time; and necessary, because its eternity and its ultimate nature could be demonstrated by logical reasoning. Aristotle especially took this view, and Spinoza's argument on behalf of the eternity of the world can be traced back to him. Plato, even though he had a doctrine of creation, was no exception, for it was Plato's belief that the creator was required to act upon an eternal, preexisting matter.

If, however, the world is created *ex nihilo* by God, as the Christians say, then obviously it cannot be eternal. And, what is even more important, it cannot be necessary. One cannot construct an argument showing that it had to exist even within a limited time span. Thomas Aquinas was forced to abandon Aristotle on this score and was among the most vehement of Christian philosophers in listing the act of creation as a mystery which has to be accepted on faith alone. Since God is a perfect being who lacks nothing, why should he bother to create a world? In fact, since he is immutable and since an act of creation, at least as understood by a finite mind, involves some sort of motion, it is impossible to understand the act of creation at all.

The traditional technical term for a fact which defies human understanding is "contingent," although existentialists often prefer the word "absurd." And in traditional terminology it was the necessary contingency of being which St. Thomas and other Christian philosophers were trying to prove. The ancients said that being was necessary because they could construct a logical argument showing that it existed from eternity. Christian philosophers, on the other hand, claimed to have constructed an argument showing that being and nonbeing are both logically possible and that human reason is incompetent to explain the fact of being.

Another proof of the contingency of being has been presented by a more recent philosophical tradition, among whose proponents the eighteenth-century English philosopher David Hume is most prominent and which includes the vast majority of philosophers in the English-speaking world today. Genuine knowledge, according to members of this movement, is always knowledge of particular beings and the relationships which obtain between them. Put slightly differently and somewhat more precisely, genuine knowledge is invariably a knowledge of a recurrent type of relationship between two or more kinds of particular beings under similar circumstances. Regardless of how this theory is stated, it is clear that being itself, or the totality of particular beings, cannot be an object of knowledge. Since being is singular rather than plural, since as the American philosopher Charles Peirce says, "worlds are not as plentiful as blackberries," being is totally unintelligible. We can know neither why it is nor what its ultimate nature is. It is simply a brute, contingent fact.

American pragmatism is one of the offshoots of this larger movement, and William James specifically related his belief in the necessary contingency of being to the experience of anguish, which he called at various times "metaphysical wonder," "ontological wonder sickness," and "cosmic fear." James states that it is precisely at the moment when a man feels he has explained all particular natural phenomena

that the craving for further explanation, the ontological wonder sickness, arises in its extremest form. As Schopenhauer says, "The uneasiness which keeps the never resting clock of metaphysics in motion is the consciousness that the nonexistence of this world is just as possible as its existence." The notion of nonentity may thus be called the parent of the philosophic craving in its subtlest and profoundest sense. Absolute existence is absolute mystery, for its relation with the nothing remains unmediated to our understanding.

Still another offshoot of the movement under discussion is positivism, one of whose most notable twentieth-century representatives, Ludwig Wittgenstein, also specifically related the necessary contingency of being to the fact of anguish. "Not *how* the world is," he writes, "is the mystical, but *that* it is. . . . We feel that even if *all possible* scientific questions be answered, the problems of life have still not been touched at all."[3]

The fact that Thomists, pragmatists, and positivists agree with the existentialists in regarding being as necessarily contingent ought not to lead us to overlook the originality of the latter's views. In the first place, the Thomists based their position upon an argument which includes among its premises certain notions about the nature of the divine being, while the pragmatists and positivists based their position upon a general theory of knowledge. If God does not exist or if he does not have the properties traditionally attributed to him, the Thomist argument loses all validity. Similarly, the argument of the pragmatists and positivists stands or falls with their theory of knowledge. The existentialists, for their part, offer no argument for the necessary contingency of being, grounding their belief instead upon intuitive insight. All of us, they say, whether we have known the experience of anguish or not, have at least a dim appreciation of the absurdity of being, just as we all have a dim appreciation of the principles of logic. The anguish of being merely makes that dim awareness explicit; and once it has been made explicit through anguish it has all of the self-evidence that the principle of identity and the principle of contradiction have reputedly had for the logician.

In the second place, the existentialists differ from the pragmatists, positivists, and Thomists in their reaction as human beings to the necessary contingency of being. Not, of course, in their initial reaction, which is invariably one of acute distress. Apparently few, if any, human beings can accept with total equanimity that being should be opaque to the human understanding. The difference arises at a secondary and reflective level, in the interpretation of the experience of anguish and in the effort to tame it.

James experienced the anguish of being, regularly and with intensity, and significantly enough, he constantly complained of a sense of unreality and hollowness which accompanied him throughout his life. None the less James decided that anguish is merely an "incidental feature" of our mental life and declared that if the philosopher cannot "exorcise" the question of being, he should either "ignore or blink it, and assuming the data of his system as something given, and the gift as ultimate simply proceed to a life of contemplation or action based upon it." Unfortunately, James did not explain how one can base a life of contemplation or action upon a fact which one ignores or blinks.

Wittgenstein went even further than James. He regarded the anguish of being as a disease or aberration for which a cure should be found. As he saw it, the anguish of being arises because we ask the question "What is being?" in the mistaken notion that this question is meaningful since other questions of the same grammatical form are meaningful. At first we think that "What is being?" is a question of the same type as "What is man?" Upon reflection, however, we see that this is not so. We may not now have a satisfactory answer to either question, but the latter is unlike the former in that we can at least conceive of the type of answer which would satisfy us. The mistake lying at the source of the disease constituted by the anguish of being is thus the logical one of assuming the meaningfulness of an interrogative sentence on the wholly inadequate grounds that it is in correct grammatical form. "The solution of the problem of life is seen in the vanishing of the problem. . . . The riddle does not exist. . . . For doubt can only exist where there is a question; a question only where there is an answer."[4] Unfortunately, Wittgenstein's therapy has not been notably successful; and like James, Wittgenstein was hounded until death by the fear of mental illness.

The Thomists share with the existentialists the conviction that every normal human being ought squarely to face the necessary contingency of being. Yet, the differences between Thomists and existentialists are at least as important as the differences between existentialists and philosophers who trace their lineage to Hume. The Thomists argued that since God is a perfect being who lacks nothing, it is impossible to discover within the divine nature a motive for creation, and that since God is an immutable being, it is impossible to understand the act of creation. God's ways are unfathomable; the being of man and the being of the world are both stamped with contingency. Side by side with the conclusions of this argument, however, stands the doctrine that the world was made for man, that man was made to worship God, and that God will reward the individual who properly worships him.

The Thomists say that God created the world and found it *good*. He placed man *within* the world, gave him dominion over the lower animals, and provided him with an abundance of good things—more than enough for his well-being and comfort. The condition of God's bounty is that man worship him by observing his natural and moral laws.   By the right use of his reason and aided by revelation, man may know these laws, and by the right use of his free will he may conform to them in his behavior.   The Thomists find a place for the doctrines of the fall and of divine grace, but as a rule these doctrines are kept comfortably in the background.   Thomists are emphatic in asserting that the fall did not affect man's essential nature, and although tradition requires them to say that grace is the one necessary and sufficient condition of salvation, they stress instead the role of rational and voluntary adherence to moral law.

It is impossible and unnecessary in a book of this compass to review the subtle and often ingenious reasoning by which Thomists have attempted to reconcile belief in a providential divine order with belief in the contingency of being.   For our purposes it suffices to point out that the existentialists, Christian and atheist alike, refuse to recognize the compatibility of these two beliefs and come out boldly for the contingency of being. To emphasize their disagreement with the Thomists, they speak, not simply of the contingency of being, but of its *radical* contingency.

The atheistic existentialists say that since God alone could conceivably give meaning to being and since he does not exist, being is totally meaningless.   The Christian existentialists say that although it is permissible to believe on faith that God exists and that for him being has meaning, the "radical incommensurability" between God and man makes it impossible for us even to guess what that meaning is.   There is no possible way in which it could be shown that the world was made for man, that man was made to worship God, or that God will reward us for obedience.   The fact of creation is not simply a mystery which surpasses human understanding; it is an unsurpassable logical paradox.   The metaphysical properties of Platonic Being which Christians attribute to God are logically incompatible with the properties of a creator.

Accordingly, the Christian existentialists place the dogma of the fall and of divine grace in the center of their philosophy, as did Augustine and Pascal.   The fall did radically affect man's nature.   Since the fall man has become an exile from the world. His natural reason has become not merely impotent to fathom God's way but also a barrier between man and God.   At the same time man cannot hope for salvation through the strained quest after moral perfection. God's grace, like the rain, falls on good and bad indifferently.

The difference between atheistic and Christian existentialists thus becomes minimal, and it is a matter of relatively little importance whether one expresses their essential similarity by saying that Christian existentialists are close to atheism or by saying that the atheistic existentialists are essentially religious. The expression "God is dead," which Nietzsche made famous, has found its way into both branches of the movement. Both branches are primarily, as one critic has said specifically of Heidegger, discourses "on the absence of God."

In sum, the anguish of being reveals the radical contingency and ultimate meaninglessness of both man and the world. To say that the *being of man* is radically contingent and ultimately meaningless is to say that man knows not why he exists and cannot rise to a knowledge of his destiny. In the language of Heidegger it is as if man were "thrown into" the world and left there. To borrow another term from Heidegger, it is as if man were "forsaken," as Christ was forsaken on the cross. The same idea can be expressed in still other language by saying that man is "alienated" from the source of his being.

To say that the *being of the world* is radically contingent and ultimately meaningless is to say that its existence is inexplicable and that there is no knowable providential order either in nature or in that larger realm of being which includes both man and the external world. More specifically, it means that there is no reason to believe that the world was made for man. It is as if man stands face to face to a world which has no point of reference beyond itself and no meaning other than that which we human beings with our finite personal cares decide to give it. Thus man is also "alienated" from the world.

The enormous significance of the anguish of being is now becoming clear. So long as philosophers believed that the individual could harmoniously relate himself to eternal and necessary beings, the temptation to locate the source of value and intelligibility in those beings proved impossible to resist. But as soon as man felt himself forsaken by God and stamped the beings once believed to be eternal and necessary with the sign of radical contingency, the source of value and intelligibility was relocated within human subjectivity.

The German philosopher Immanuel Kant declared in the late

eighteenth century that he had effected a Copernican revolution in philosophy by showing that the so-called universal and necessary laws of nature are not out there in things themselves, but are rather patterns of human thinking imposed upon things. To mark the distinction between things as they are in themselves and things refashioned by the human mind, Kant introduced the terms "noumena" and "phenomena." The noumenal world is the world of things in themselves, and of it Kant declared that we can know nothing except that it exists. The phenomenal world is the world actually present to the human mind, the world of the ordinary man. Even space and time were regarded as mere forms of human sensibility, and consequently determinations of phenomena or what appears to the human mind, but not of noumena or ultimate realities.

Kant's conception was truly revolutionary when it was advanced, and it is an important milestone along the route by which modern man has come to attach more and more importance to his own subjectivity. But for the twentieth-century philosopher who has felt the impact of existentialist thinking Kant's pretension to have completed the revolution is a source of merriment. Had Kant been able to foresee the extent to which man would retreat from God and the world to seek after meaning and value within the tortured appreciation of his own individual forsakenness, he would have recoiled in horror. Certainly, he was not ready to embrace the nightmare world of Franz Kafka, who better than anyone else has illustrated in literary fashion man's alienation from the world and from the sources of his being.

The distance which separates Kant from modern-day existentialists can most clearly be seen by contrasting Kant and Sartre. Kant saw man as comfortably installed in the phenomenal world. Since the laws of nature derive from forms of human sensibility and categories of the human understanding which are permanent and irremovable parts of all human beings' mental equipment, they hold necessarily and universally for the phenomenal world. And since the noumenal world is in principle beyond the reach of human consciousness, there is no danger that it will ever erupt into the phenomenal world to upset its orderly pattern.

In Sartre's system the noumenal world, or world of things in themselves, is named "being-in-itself" or sometimes simply "the in-itself," the term "world" being reserved exclusively for Kant's phenomenal world, or world created by the activity of the human mind and sensibility. Sartre, however, does not see man as comfortably installed in the world. This is partly because, according to Sartre, each man lives in his own world, there being as many worlds as there are individual human beings. But there is a second reason, more germane to the present discussion. If Sartre is right, the in-itself (what Kant called the noumenal world) constantly threatens to explode our individual worlds. All of us, says Sartre, have a "pre-ontological comprehension" of being-in-itself, that is to say, an opaque, inarticulate, but very real sense of its presence and nature. The world is but a "varnish" on the surface of being-in-itself; or, changing the metaphor, the world is but a "thin crust" of meaning which we impose upon being-in-itself. Ordinarily this thin crust of meaning conceals the in-itself and obscures our awareness of it, but the anguish of being is always there just below the surface of daily consciousness, and from time to time it breaks through to the surface, presenting being-in-itself without disguise.

Sartre has two apparently contradictory descriptions of the in-itself. In the novel called *Nausea* and sometimes in *Being and Nothingness* the in-itself is represented as a soft, shapeless dough or paste, something ugly and even obscene which threatens to engulf us. Other times, Sartre describes the in-itself as a solid and impervious mass, something hard and impenetrable before which we can only stand agape. The former description explains his reference to the world as a "thin crust of meaning;" the latter his reference to the world as a "varnish" on the surface of being-in-itself. The explanation of this apparent contradiction will be given later. The point of importance here is that the in-itself is not a neutral something like Kant's noumenal world from which man has nothing to fear. It is rather an absurd or contingent being of which we are constantly aware, be it only dimly, and which poisons our existence, as Sartre's choice of the word "nausea" to designate the anguish of being sufficiently indicates. The hero of the novel *Nausea* is made to say of this experience: "It took my breath. ... At one blow it was there. ... The diversity of things, their individuality, was nothing but an appearance, a varnish. This varnish had melted. What was left were monstrous soft masses in disorder, naked in frightening nudity."5

By a curious twist Sartre's in-itself, though remaining radically contingent, takes on two traditional properties of Platonic Being: timelessness and immutability. The reason is that, like Kant, Sartre regards time and space as properties of the man-made world rather than of being-in-itself. But in common with all existentialists, Sartre denies that man can harmoniously relate to the timeless and immutable being whose existence he recognizes. Human existence, which is essentially an affair in time and space, is radically different from the timeless and immutable being of the in-itself. The encounter between man and the in-itself cannot therefore be comfortable; it will necessarily involve tension.

By another curious twist Sartre has his own problem of creation. Man, he says, must be posterior to the in-itself and emerge from it; but the means by which this occurs is wholly incomprehensible. To produce man the in-itself would have to have the property of consciousness, which it cannot have since consciousness is by nature temporal and the in-itself is timeless. To say, therefore, that man arises from the in-itself is to become involved in a self-contradiction, which Sartre himself calls "profound." In his cautious moments, therefore, Sartre limits himself to the declaration that "it is as if" man arose from the in-itself.

So far the emphasis has been upon the dread produced by the anguish of being. By implication, however, the positive side of the experience has already been presented. If eternal and immutable beings do not exist or if they are opaque to the human understanding, then man becomes the source of value and meaning. The place formerly held by God or Nature is assumed by individual human beings. Man is exalted. He takes on the dignity of a being responsible to himself alone. Nietzsche has best expressed this point:

> All the beauty and sublimity which we have attributed to real or imaginary objects I claim as the property and creation of man. They are his most beautiful justification. Man the poet and the thinker! Man as God, as love, as power! With what royal generosity has he impoverished himself and made himself feel miserable in order to worship things. Up to now his greatest baseness has been that he admired and venerated things, forgetting that it was he who had created what he admired.
>
> Reject the humble expression "Everything is subjective." Say rather: "It is our work! Let us be proud of it."

Anguish Before the Here and Now

The second form of anguish is anguish before the fact of human particularity. An apt name for it would be anguish before the here and now. Among the existentialists Gabriel Marcel most emphasizes this form of anguish. Why, he asks in extreme wonder, does he exist as an author at a particular point in the space-time of the modern world writing a book on philosophy? Why is he not rather a leper at a point of space-time in the medieval world ringing his warning bell as he approaches a walled city? The classic statement of this form of anguish is a text by Pascal:

> When I consider the short duration of my life, swallowed up in the eternity before and after, the little space which I fill, and even can see, engulfed in the infinite immensity of space of which I am ignorant, and which knows me not, I am frightened. I am astonished at being here rather than there. Why now rather than then!

The feature of the human condition which this form of anguish reveals can be expressed either negatively or positively. Negatively, it means that even if eternal objects exist, man cannot participate in their eternity. Positively, it means that man is by nature a temporal being with an individual history confined to a limited historical epoch and a limited region of space.

In one sense it is a mere truism to say that individual persons always live at a particular historical epoch and in a limited region of space, and in the same sense it is a mere truism to say that man is cut off from the eternal. It is precisely because these statements can be taken to stand for certain obvious facts that traditional philosophers sought so desperately for a means of extricating themselves from the limitations of historical existence. The statements cease to be truisms only when interpreted to assert the total impossibility of escape, and it is, of course, in this sense that the existentialists intend them to be taken.

Plato and Aristotle thought they had found an escape from the world of becoming to the world of eternal being through the mind or the intellect. A concrete individual object apprehended by the physical senses, such as a chair or a man, comes into existence and passes out of existence, and while in existence suffers many changes. But the Idea or essence of these objects, apprehended by the intellect alone, neither comes into existence nor passes out of existence and is always the same. Ideas or essences are therefore eternal, and the human mind can behold them.

Spinoza and Hegel also believed that they had found access to the eternal through the mind. But for them the eternal object was the totality of what is, rather than Ideas or essences, and the argument by which they attempted to show that man could rise to a knowledge of the whole of things is neither so simple nor so plausible as the argument by which Plato and Aristotle tried to show that man has access to the eternal. In fact, one is tempted to say that they did not argue their case at all.

Spinoza calls the type of knowledge which allegedly presents God or Nature to our mind *scientia intuitiva*; but his remarks about *scientia intuitiva* are so scant and so vague or confused that it is still a highly controversial problem for his interpreters. Moreover, Spinoza had little to say about the temporal or historical character of human existence, which the existentialists believe to be one of the crucial barriers to any view of being *sub specie aeternitatis*. If Spinoza did not provide a clear and explicit argument demonstrating that man can rise to a knowledge of all of being, it is probably because he did not fully realize how great his break with Plato and Aristotle was and consequently how urgently he needed an original argument to prove that the eternal as he conceived it could be reached by the human mind. The philosophic tradition initiated by Plato and Aristotle had so roundly affirmed for so long that eternal and immutable objects are knowable that this proposition had become very nearly an axiom. The fact that the eternal and immutable objects of Plato and Aristotle were very different from Spinoza's Nature and that Plato and Aristotle had used an argument to establish their point was simply forgotten.

Spinoza's recognition that a vision of being *sub specie aeternitatis* requires a special type of knowledge strongly suggests that he was not, as has sometimes been said, simply pushing to the limit the case for an indefinite extension of scientific knowledge, even though the mental vision of the scientist does extend far beyond the range of our physical vision. Hegel differs from Spinoza in that he does explicitly recognize historical process, the Absolute Spirit itself being engaged in a temporal process of self-unfolding. But, as in the case of Spinoza, one searches in vain for a clear argument demonstrating that the individual can acquire knowledge of the Absolute Spirit. To be sure, historians have reconstructed large areas of the historical past through the use of their intelligence, and successes in the prediction of the historical future are not totally unknown. It is, however, as unlikely that Hegel would have wanted to base his case upon facts of this kind as that Spinoza would have wanted to base his case upon the fact of scientific knowledge. Scientism, as the unlimited faith in the power of the scientific understanding is sometimes called, has other origins. Just as Spinoza declared that *scientia intuitiva* was a different kind of knowledge from scientific understanding, so Hegel declared that science was merely a handmaiden of philosophy. The explanation of Hegel's failure to argue directly for the possibility of knowing the Absolute Spirit is probably the same as that suggested for the comparable omission of Spinoza.

The vigor, though not the logical structure, of the existentialist attack upon the mechanism of escape from the historicity of the human condition typified by these thinkers in the Platonic tradition is beautifully expressed in the following passage from Kierkegaard, who habitually referred to his archenemy Hegel as Herr Professor:

> Can the principle of mediation . . . help the existing individual? . . . The poor existing individual is confined to the straight-jacket of existence. . . . How can it help to explain to a man how the eternal truth is to be understood eternally, when the supposed user of the explanation is prevented from so understanding it through being an existing individual, and merely becomes fantastic when he imagines himself to be *sub specie aeternitatis*? What such a man needs instead is precisely an explanation of how the eternal truth is to be understood in determinations of time by one, who as existing, is himself in time, which even the worshipful Herr Professor concedes, if not always, at least once a quarter when he draws his salary.[6]

Of course, rhetoric cannot pass as argument, and an appallingly large proportion of the existentialist literature dealing with this problem is pure rhetoric.   None the less behind the rhetoric, or wedged in between the purple passages, several respectable arguments will be discovered.

The first of these is directed especially at Spinoza, Hegel, Marx, and the advocates of scientism, the existentialists normally regarding scientism as a part of the Spinozistic tradition.   This argument consists in pointing out that all these thinkers tend to gloss over the duality of man the observer or viewer and man as part of that which is observed, be it nature or historical process.   Spinoza, for instance, apparently believed that man could exist simultaneously as a part of nature and as a spectator of nature.   Had he not believed this, he could not logically have urged the individual to adopt a perspective on the whole of being in order to reconcile himself to his role in the natural scheme of things.   The existentialists, on the contrary, say that the duality of man the viewer and man the observed cannot be overcome and that consequently man can never rise to a vision of things *sub specie aeternitatis*.   In so far as man is a part of nature he is actively engaged in natural processes and cannot sufficiently detach himself from his involvement in these processes to adopt a perspective on the whole of things.   And in so far as man does detach himself from nature to exist as observer or spectator, he still fails to gain a vision of the whole of things since he as observer or spectator could not possibly be included within that vision.   To reinforce this argument several contemporary existentialists have made capital out of developments in modern physics, such as Einstein's theory of relativity and Heisenberg's principle of indeterminacy, which amply demonstrate that the experimenter modifies the experimental situation in such a way that many laws of nature formulated without regard to the position of the observer in space and time lose much of their validity.

A second argument is directed especially at Plato, Aristotle, and their followers, who believe that man has access to the eternal through communion with Ideas or essences.   For reasons which are not at all clear the ancients took as axiomatic the proposition that only like could know like.   If, therefore, the Ideas or essences are eternal, the faculty by which the Ideas or essences are known, namely reason, must also be eternal.

From this doctrine, together with the classical definition of man as a rational animal, it follows that man is immortal.

But, say the existentialists, what reason is there for defining man as a rational animal? The eminently quotable Unamuno expressed his doubts on the subject in the following text: "Man is said to be a reasoning animal. I do not know why he has not been defined as an affective or feeling animal. Perhaps that which differentiates him from other animals is feeling rather than reason. More often have I seen a cat reason than laugh or weep. Perhaps it weeps or laughs inwardly—but then perhaps, also inwardly, the crab resolves equations of the second degree."[7] In any case, whether man can be correctly defined as a rational animal or not, it is not merely man the rational being who experiences the anguish of the here and now. It is man the feeling being who is tortured by the realization of his limits in space and time. Even, therefore, if he could transcend these limitations through the exercise of the intellect, he would not find in that act of transcendence the salvation he seeks. His body and his passions are also a part of his nature, and he cannot be content with immortality of the mind alone. If he could be so satisfied, he would not be subject to the anguish of the here and now.

The same point can be made in a slightly different way. According to Aristotle, and after him Spinoza, the immortality which man achieves through the mind or intellect is universal and impersonal in character. Since like alone knows like and since the essences or forms known by the mind are universal and impersonal entities, the mind or intellect to which immortality is attributed must itself be a universal and impersonal thing. Immortality is not a characteristic of the concrete body and soul of the individual man; immortality belongs to Mind conceived as a universal and impersonal entity of a metaphysical order. In other words, it is man in the abstract, not the concrete individual person, who is immortal. And how, ask the existentialists, can a knowledge of man in the abstract possibly help the existing individual? The gap between the abstract and the concrete is so enormous that the individual can rarely close it. By virtue of his preoccupation with himself as a whole person, he almost never succeeds in realizing that the characteristics of man in the abstract actually apply to him. He simply does not see himself as a member of a species. He is not concerned with man in general. It is he himself as an individual whom he wishes to know and understand.

This observation applies even if the abstract characteristic of man in general which comes under consideration is mortality rather than immortality. In Tolstoy's story "The Death of Ivan Ilych" this aspect of existentialist doctrine is illustrated with uncommon clarity. "The syllogism he had learned from Kiezewetter's Logic: 'Caius is a man, men are mortal, therefore Caius is mortal,' always seemed to him correct as applied to Caius, but certainly not as applied to himself. That Caius—man in the abstract—was mortal, was perfectly correct, but he was not Caius, not an abstract man, but a creature quite, quite separate from all others."[8]

The last major argument by which the existentialists attempt to show that man cannot escape his historical limitations through knowledge is directed primarily against the same antagonists as the first. If, they say, man has freedom of choice, then it is impossible for either the individual or the race by collective labor to rise to a knowledge of things *sub specie aeternitatis*, for the simple reason that the future is largely undetermined, especially in those areas which most vitally concern us. Although the inspiration of this argument lies rather in the anguish of freedom than in the anguish before the here and now, the two forms of anguish are not ordinarily independent of one another and in any case tidiness requires that it be mentioned briefly here. The link between the two forms of anguish should also be noted. The corollary of the doctrine of human particularity is that man is in some sense a part of history, a being actively engaged in historical process. As such, he is necessarily a part, not wholly reducible to other parts, of history. By his own activity he helps to decide the outcome of historical processes. The logical consequence of denying to man an original role in the shaping of history is to exclude him from history altogether and to attribute to him, as some of the advocates of scientism explicitly did, a purely marginal status in being. In technical language man becomes an "epiphenomenon"; he is merely carried along on the surface of history like a piece of flotsam.

Not all men have sought escape from their individuality through knowledge. A second mechanism of escape is through some sort of identification with the race of mankind or a large social unit such as the nation. Humanism and theoretical communism are instances of attempted identification with mankind; fascism and other forms of virulent patriotism, instances of attempted identification with larger social groups. For the sake of simplicity, the following exposition will deal exclusively with the existentialist attitudes towards humanism. Since the arguments against humanism can be adapted without difficulty to other manifestations of the same human propensity, nothing will be lost by this procedure.

If, of course, by humanism one understands a doctrine according to which individual persons are the source of value and intelligibility, then existentialism is itself humanistic, as Sartre went to great pains to show in a pamphlet entitled "Existentialism Is a Humanism." In this context, however, humanism is taken to mean the doctrine mentioned in the last chapter according to which the individual can and should identify with the species mankind, putting the interests of mankind at large above his own or those of any other single individual.

Humanism emerged as an important historical force in the nineteenth century. Although its immediate source was the set of ideas associated with the eighteenth-century Enlightenment, its seeds were planted by Aristotle. Aristotle's influence was felt in two ways. First, when Aristotle brought Plato's Ideas down from their transcendental heaven to the world of becoming and decided to call them essences, he preserved their eternity and immutability by pronouncing the doctrine of fixed species. Horse in the abstract and man in the abstract were immortal, even though individual horses and men were mortal. At the same time, by settling upon reason as the distinguishing characteristic and highest function of human nature and by making of eternal essences the principle object of reason, he opened the way to the view that the individual can achieve a desirable form of immortality through identification with the species.

Second, it was Aristotle who opened the way to the doctrine of human equality which is so dear to the humanists and their predecessors, the gentlemen of the Enlightenment. The doctrine of human equality was implicit in Aristotle's doctrine of substantial forms. Every existing thing, said Aristotle, is composed of matter and form, "form" being here a rough synonym for "essence." The material component is different for each individual, but the form is always the same. Since reason is the form or essence of man, every man's reason must be like his neighbor's, and individual differences will have to be attributed to accidental material properties. In modern language one would say that individual differences are a product of external environmental influences. Aristotle was not greatly interested in drawing political implications from these ideas, but even so he found some difficulty in reconciling them with his belief in the natural inferiority of slaves. In one passage he came close to suggesting that slaves be regarded as a separate species. The historical influence of Aristotle's doctrine of essential equality among all members of the same species was enormous. Even Descartes, the revolutionary founder of modern philosophy, subscribed to it. "Good sense," he wrote, "is of all things in the world the most equally distributed. . . . In this I follow the common opinion of philosophers, who say that the question of more or less occurs only in the sphere of the *accidents*, and does not affect the *forms* or natures of the *individuals* in the same species."

At the time of the Enlightenment the political implications of this doctrine were explicitly drawn, many philosophers formally declaring their faith in the natural equality or equal ability of all men and urging that everyone be given equal education and equal social opportunities. Fourier's belief that when French society was properly organized France would produce thirty million scientists as great as Newton and thirty million poets as great as Shakespeare dramatically illustrates the Enlightenment confidence in the doctrine of natural equality. And a text from Helvetius clearly indicates the true parentage of this faith: "Who can be sure that differences of education do not produce the differences we find between minds; that men are not like those trees of the same species whose seed, indestructible and absolutely the same, never being sown in exactly the same soil, nor exposed to precisely the same winds, or the same sun, or the same rain, must necessarily in developing assume an infinity of different forms!"

When in the middle of the nineteenth century Darwin exploded the doctrine of fixed species and when still later conclusive evidence was adduced showing that individuals vary enormously in native abilities, humanism as a philosophical doctrine suffered blows from which it has never recovered. None the less in modified versions it has persisted up to the present time.

In later versions mankind is regarded, not as an Aristotelian essence, but as an historically evolving chain of generations. The means by which the individual identifies with the race is no longer intellection, but imagination or empathy. The satisfaction promised to the individual is not an Aristotelian type of intellectual immortality, but an emotional satisfaction accompanying universal love. Finally, the individual is urged to submerge his interests and those of other individuals in the interests of mankind at large, not because all individuals are equally well endowed in natural ability, but rather because all individuals are assumed to be equal in *moral* worth.

The basis of the existentialist attack upon humanism is quite clearly the anguish of the here and now. If man is tied to a limited region of space and time, then he cannot identify with mankind at large, even if there were a moral obligation to do so and even if personal satisfaction could be thereby derived. The Aristotelian concept of mankind is an empty abstraction; there can be no vital relationship between a concrete individual and an empty abstraction. And the situation is not improved by conceiving of mankind historically as a succession of generations; for in so far as the destiny of mankind so conceived is still hidden from the gaze of the particular individual, the concept is indeterminate. The future of mankind is unknown, and the individual cannot identify with the unknown. Neither is the situation improved by substituting imagination or empathy for intellectual understanding as the means by which the union between individual and mankind is effected. The human power of imagination is even narrower in scope than the power of intellection. We may know abstractly a great deal about a foreign people with whom we have had no personal contact; but it is next to impossible imaginatively to recreate the conditions of their life without personal contact. There is hardly a single great novel whose locale and characters are not of a kind well known to the author through personal contact.

As for universal love, how can the individual love beings he does not personally know? The humanists are right in saying that universal love would depend upon some kind of imaginative identification with others; but the things we imagine best are the things nearest to home, since imagination is a concomitant of passion, and passion the result of personal concern. Rousseau once posed the case of a man given the power to secure enormous benefits for himself and immediate associates by merely willing the death of a Chinese mandarin of whom he knew nothing. Granting that there is no possibility of detection, who, he asks, would fail to use this power!

Universal respect is equally impossible, and for similar reasons. How can we respect beings we do not know as individuals? And how could we put the interests of mankind in general, i.e., of a multitude of beings we do not know, above our own? We cannot know their interests. To think that we can is to betray an unjustifiable pride in the human intellect and at the same time to deny by implication the one universal feature of human beings which might conceivably entitle all equally to respect, namely their freedom of choice.

The existentialist attack becomes even more impressive when to the considerations stemming from the experience of anguish are added considerations based upon the existentialist value orientation, especially the contention that only an honest recognition of human limitations will permit us to experience those values which our condition permits. The man, for instance, who ignores the limitations of the here and now by pretending to respect all mankind succeeds only in depriving individual men of even the possibility of respect. As Nietzsche pointed out, respect is by nature recognition of superior merit, and if all men are equally respected, then nobody is respected. To respect everybody is to respect nobody, not even the man of superior worth. The only possible effect of preaching universal respect is to introduce an era of mass culture in which everybody is the loser—the men of merit because ordinary men will attack them with insane fury in a hopeless effort to prove their equality, and the ordinary men themselves because the men of merit will return the attack and enslave them.

Similar remarks can be made about love. Marcel and Jaspers have repeatedly asserted that he who loves mankind does not love at all. Love is by definition a personal relationship between two concrete beings. There can be no personal relationship between an individual human being and the abstraction humanity. The person who in the name of humanity sacrifices himself or others is not acting out of universal love;

he is merely betraying his own incapacity for personal love. In *The Brothers Karamazov* Dostoyevsky posed the following problem: If God offered the whole of mankind eternal salvation on condition that a single, innocent child suffer eternally, ought mankind to accept the bargain? How can the person who has so little love for this child that he will condemn her to eternal torment cast his vote in favor of the bargain and claim that his motivation is universal love of mankind?

Anguish of Freedom

The expression "anguish of freedom" may seem puzzling. Is not freedom something wholly desirable? The bafflement will be largely dispelled by fixing firmly in mind that the type of freedom before which the existentialist stands in anguish is not the ability to achieve chosen goals. If one has decided to be a doctor and is free to do so in the sense that there are no obstacles in his way (he has the money, a good medical school has accepted him, there are no other commitments which take priority, etc.), it would be silly to speak of anguish. But even with this qualification the expression may still seem puzzling. Why should anyone be anguished simply because he has the ability to choose? The wider the range of choice, the more possible lines of conduct from which the individual may select, the greater will be his sense of power and mastery. The answer to this last question is that "anguish of freedom" is a somewhat misleading expression. What is called the anguish of freedom would more accurately be called "anguish before the necessity of choosing." The anguish of freedom is really anguish over the fact that one *must* choose. And this is something that everybody can understand. Important decisions affecting the entire course of one's life are rarely made without some form of mental distress; and it is a commonplace of contemporary social criticism that modern-day men try very hard to escape this form of distress by having others (the state, public opinion, or the corporation) make decisions for them.

This does not mean, however, that the anguish of freedom is to be identified with the mental distress which a responsible person experiences when he is obliged to make a crucial decision. The anguish of freedom arises only with the realization that one must always decide for oneself and that efforts to shift the burden of responsibility upon others are necessarily self-defeating. Not to choose is also to choose, for even if we deliver our power of decision to others, we are still responsible for having done so. It is always the individual who decides that others will choose for him. At times he may dull the awareness of his original and inalienable responsibility, but he can never wholly suppress that awareness. It will always be there even on the surface of consciousness as a vague sense of guilt or uneasy feeling of personal inadequacy.

The relationship between the anguish of freedom and the other two forms of anguish are subtle and complex. As already seen, the anguish before the here and now leads inevitably to the anguish of freedom. Since the individual is tied to a limited portion of space and time and since he is actively engaged in the historical process as a unique and irreducible factor, he must be free. For the existentialists freedom of choice means autonomy of choice, and autonomy of choice means undetermined choice. But what does it mean to say that man's choices are undetermined if not that he is a unique and irreducible part of the historical or social scene? If man makes history, it is because man himself is not made by history.

The relationship between these two forms of anguish also works in reverse. If man is free to choose, then he cannot merge with the whole of being. "Every choice is a choice of finitude," as Sartre says, since every choice involves elimination. The voracious appetite for being displayed by Spinoza and Hegel cannot coexist with respect for human freedom. If one chooses to be a doctor, then one chooses the world of a doctor. Everything about one's life—the source of one's income, one's daily work, daily surroundings, relationships with others, even the odors one breathes—has a particular character and will separate one from the world of those who have made a different choice. The doctor cannot see things *sub specie aeternitatis* without ceasing to be a doctor. His attention will have to be focused on individual human beings and their specific ailments.

The relationship between the anguish of being and the anguish of freedom is also reciprocal. In rough and general terms it can be put this way: To the extent that man is free, it is by his choices or decisions that the natural and social world becomes meaningful. A shivering lump of human flesh in the agonies of death means one thing for the doctor who has chosen to take a professional interest in it, but something very different for the man who has decided to call that lump of flesh his wife. It follows from this that in so far as a man is conscious of his freedom, his natural and social environment will take on the character of a brute fact, something contingent, absurd, alien; for consciousness of freedom is also consciousness of the fact that meaning comes to being through us. In Sartrean terms the consciousness or anguish of freedom is the means by which "the world" dissolves and "being-in-itself" is revealed. Conversely, the consciousness or anguish of being is the means by which we take cognizance of our freedom; for it is only when the world dissolves and being-in-itself stands revealed to us that we understand the utter emptiness of our own being as persons in so far as we are not engaged in a process of choice, i.e., in so far as we fail to construct for ourselves a habitable world.

Of all the existentialists Sartre has most stressed the anguish of freedom. The manner in which he has developed the set of ideas connected with this form of anguish has, therefore, a special interest. Sartre's major antagonists are the Thomistic-minded Christians and the Marxists. For them, as for determinists of every variety, man is so made by God or Nature, as the case may be, that he automatically pursues certain goals. He has a given nature which determines him to realize certain ends. The motives of his acts are, so to speak, "ready-made and prehuman." According to Sartre, however, man freely chooses his own goals and in terms of his choice of goals confers upon the ready-made and prehuman whatever meaning it may possibly have. The determinist asks Sartre: If my action "cannot be understood either in terms of the state of the world or in terms of my past taken as something irremediable, how can it possibly not be gratuitous?"[9] Sartre counters by asking: If the world and my past are not understood in terms of my personally chosen projects, how can the world and my past possibly not be gratuitous? The determinist, in other words, says that man's life would be vain and meaningless if it did not have a place in an objective and meaningful scheme of things. Sartre says the universe would be vain and meaningless if man did not endow it with meaning by an unceasing act of choice.

It follows from Sartre's fundamental contention that "no state of fact, whatever it may be (political or economic structure of society, psychical 'state,' etc.), is by itself capable of motivating any act whatsoever."[10]   He invites us to consider the case of the individual who revolts against certain bitter material conditions in his life.   According to the common-sense point of view, in this respect similar to that of the determinist, these objective conditions constitute in themselves a sufficient cause for the action of the individual.   But common opinion, if pressed, will recognize that the objective situation stimulates action only to the extent that the individual is aware of a better state of affairs in terms of which the actual circumstances of his life are seen to be unsatisfactory.

In order to reconcile the recognition of this fact with the belief that external circumstances are sufficient to cause action, the determinist and the common man tend to explain the awareness of a better situation to be realized in the future as itself a strict causal consequence of the objective situation. Sartre, however, finds it necessary to "invert the common opinion and recognize that it is not the severity of a situation or the sufferings it imposes which give rise to the conception of another state of affairs . . .; on the contrary, it is from the day we conceive a different state of affairs that a new light falls upon our misery and our sufferings and that we *decide* they are no longer tolerable."[11]   In so far as man is a part of nature or "sunk in the historical situation, it will not even occur to him to conceive the defects or the insufficiencies of the given political or economic organization. . . . He grasps it in its fullness of being and cannot even imagine that it could be different."[12] The worker subjected to extreme hardship "will have to go beyond the objective situation and his suffering, to put a distance between himself and it and to effect a double nihilation: on the one hand he will have to pose an ideal state of affairs as a pure nothingness with respect to the present; on the other hand he will have to pose the present situation as a nothingness with respect to that ideal state of affairs."[13]

Resuming this argument briefly, human action is always to be interpreted as a reaction against an existing state of affairs and an effort to establish an ideal state of affairs. It implies both the recognition of a given situation as undesirable and the conception of an ideal situation as desirable. These two factors appear simultaneously, complementing one another; but neither of them can be determined by the objective situation in itself, since "no state of fact can determine consciousness to grasp it as a negative quantity or as lack."[14]

In order to advance further into Sartre's thinking it will be necessary to introduce a bit of his technical terminology and to clarify his conception of man. Opposed to the being of fact or being-in-itself stands the being of consciousness, which Sartre also calls "being-for-itself." The choice of the term being-in-itself for objective fact is easily understood, since this region of being is merely a network of undifferentiated things and objects which point to no ideal value, which refer dumbly and meaninglessly to themselves alone. The choice of the term being-for-itself is also easily understood, since for the existentialists consciousness is fundamentally characterized by purpose or intention. As the names of these two regions of being indicate, they are radically opposed to one another. The in-itself has the properties of Platonic Being: its timelessness, self-sufficiency, and immutability. It is being par excellence. The for-itself, on the other hand, is a temporal being with all the properties of Platonic Becoming. Its existence is derivative and unstable. In the full sense of the term it *is* not. It merely exists. Etymologically, the term "existence" means to stand out of, and to mark their close adherence to the etymological meaning of the term existentialists frequently hyphenate the word, writing "ex-istence" instead of "existence."

Despite the radical duality of the in-itself and the for-itself, man or the "human reality," to use Sartre's favorite expression, is itself made up of this duality. Whereas the in-itself is defined as a being "which is what it is," man or the human reality is defined as a being "which is what it is not and is not what it is." Man is, as the determinists say, an empirical being born at such and such a time and living under such and such conditions. In this sense, he is what he is. But in another sense man is not this empirical being living in a given situation, assuming a place in a chain of empirical facts going back to his birth or further. He is also a complex of desires or pattern of values which does not empirically exist, which empirically is not, since its factual being, if it ever has one, must await realization in the future. In this sense, man is not what he is.

It is important to realize that although the Sartrean definition of human reality is most definitely paradoxical, the paradox is largely verbal. It can best be understood as a forceful rhetorical device for illustrating the irreducibility of the distinction between the being of fact and the being of ideals or values and for emphasizing that it is man's fate to be simultaneously both types of being. It is especially important to bear this in mind in interpreting a second, but strictly convertible, Sartrean definition of man. Man, says Sartre, is a "nihilating nothingness." If again we follow the common-sense approach and take as the primary definition of being the being of fact, that is, the being which points to no ideal goal and which is simply what it is without reference to any system of values, then conscious human existence is pure nothingness; for consciousness is nothing more than a complex of desires tending toward the realization of an ideal state in the future. This ideal state of affairs being nonexistent, the desire or motive behind it is likewise nonexistent, the desire and its ideal value being but two aspects of a single phenomenon. "The motive can only be understood by its end, that is to say, by a nonexistent; the motive of action, therefore, is in itself a negative quantity."[15] But this nothingness of desire and of value, of motive and end of human behavior, can only exist for the individual in so far as he nihilates the being which he is, i.e., the objective situation and the conditions which constitute his being of fact, by posing a better ideal world in terms of which the objective situation and his empirical being are viewed as nothingness. In other words, to exist, man must perpetually transcend himself.

If this theory is correct, it necessarily follows that we must abandon all hope of attaining a secure and harmonious integration with the surrounding objective world. In desiring, valuing, and existing we necessarily reject the world in which we live. All projects which are turned toward acceptance of the world as constituted imply a diminution of our being and a loss of self-respect in so far as they tend to reduce the tension which constitutes the necessary condition of free human action. Freedom is a "lack of being with respect to a given being."[16] In technical language Sartre expresses this fact by saying that the human reality is a "detotalized totality" of in-itself and for-itself. Man is both in-itself and for-itself, but the two dimensions of his being are radically different. There is a deep rent in his being, and it will never be closed.

If Sartre's theory is correct, it also follows that "man is the foundation without foundation" of his values. "Nothing," says Sartre, "absolutely nothing, justifies me in adopting this or that value, this or that scale of values. As the being through whom values exist, I am incapable of justification."[17] The price of human existence is alienation—from God, from nature, and from society. Man is "condemned to freedom."

At this point the following problem arises. Let it be granted that man is both an empirical being and a bearer of values, that the human reality is a detotalized totality, and that only through undetermined choices by the for-itself do values and meanings arise. Let it even be granted that a realization of all this will inevitably produce psychic distress. Need we be quite so distressed about it as the existentialists would apparently have us be? Many people have faced up to the responsibility of choosing for themselves without making all this commotion about the anguish of freedom.

Sartre's answer to this question will lead us to his most thoroughly pessimistic conclusions—but also to his theory of salvation. Although Sartre denies that man has an essence or nature if by this one means that God or Nature has predetermined him to pursue certain goals to the exclusion of others, he does not deny that man has an essence or nature if by this one means that it is possible to discern certain universal and necessary structures within the human condition. Two of these structures are revealed through the anguish of freedom. Through this form of anguish man learns not only that he is free but also that his existence as a free being is characterized by precariousness and lack. It is no more solid than the thin crust of meaning which we call the world. At the root of our being as freedom is nothingness. We cannot, therefore, totally renounce the aspiration to participate in the security of the in-itself, its wholeness, its massiveness, its positivity. Dread of our freedom and desire to coincide with the in-itself is a fundamental structure of our being and must somehow manifest itself in every project of being, however personal and individual it may be in other respects. Metaphysically stated: "The for-itself is the being who is to himself his own lack of being, and the being which the for-itself lacks is the in-itself. The for-itself comes into being as a nihilation of the in-itself, and that nihilation must be defined as a project toward the in-itself: between the nihilated in-itself and the projected in-itself stands the for-itself and nothingness. Thus the goal and end of the nihilation that I am is the in-itself. Thus the human reality is desire of being-in-itself."[18]

The second universal and necessary structure of the human condition is complementary to the first, but tends to cancel it out. On the one hand, as we have seen, anguish reveals a dread of one's necessary existence as freedom and thus a desire to coincide with the in-itself. But at one and the same time anguish reveals a dread of being swallowed up by the in-itself. Because in anguish man sees the in-itself for what it is, he realizes that its security is a brute fact, contingent, gratuitous, meaningless, and therefore valueless. The in-itself does not have the consciousness to appreciate its positivity and fullness of being; it cannot experience it as security or value. It can, in fact, experience nothing. It is quite simply what it is. Man, therefore, whose very existence is derived from his being as projector of values, cannot desire the in-itself as such. He stands in dread before the brute fact of the in-itself, his whole existence being a revolt against it, a nihilation of its contingence and absurdity. The in-itself which the for-itself desires "could not be pure in-itself, contingent and absurd, in every way comparable to that which it meets and which it nihilates."[19]

It is precisely this ambivalence in our attitude toward it which explains the ambiguity in Sartre's descriptions of the in-itself. By virtue of our yearning for it, it takes on a soft and voluptuous aspect like the womb of Mother Earth. But in the act of recoiling against it, we project our firm determination to safeguard freedom and construe it as a hard and resisting solid.

What man really desires is the in-itself as a value. Man wants to be a fact-value, an in-itself-for-itself without duality. It is not enough for him to be a detotalized totality; he wants to be a totality without fissure. He wants consciousness without risk, security with the consciousness to appreciate it. He wants to have, like God the Father, the properties of serenity, eternity, and immutability, but he also wants the intensely human properties and capacity for suffering of God the Son. "The being which constitutes the object of desire of the for-itself is, then, an in-itself which would be to itself its own foundation. . . . Thus one may best describe the fundamental project of the human reality in saying that man is the being who projects to be God. . . . And if man possesses a preontological comprehension of the being of God, it is neither the great spectacle of nature nor the power of society which have given it to him. Rather God . . . represents the permanent limits in terms of which man understands his being. To be man is to strive to be God, or, if one prefers, man fundamentally desires to be God."[20] Man is "haunted" by the ideal of the "*ens causa sui* which the religions call God."[21] In still other language: "It is as if the world, man and man-in-the-world express an abortive attempt to become God. It is as if the in-itself and the for-itself reveal themselves in a state of disintegration with respect to an ideal synthesis. Not that the integration has ever taken place, but precisely on the contrary because it is permanently suggested and permanently impossible."[22] Unfortunately, "the idea of God is contradictory and we lose ourselves in vain: man is a useless passion."[23]

For obvious reasons the attempt to escape these fundamental aspects of the human condition through the classical philosophical devices will necessarily fail. And so will the attempt to escape them through the pursuit of wealth, pleasure, and prestige. The specific desires or projects of man invariably exemplify the fundamental desire to be God. "The desire of a particular object is not the simple desire of this object; it is the desire to be united with the object in an internal relation."[24] Love, for instance, "is a fundamental relation of the for-itself to the world and to itself . . . through a particular woman; the woman represents only a conducting body which is placed in the circuit."[25] The same thing holds for the acquisition of wealth. "Appropriation is nothing save the symbol of the ideal of the for-itself or value. The dyad, for-itself possessing and in-itself possessed, is the same as that being which is in order to possess itself and whose possession is in its own creation—God . . . My original desire of being my own foundation is never satisfied through appropriation any more than Freud's patient satisfies his Oedipus complex when he dreams that a soldier kills the Czar."[26]

This conception of the human condition is by no means specifically Sartrean. Sartre, as the most recent of the great existentialist figures, has developed it most fully and has devised the most elaborate technical terminology to express it. The conception, however, was already present in Kierkegaard, the so-called father of existentialism, for whom "the predicament of the existing individual" arises "from his being a synthesis of the temporal and eternal."²⁷ For Kierkegaard, no less than for Sartre, the temporal and the eternal are contradictory categories, and a being who is simultaneously both is indeed in a predicament. He cannot but desire the completion of being which God alone possesses, but at the same time he cannot but cling passionately to the pleasures and pains of finite existence. This paradox in man's nature approximates to the God-Man paradox, i.e., the paradox of Christ, which is at the very center of Kierkegaard's philosophy. It is impossible that a perfect and immutable being who lacks nothing should create; but it is even more impossible that a perfect and immutable being who lacks nothing should be incarnated in flesh, walk the earth, suffer, and die. Yet if Christ is not wholly divine and wholly human at one and the same time he fails to be a fit object of worship, precisely because man himself aspires to be wholly divine without loss of his humanity. Sartre's views up to this point are hardly more than a secularized version of Kierkegaard.

It is difficult to conceive of a blacker picture of the human condition; but Sartre can no more resist the temptation of appending a theory of salvation to his analysis of the human condition than the Christians and the Marxists. Unfortunately the analysis of Sartre's theory of salvation is somewhat complicated by the fact that the theory has not to date been treated systematically and at length. It was presented dramatically in Sartre's play *The Flies*, where the hero Orestes defies Jupiter in the name of freedom and heroically takes upon himself the burden of the human condition. It was also sketched briefly in the last pages of *Being and Nothingness*, where Sartre promised a separate work dealing exclusively with his "ethics of deliverance and salvation." But the promised book has not yet appeared, and the brief sketch in *Being and Nothingness* is couched in somewhat cautious terms. In fact, the clearest statement of it to be found there is in interrogative form.

Briefly, the theory is this: Man's project to be God is a

universal structure of his being and a necessary motive of his behavior, but it is not necessarily the final motive of his behavior and it is not an absolute or exclusive structure of his being. Man is capable of refusing to be "an accomplice" of the cosmic process; man may defy God and the values which haunt him. In doing so, he finds his salvation. The explicit consciousness of the human situation and of man's total freedom as revealed in anguish gives to the individual a new perspective in terms of which the fundamental structure of his being may be completely altered through a "radical conversion." As Sartre himself puts it in the last pages of *Being and Nothingness*, the analyses which he has there made should

> reveal to the moral agent that he is the being by whom values come into existence. It is then that his freedom will become conscious of itself and will reveal itself in anguish as the unique source of value and the nothingness through which the world exists. As soon as the search for being and the appropriation of the in-itself stand revealed as his possibilities, it (the for-itself) will grasp in and through anguish that these possibilities imply a background of other possibilities. But up to this point, although possibilities may be chosen and revoked *ad libitum*, the theme which made the unity of all his choices of possibilities was the value or ideal presence of the *ens causa sui*. . . . Is it possible that freedom take itself as value in so far as it is the source of all values or must it necessarily define itself with respect to a transcendent value which haunts it?[28]

Rather than follow Sartre further in his own words it will be best to adopt an unorthodox procedure and quote Mlle. Simone de Beauvoir as to what happens when freedom chooses to emancipate itself. Her statement of the doctrine, appearing in dogmatic terms some years after the publication of *Being and Nothingness*, has the advantage of brevity and may safely be accepted as a faithful reflection of Sartre's own belief. Mlle. de Beauvoir states:

> In his vain endeavour to be God, man causes himself to exist as man; . . . if he accepts to be satisfied with this existence, he coincides perfectly with himself. He is not permitted to exist without tending toward that being which he will never be, but it is possible for him to will that tension itself with the failure that it involves. His being is lack of being, but precisely this mode of being is existence. In Hegelian terms one might say that there is here a negation of the negation through which positivity is re-established; man causes himself to be lack,

but he may deny the lack as lack and affirm himself as positive existence. He assumes failure. And the action condemned as effort to be recovers its validity as manifestation of existence. However what is involved here is not so much a Hegelian synthesis as a conversion. In Hegel the terms overcome are conserved only as abstract moments, whereas we hold that existence still remains negativity in the positive affirmation of itself. . . . The failure is not overcome, but assumed; existence affirms itself as an absolute which must seek in itself its justification. . . . In order to attain his truth man must not attempt to dissipate but on the contrary to accomplish the ambiguity of his being. He finds himself only to the extent that he consents to remain at a distance from himself.[29]

Here again we find in technical Sartrean language the fundamental existentialist conviction that although life is inescapably tragic and man necessarily doomed to frustration, values sufficient to make life worth the effort are available to him within the very heart of despair.

Among the chief sources of Sartre's views are the Hegelian analysis of the unhappy consciousness and the Hegelian concept of finite life as marked by inevitable contradictions and conflicts. Whereas, however, Hegel regarded the unhappy consciousness as merely a stage in the progress of the human spirit and the conflicts of finite life as mere surface phenomena which the immutable Absolute Spirit ultimately mediates, Sartre allows no surpassing of the unhappy consciousness and totally rejects the notion of an Absolute Spirit. The whole of things does not form an integrated totality and there is no ground of finite being which finally reconciles its contradictions.

Another and much more important source of Sartre's views is Nietzsche. In the later development of his thought Nietzsche hit upon the notion of the Eternal Return. Since the number of elements in the universe is finite and since time is infinite, it follows according to Neitzsche that every existing combination of elements will necessarily recur over and over again in the future. Each of our individual lives with all its frustrations, dangers, and heartbreak will be indefinitely repeated. This is our fate, and it is a hard one. But, says Nietzsche, man must become a "holy yea-sayer"; he must learn to love his fate. The doctrine of the Eternal Return and the doctrine that struggle and danger are necessary facts of life were thus joined with the doctrine known as *amor fati*, or love of fate.

The originality of Sartre's and Nietzsche's position can best be seen by contrasting it with the position of the Stoics and of Spinoza. The existentialists agree with the Stoics in urging man to abandon the hope of fulfillment through finite desires, but unlike the Stoics they do not urge the abandonment of desire itself. On the contrary, the abandonment of finite desire is neither possible nor praiseworthy, desire being not only an essential structure of human existence but also a necessary condition of value. To abandon desire is to reduce the tension which constitutes our dignity as human beings. The existentialists also agree with Spinoza in urging man to accept without regret the ultimate and inescapable realities of life and to seek a kind of fullness of being or coincidence with himself. But for Spinoza the ultimate reality was the whole of things conceived as an harmonious and stable unit, and man achieved fullness of being or coincidence with self by merging his finite personality with infinite being, the true ground of his being as self. The existentialists, on the contrary, conceive of being dualistically, and for them coincidence with self or fullness of being consists in joyfully accepting or assuming one's finitude.

III. Reason and Unreason

From almost all sides existentialism has been proclaimed a movement of irrationalism. Political liberals contemn the movement on this ground above all others. They will not forget Heidegger's brief involvement with Nazism and sometimes argue that fascism would be the logical outcome if the tenets of the movement were widely accepted. At the same time Marxists often see in existentialism a last desperate effort of the *petite bourgeoisie*, a group doomed by the objective march of history but anxious for one last fling. One Marxist, taking up this line of attack, called existentialism a "carnival of subjectivity," a charge which infuriated Sartre and which his latest major work, *Critique of Dialectical Reason*, was designed to answer.

On the other hand, a relatively large group of artists, writers, intellectuals, and others have given unstinting praise to the movement precisely because of what they take to be its irrationalism. Members of the beat movement, which is a degenerate form of existentialism for the weak-minded and weak-willed products of America's educational institutions, presently prefer soporific dope to kicks, the in-itself to the for-itself, Buddha to Sartre. But the Beats' sympathy for continental existentialism in so far as they see in it a sanction for incoherence and self-pity will not be questioned.

It would, of course, be idle to deny the legitimacy of regarding existentialism as in some sense irrationalistic. Kierkegaard is certainly no blood brother of the Beats, but neither was it a country cousin who cried: "Oh, the sins of passion and of the heart—how much nearer to salvation than the sins of reason. . . . Yes, I believe that I would give myself to Satan so that he might show me every abomination, every sin in its most

64

frightful form."[1] Nor have they any reason to feel great hostility toward Sartre, who found Jean Genet, France's latest self-styled "black saint" (homosexual, petty criminal, police informer, etc.), worthy of seven hundred pages of close and sympathetic analysis.

The antipathy of liberals and Marxists, whose faith in reason is closely allied to their faith in the behavioral sciences and historical progress, is at least as well grounded from their standpoint as the sympathy of the Beats is from theirs. None of the existentialists profess sympathy for liberalism, and Sartre alone among them professes sympathy for Marxism. In the *Critique of Dialectical Reason*, however, Sartre himself attacks Kierkegaard and Jaspers as belonging to "a certain element of the European bourgeoisie which wishes to justify its privileges by claiming a spiritual aristocracy, by fleeing . . . into an exquisite subjectivity and allowing itself to be fascinated by an ineffable present in order to ignore its future."[2] Moreover, his own attempt in the same work to reconcile the ideas propounded in *Being and Nothingness* with his personal brand of Marxism is incomplete and less than satisfactory as far as it goes.

So much granted, however, it remains to be said that the terms "rationalism" and "irrationalism" are among the most ambiguous in the vocabulary of every civilized people and that absolutely nothing of any real interest has been said so long as the sense in which these terms are used is unspecified. Empiricism, the philosophical movement whose present-day members are most vociferous in denouncing existentialism as antirationalistic, was not long ago denounced in the same terms; and while some early empiricists bore the label of antirationalist with a strident pride very much as Kierkegaard and sometimes Jaspers have done, others adopted Sartre's tactic and claimed to be defending *true* rationality. It is interesting to speculate whether future descendants of the existentialists will not have to carry the banners of reason against some new enemy who dares to conceive the truth differently from them.

In order to make any sense at all out of the controversies which rage around this issue it will be necessary to consider three questions. First, what and how much can mankind expect to know? The answer to this question will depend largely upon one's theory of being, or ontology. Second, what are the methods by which men may acquire whatever knowledge is possible? The answer to this question will depend upon one's theory of knowledge, or epistemology. Third, how valuable would the knowledge which man can hope to acquire be to a living human being? The answer to this question will depend upon one's theory of value, or axiology. In general the type of answer given to any one of these questions is accompanied by a specific type of answer to the others. By limiting the discussion to only the major historical positions and by remaining at a fairly high level of generality, it will thus be necessary to consider only three major movements: the movement known technically in the history of philosophy as rationalism, running from Plato through Descartes to Spinoza and Hegel; the movement known technically as empiricism, running from the seventeenth-century English philosophers Bacon, Hobbes, and Locke up to present-day philosophizing in the Anglo-American world; and finally existentialism itself.

Philosophical Rationalism

To the first question, "What and how much can man expect to know?" the rationalists answered: Whatever is eternal, necessary, immutable, and universal. The temporal, contingent, mutable, and particular cannot be known. To the second question, "What are the methods by which men may acquire knowledge?" the rationalists answered: Through the mind or intellect. Through the physical senses almost nothing can be known, their role is wholly subsidiary. To the third question, "What value has knowledge for the living individual?" their answer was twofold: Knowledge, they say, is valuable in its own right. Through knowledge, be it the contemplation of eternal Ideas and Aristotelian essences or a vision of things *sub specie aeternitatis*, the individual experiences the greatest pleasure of which he is capable and becomes immortal. But also knowledge is valuable because through it man learns how to conduct himself in the world of becoming. A good life, like a good political state such as Plato's Republic, is one modeled upon or patterned after eternal and universal forms.

Two major arguments have been used to prove the existence of eternal objects knowable only through the mind. The first and most important of these is drawn from reflection upon mathematics. The great mathematical invention of the Greeks, who were perhaps the most visually minded people in history, was systematic geometry. In the development of systematic geometry the Greeks were led to adopt the notion of perfect geometrical figures (perfect circles, perfectly straight lines, etc.). These, it was said, were the objects of the mathematician's study, and since systematic geometry actually existed as a science, these objects must exist. Moreover, the science of geometry could not be as exact as it is if the objects under study were constantly changing.

But what is the ontological status of these objects? Where do they exist? They cannot exist in nature or the world of becoming, conceived as the world revealed to the physical senses. All the spherical shapes and straight lines in nature are imperfect. At the same time, it is perfectly obvious that all bodies in nature are subject to change; wind, rain, the touch of human hands, or some other natural event is bound to affect them.

Do they, then, exist in the human imagination? Again the answer is no. For one thing, images in the mind are invariably images of physical realities. The imagination is limited to reproducing elements in the physical world. The blind man cannot imagine colors, and the deaf man cannot imagine sounds. The imagination is free only in the sense that it can combine images of physical things in ways that nature has not done—constructing, for instance, an image of Pegasus by combining the image of a horse and the image of wings. For another thing, the geometer's objects include figures for which there are not even imperfect copies in nature or in the imagination. The geometer, for instance, knows an abstract triangle, a triangle which is neither a right triangle nor a scalene triangle nor an isosceles triangle. But who can form a mental picture of such a triangle? Similarly, a chiliagon or thousand-sided figure is an object of mathematical calculation; but how does the image of a chiliagon differ from the image of a centagon or hundred-sided figure? Clearly, the imagination cannot draw distinctions as sharp as those of the geometer. Consider also the concept of zero. Surely, zero does not exist either in nature or in the imagination. We can, of course, visualize the figure "0" or the word "zero," but not the thing for which it stands.

Are the objects of mathematical study, then, concepts or ideas, as opposed to images? Do the objects of mathematical speculation reside in the human intellect, as opposed to the human imagination? Again the answer is no. The human mind, as human, is finite and mutable, whereas the objects of mathematical speculation are eternal and unchanging. That the human mind is mutable is sufficiently evidenced by the fact that in order to make inferences it must proceed stepwise. It acts, as the expression "operations of the mind" indicates. In technical language, the human intellect is "discursive." Besides, if the objects of mathematic speculation were within the human mind, as marbles are within a box, if we already possessed them, why do we speak of grasping or seizing them, of making them ours?

There are only three places where the objects of mathematical knowledge may be located. The first is the heaven of eternal Ideas, a realm which transcends both individual men and nature. This, of course, was Plato's belief. The second is a nonhuman, nondiscursive, and universal mind such as that in which Aristotle said human beings can participate or such as the Christians believed God's mind to be. St. Augustine, for instance, eliminated Plato's transcendental realm of Ideas by conceiving of the Ideas as absorbed in the divine intellect. Thirdly, they might be located in nature—on condition that nature be conceived, not as the world directly revealed to the physical senses, but as a world lying behind or beyond the world revealed to the senses and itself accessible only to the intellect. This was roughly the position of Aristotle. In the last chapter it was said that Aristotle located his essences in the world of becoming, but this is not strictly correct if by the world of becoming one means the world revealed to the physical senses. The essences, according to Aristotle, could not be directly apprehended by the senses. This was also the position of Descartes, who was much clearer on this score than Aristotle. The real sun, said Descartes, is the sun of the mathematician or scientist. The sun which appears to the senses, an object of small dimensions and changing colors, is merely an illusory appearance. This was also the position of Spinoza, Leibniz, Hegel, and nineteenth-century scientism.

Having established to their satisfaction that the objects of mathematical knowledge are eternal and immutable objects, the rationalists did one of two things. Either they declared that all genuine knowledge is mathematical in character or else they declared that nonmathematical knowledge is similar to mathematical knowledge in that its proper objects are eternal and immutable entities which transcend the world and to which man has access only through the intellect.

To support this latter view the second major argument was invoked. This second argument consists in observing that words are singular whereas the physically observable things for which words are commonly said to stand are plural, and that words are constant in meaning whereas the physical objects to which words are applied are mutable. The clearest formulation of this doctrine is found in several of the early Platonic dialogues wherein Socrates attempts to explicate the meaning of words such as "courage" and "temperance." "Courage," he says, is one word with a constant meaning; but courageous men and courageous acts are many and changing. The meaning of the word cannot, therefore, be found in the mutable and particular world of becoming. Particular beings are referred to by a word only in so far as those particular beings resemble or in some way participate in the object which constitutes the true meaning of the word; properly speaking, the meaning of the term is never to be found in the physically observable world.

It will be noted that as the role of the physical senses is diminished, so is the role of the sensuous world of sights and sounds in which we normally live and about whose reality alone the ordinary man seems to care. But the physical senses and the ordinary man's world do still have some importance. Aristotle and St. Thomas both declared that nothing is in the intellect which is not first in the senses. The point of this declaration is that man can intuit universal essences only through physical exemplifications of them. Aristotle called this process of intuiting universal essences through individual instances induction, and it is not uncommon for beginning students of Aristotle to seize upon this word "induction" in

order to make an empiricist out of him.   In fact, however, the
Aristotelian use of the word "induction" is wholly different
from that of modern-day empiricists.   Though he uses the
term "induction" and talks a good bit more than Plato about
knowledge through the senses, Aristotle, and St. Thomas after
him, remain squarely within the Platonic tradition.

This last point is worth elaborating upon.   Plato was a
believer in preexistence, and according to him at some point
prior to physical birth we witnessed the eternal Ideas directly.
Unfortunately, just before physical incarnation we passed
through the waters of forgetfulness, and in our present physical
state as prisoners within the body we remember these Ideas only
when we behold their imperfect physical copies.   This is the
substance of Plato's famous doctrine of "knowledge through
reminiscence."   The description in the *Symposium* of our
ascent to the Idea of beauty through love of beautiful bodies
and beautiful souls is but an application of it.   The Christian
rationale for the use of images as an aid to meditation and the
Christian doctrine of the mystic ladder by which we mount to
God through contemplation of the various degrees of perfection in nature also derive from this source.   And so does
Aristotle's doctrine of induction, according to which we must
grasp essences through particular physical beings which
exemplify them.   In every case the physical object has worth,
less in itself than as a symbol or indicator of something beyond
it.   According to one very old Christian doctrine the physical
world is but a system of signs all of which point to God.

The chief difference between Plato, Aristotle, and St. Thomas
turns on the nature of the something toward which physical
objects ultimately point: transcendental Ideas, universal
essences, or God.   There are, however, other significant
differences in this connection.   One is that whereas Plato was
by traditional interpretation an extreme dualist who boldly
contrasted Being and Becoming, Aristotle and St. Thomas
tended to think in terms of degrees of being.   For Aristotle
essences may be graded according to degree of inclusiveness,
from the smallest species to the widest genus.   St. Thomas says
that God alone truly *is*; he alone has the full ontological
dignity of Being.   After God come the angels, and then man,
who is a little below the angels and a little above the beasts.
This doctrine of the degrees of being is also known as the

doctrine of "the great chain of being." Significantly, matter is invariably the last and least of the links in the chain.

Another area of disagreement finds Plato and Aristotle opposed to St. Thomas. Plato and Aristotle stated unequivocally that the rational intellect is man's highest faculty and that through the intellect man can come to participate in immortality while yet in the body. St. Thomas, as a Christian, could not go this far. Some of the Christian mystics claimed a kind of personal participation in the divinity, but the participation was not ordinarily effected through the intellect and in any case the Catholic Church has constantly denounced mysticism of this type as heretical. The creature cannot merge with the creator. St. Thomas contented himself with listing the intellect as the highest of man's *natural* faculties, the so-called theological virtues or faculties of faith, hope, and love being higher still. Through the intellect one can have partial access to God, but the intellect is neither the only mode of access nor in itself a sufficient one. None the less, St. Thomas must be counted among the rationalists. He did not, like St. Augustine, argue that since the fall reason will serve the individual only to the extent that the will has antecedently been turned toward the light by God's grace. According to St. Thomas the independent exercise of God-given reason can take man a considerable distance along the path to God.

For the inferior grade of knowing which has as its object the mutable, singular, and temporal things in the world of becoming, rationalists employ the term "opinion," the term "knowledge" being used narrowly and exclusively for the superior grade of knowing. As being is to knowledge, so becoming is to opinion. Knowledge is necessary, certain, and universal. Opinion is probable, uncertain, and particular.

Still another set of terms used to distinguish between the two types of knowledge is "a priori" and "a posteriori." A proposition, regardless of how we are led to entertain it, is said to be a priori if its truth or falsity can be certified without recourse to sense experience. The qualification "regardless of how we are led to entertain it" is important, since even according to the rationalists sense experience will often lead us to entertain a proposition without thereby rendering the knowledge of its truth or falsity any the less a priori. If, for instance, one is led to assert that all men are mortal because one has observed

Socrates and other individuals die, it does not necessarily follow that the proposition "All men are mortal" is not a priori. It suffices that the fact of death as observed through the physical senses not be needed to prove its truth. Propositions which are not a priori are, of course, a posteriori. A synonym for a posteriori knowledge is empirical knowledge.

A priori propositions fall into two classes. They are either immediately intuited or else deduced by principles of logic from immediately intuited propositions. According to classical rationalists the statements "Two parallel lines extended indefinitely will never meet" and "Either Socrates is mortal or Socrates is not mortal" are examples of immediately intuited a priori truths. The conclusions of any proof in a mathematical or logical system would be examples of deduced a priori truths.

The distinctive claim of the rationalists, however, is that there are many a priori truths, either directly intuited or deduced, other than those found in mathematical or logical systems as these are ordinarily conceived. Descartes, for instance, claimed "I think" is an immediately intuited a priori truth and he claimed that logical principles alone compel us to infer from it "I am." "I think, therefore I am," or *cogito, ergo sum*, is one of the cornerpieces of his philosophy. And by arguments which he believed to be of exactly the same type, though more complex, Descartes claimed to have proved the existence of God, the existence of an external world lying behind the veil of sense appearances, and the fundamental laws of nature which govern the external world. Aristotle claimed to intuit the essential properties of animal species, including man. Spinoza's chief work, *Ethics*, consists of a set of definitions, axioms, and theorems after the manner of Euclidean geometry. And Leibniz actually claimed that the day would come when instead of arguing about right and wrong we would simply "sit down and calculate."

If it can be established that the knowledge of mathematicians has as its basis eternal objects, why should not all knowledge be of the same kind? And if it can be established that words are constant and unchanging in meaning, then it is clear that the true meaning of words cannot be the physical objects to which they are applied. Their true meanings must also be eternal objects.

Empiricism

To the question "What can man know?" the empiricist answers: Particular beings and the relationships which obtain among them. To the question "How does man know?" the empiricist answers: Through the physical senses. To the question "Why should man want to know?" the answer is: For the sake of power, specifically power to transform the natural and social environment.

The empiricist movement is so overwhelmingly Anglo-American that the expression "British empiricism" for its early stages is almost redundant. During the eighteenth century empiricism was adopted enthusiastically by the Enlightenment thinkers, but they added nothing of importance to the doctrine and it never really took hold on the Continent. In the nineteenth and twentieth centuries Enlightenment ideas were incorporated by continental thinkers into systems such as humanism, Marxism, and scientism—all of which are more rationalistic than empiricistic.

The originators of empiricism are Francis Bacon, Thomas Hobbes, John Locke, and George Berkeley. The movement achieved maturity with David Hume in the mid-eighteenth century and has survived with vigor up to the present day. All of the important philosophical movements in twentieth-century England and America—pragmatism, positivism, phenomenalism, and the more recent movement known as analytic philosophy—are among its offspring. In its earlier stages empiricism was much more rationalistic than its innovators believed, and at times it has veered toward scientism. From the perspective of the present day, however, its major outlines and its true direction are unmistakable.

It was David Hume who first clearly and without compromise declared that there can be no genuine a priori knowledge outside the field of mathematics or logic and that all knowledge of fact is knowledge of particular beings or the relationships between particular beings. In the peroration to one of his major works Hume tells us that when we pick up a book of philosophy we should look to see whether it contains statements of empirical fact or abstract reasoning in mathematics or logic. If not, he says, "commit it to the flames," for it can contain nothing but "sophistry and illusion."

It was also Hume who first drew from these premises the logical conclusion that the totality of being was contingent in the sense that man cannot know why it is and cannot rationally attribute to it design or purpose.

Again, it was Hume who most loudly defended the view that all general knowledge of fact is ultimately based upon simple induction, i.e., observation of a repeated or recurrent relationship between two or more kinds of things under similar circumstances. For instance, we know that fire burns because we have observed what happens when we put a match to a piece of paper or put our hands in an open fire. We could never know this simply by intuiting the essence of fire, as Aristotle presumably believed. Nor could we know that this was generally the case from a single experiment, as Aristotle also appeared to believe. If the event fire had been conjoined to the event burning only once in human experience there would be no way of knowing whether this was the result of a law of nature or whether it was a mere accident. It is only because fire and burning have been observed to be regularly or repeatedly conjoined in experience that we can establish the truth of the general proposition that fire burns.

Finally, it was Hume who most insisted that all general knowledge of fact, knowledge of the so-called laws of nature, is merely probable. Even if two kinds of events have always been regularly conjoined in the past, there is no guarantee that they will continue to be conjoined in the future. The principle of induction by which we infer that types of events conjoined in the past will continue to be conjoined in the future is the foundation of our reasoning, but as Sartre said of an individual's choice of values it is a "foundation without foundation." The principle itself cannot be justified. We cannot know that being or nature is necessary or eternal, as Aristotle believed. And although there may be a God, we can have no knowledge of him or his purposes. We cannot, therefore, appeal to him, as did Descartes, in order to guarantee that the course of nature will remain uniform throughout all time.

The chief contribution of later empiricists was to provide a more plausible answer than Hume to the arguments whereby rationalists attempted to prove the existence of eternal objects or universals knowable only to the intellect. Elements of the answer can be found among the earlier empiricists, but it is chiefly twentieth-century empiricists, especially twentieth-century logical positivists, who worked out the final answer.

The first of the rationalist arguments was based upon the actual existence of mathematical and logical systems whose objects are neither physically observable things nor entities in the human mind and whose propositions are eternal and necessary truths. The second of their arguments was based upon the observation that the meaning of words is one and unchanging whereas the physically observable things which in ordinary life are denoted by these words are many and mutable. The empiricists answer both arguments in roughly the same way, but it will simplify the exposition to consider them separately and to begin with the answer to the second argument.

One part of the empiricist answer consists in pointing out that the rationalists have their facts wrong. The meaning of words is not necessarily either one or unchanging. Words are frequently ambiguous and they often take on new or different meanings in the course of time. The modern concept of courage is very different from that of the Greeks; and for the Greek term translated into English as "temperance" or "moderation" there is no precise equivalent in any of the modern languages. Had Socrates not been so convinced that every word had one unchanging meaning, he would perhaps have seen that the word "meaning" itself is ambiguous and that once one of the ambiguities in this term is cleared up, there is no longer any reason for assuming that words refer to eternal objects.

The ambiguity in question is that between meaning as "intension" and meaning as "extension." Roughly speaking, the extension of a term is the set of objects denoted by the term; the intension of a term is a human conception of some set of properties regarded as common to the objects denoted by the term and setting them off from other objects. The term "swan," for instance, means extensionally all of the individual birds which the term is used to refer to, while the intension of the term is our conception of some set of properties common and unique to these birds by virtue of which we consider ourselves justified in using the term "swan" to refer to them.

The extension of the term "swan" is obviously multiple and changing, but so is the intension. For a child the intension of the term "swan" probably consists of a set of properties such as whiteness, having a long neck, floating on ponds in public parks, etc. For the zoologist, on the other hand, the intension will be an altogether different set of properties. Moreover, if the zoologist found a more convenient principle of classification than the one currently employed or if through a slow evolutionary process the beings we now call swans were to change their fundamental properties, even the zoologist's intension of the term would change.

None the less the intensional meanings of a term are ordinarily many times fewer than the extensional meanings; and the intensional meanings of a word ordinarily long outlast the lifetime of any individual object comprised in its extension. Swans have a very short life span; the current biological intension of the term "swan" has outlasted many generations of swans and will probably outlast many more. Socrates' mistake, therefore, was to have failed to distinguish clearly between the extension and intension of a term and to have attributed absolute constancy and uniqueness to the relatively constant and relatively unique intensional meaning of a term.

An understanding of the empiricist position with respect to Aristotle's theory of definition will further clarify the issue. Aristotle originated the idea that a proper definition will provide a list of properties common to all the objects denoted by a term and which, if taken jointly, exclude from the extension of the term all other objects. His own definition of man as a rational animal is of this sort. All men are rational animals, and no beings but men have both the properties of animality and rationality. This kind of definition is known as definition by genus and specific difference. The class of animals is the genus to which men belong and rationality is what makes them different or sets them apart from other animals. Up to this point the empiricist finds nothing objectionable. When, however, Aristotle goes on to say that the specific difference is the necessary and eternal essence of whatever is being defined and that the specific difference of a thing is that property without which it would cease to be what it is, the empiricist raises his voice in protest.

In the first place, evolutionary theory has once and for all exploded the doctrine of fixed species; present-day human beings are the offspring of irrational animals and there is no guarantee that our own offspring will not revert to a state of irrationality. No class of beings has necessary or eternal properties in this sense.

In the second place, it is pure nonsense to say that the essence of a thing is that without which it would cease to be what it is, if one means thereby that things have a given and predetermined nature which could not conceivably be altered. To say that a thing would cease to be what it is if it lost a certain property is either to utter nonsense or to express awkwardly the simple fact that we have so chosen to use a word that if something failed to possess that property the word would no longer be used to designate it. It may well be, to stay with the example of man, that if we encountered a being otherwise like man but without reason we would refuse to use the term "man" to refer to it. Similarly, if we knew that the present race of human beings would revert to irrationality, we might very well say that man will cease to be man. But in neither case would we be saying anything about an eternal or unchanging property of the beings presently comprised in the extension of the word "man."

In the third place, most things have more than one specific difference. The beings denoted by the word "man" are distinguished from other animals by a large variety of properties other than rationality. Man is the only animal who cooks his own food, the only animal who can make love all the year round, the only animal who knows he is going to die, the only animal who makes promises, the only animal who laughs, and so on. Who, then, is to say which of these various specific differences is the essence of mankind and on what grounds? For Gabriel Marcel, in whose system the notion of fidelity is central, a definition of man as the being who makes promises would be more adequate than a definition of man as a rational animal. For Adam Smith man was the bartering animal; never, he said, had he observed two dogs get up on their hind legs and exchange bones. Ontological considerations alone can never decide which of the various specific differences that characterize man ought to be regarded as the essential or defining property of the human species.

To say, therefore, that the essence of man is rationality can mean only some one or some combination of three things. (1) The beings ordinarily denoted by the term "man" have been observed to possess the property of rationality as a specific difference. (2) The speaker or other users of the term "man" would refuse to apply it to beings who lacked rationality. (3) Of all the properties which set man off from other animal species rationality is the one which the speaker, given his value orientation and his fund of knowledge, regards as most important, most interesting, or most valuable. To use the term "essence" to mean anything else would be to commit a gross logical blunder.

The empiricist answer to the argument based upon mathematics and logic is similar, but slightly more complex. Berkeley was the first of the empiricists to deal clearly and consistently with the problem of mathematical terms. According to Berkeley mathematical terms *do* stand for particular images or ideas and through them for particular physical objects. When for instance, we pronounce the word "triangle," an image of a triangle is evoked in the mind, and by virtue of that image we are able to apply the term properly to things in the world. The fact that mental entities, ideas or images, are always particular does not have the importance rationalists attribute to it. To serve as a symbol of the many different triangles in nature it is not necessary that the mental image be exactly identical to each or all of the triangles in nature. Nothing prevents us from using a particular image of a triangle to stand for an indefinite number of physical triangles which only roughly approximate to the image, and nothing prevents us from annexing an image to a word. The word, the particular image in the mind, and the innumerable triangles in nature can be linked together by a personal decision or by social convention.

Later empiricists have pointed out many inadequacies in Berkeley's answer to the rationalists. One of these is that he has not explained the meaning of mathematical terms which do not have and apparently cannot have any image or physical object annexed to them either by convention or by personal decision. The term "zero" is one of these, and in logic there are many others, especially words like "not," "or," and "and." Another inadequacy is that frequently when we employ mathematical terms there is no mental imagery at all, even though there might be. In fact modern-day mathematicians are notoriously poor visualizers. None the less, Berkeley's largely undeveloped suggestion that human conventions or personal decisions are the clue to the meaning of mathematical terms is at the root of the modern-day empiricist answer to the problem.

According to contemporary empiricists, mathematical and logical propositions are necessarily and eternally true, not because they deal with necessary and eternal objects, but because human beings have decided that they will be necessarily and eternally true. In technical language, a priori truths, i.e., truths established without recourse to sense experience, are necessarily and eternally true because they are tautological or analytic, i.e., they say nothing about the world. They merely express a resolution or decision on the part of some individual or some group to use terms in certain ways. William James put the matter well when he said that a priori truths are *merely* eternal. Like Kant, the empiricists discover the source of universal and necessary truths in human subjectivity, but like the existentialists though in another sense they have pushed this Kantian view in a direction Kant would have found most distasteful. Kant retained the rationalistic conviction that the human mind was essentially the same in all individuals. The empiricists do not. It is not mankind as such, but individuals and groups within mankind who are responsible for there being necessary truths.

An example will help to make the empiricist position clear. The statement "All bachelors are unmarried men" is an a priori truth; nobody would conduct a survey of bachelors to verify it. At the same time it is an analytic truth or tautology; it gives us no information whatsoever about bachelors. Furthermore, it is *because* the statement is analytic or tautological that it is a priori; obviously recourse to experience is not required to verify a statement which says nothing about experience. In what sense, then, is this statement eternally and necessarily true? According to the rationalist, it is eternally and necessarily true because there is an idea or essence of bachelorhood and because an examination of that idea or essence reveals that it contains within it as components the ideas or essences of manhood and celibacy. According to the empiricist, all that one can possibly mean by saying that this statement is eternally and necessarily true is that social convention has decreed that the term "bachelor" be used to designate only unmarried men and that the person who denied that bachelors are unmarried men would be very rudely received.

Nothing absolutely prevents society from deciding to change the meaning of words. There is, of course, no good reason that society should change the conventions governing the use of the term "bachelor." But there are many cases in which society does decide to change the meanings of words, with the result that statements which were once a priori truths cease to be true a priori. An example is the expression "pure water." Once by this expression nothing was meant except that the water was clear or not muddy. Since the time of Pasteur, however, "pure water" has come to mean water free of germs noxious to the human organism. With this shift of meaning the statement "Pure water is clear water" has ceased to be true a priori. Today, even muddy water could properly be called pure.

Consider now an a priori statement which exemplifies a logical truth. An example would be: "Either John was born in 1950 or he was not born in 1950." This statement, like "All bachelors are unmarried men" is obviously a priori; no one would think of examining John's birth certificate in order to prove it. It is no less clearly analytic or tautological; it tells us nothing about John or the world in general. Again, the statement is a priori *because* it is tautological; since it tells us nothing about the world, empirical investigation could not possibly establish its truth. What, then, is meant by saying that this statement is eternally and necessarily true? The empiricist answer to this question is much the same as their answer to the similar question about "All bachelors are unmarried men." Any statement of the form "Either A is B or A is not B," say the empiricists, is true simply because of the rules governing the combination of words into sentences and the conventional usage of terms like "either," "or," and "not." Statements of this form are not true because eternal Ideas or Aristotelian essences are related to one another according to some ontological pattern which we intuit. The person who denied the truth of "Either John was born in 1950 or he was not born in 1950" should not be accused of lack of insight into eternal verities, but rather of misunderstanding or misusing language.

This last example permits us to understand the empiricist position on logic and mathematics. Logical and mathematical systems are nothing more than sets of verbal symbols manipulated according to man-made rules. Aristotelian logic and Euclidean geometry are only two of these systems. In the nineteenth and twentieth centuries a large number of others have come into existence, and there is no limit to the number which could be constructed. But all of them are alike in that they are analytic or tautological. They say nothing about the world, at least not so long as they remain purely logical or mathematical. Not all of them, of course, abide by widespread social conventions; some of them are highly idiosyncratic creations of individual men. But they are all alike in that what makes them a priori is some sort of human decision to use symbols in a certain way.

It is a tribute to the power of the rationalist tradition that talk about eternal and necessary truths still remains in vogue, even among empiricists; but it would conduce to clarity if the empiricists would simply quit using such language altogether and instead of telling us what the terms "eternal" and "necessary" really mean flatly declared that even a priori, analytic truths are neither eternal nor necessary. Their position, however, is clear. There are words, there are usages for these words determined by convention or individual decision, and there are things in the world. There are also sentences and human rules for the formation of sentences. And to understand the meaning and import of a priori truths it is these things alone which should be taken into account, not Platonic Ideas, Aristotelian essences, the divine intellect, or some mysterious order behind the flux of observable events.

If some a priori truths and some logical or mathematical systems appear to be eternally and necessarily true, it is only because the social conventions which make them true are so firmly established and their practical utility so evident that we cannot easily imagine a change in those conventions. As the wheel is an early invention of mankind much needed for purposes of transportation, so are certain logical and mathematical systems early inventions of mankind much needed for purposes of communication and calculation; and if those systems are eternal and necessary, it is only in the sense that the wheel is eternal and necessary. It is conceivable that someday man could dispense altogether with the wheel; similarly, it is conceivable that someday man will be able to dispense with Euclidean geometry for purposes of land survey. A better system might be discovered. Already man has learned that Euclidean geometry is not a satisfactory instrument for the exploration of astronomical space, any more than the wheel is a satisfactory instrument for transportation by sea.

With this summary of empiricist epistemology in mind, it is time to turn to an examination of empiricist ontology. As noted earlier, empiricism has often veered toward scientism, but its epistemology demands that it move in another direction and in fact it has. Scientism holds that the world revealed by the senses, the world of colors and sounds and of everyday objects like tables and trees, is an illusory appearance. The true world is very different from it. Colors and sounds are not *really* qualities of objects; they are vibrations in the ether. Tables and chairs are not *really* solid objects; they are collocations of atoms occupying a certain region of space which they do not even begin to fill. This doctrine can be traced back to the philosophical school of antiquity known as atomism, but it entered the modern world through seventeenth-century science.

Descartes gave the doctrine its clearest and most logical formulation. God, said Descartes, is not a deceiver. Whatever, therefore, can be clearly and precisely conceived must exist, and whatever cannot be clearly and precisely conceived cannot truly exist. The human mind cannot clearly and precisely conceive physical objects with qualities such as color and heat; the human mind is so made that it can conceive clearly and distinctly nothing but entities susceptible of mathematical calculation. Heat, therefore, must be a mathematically measurable motion of molecules, colors and sounds measurable vibrations in the ether, and so on for the other directly unmeasurable qualities of objects observed through the physical senses. Galileo held to much the same doctrine. God, he said, is a master mathematician, and mathematics the language of the world. Since you cannot square or take the cube root of blue, blue is not in the world. It is only a subjective impression in us.

The essence of scientism is that the real world is not the world revealed to the physical senses, but a world more congenial to the mathematical or rational intellect of man lying behind the physically observable world and into which we can see only with the mind's eye.

The later and more popular forms of scientism are nineteenth-century materialism, for which many philosophers reserve the term "scientism," and Marxism. Marxism is scientistic not only through its alliance with nineteenth-century materialism, but also through its faith in the existence of a pattern of historical development which is not directly observable and which cannot be known by simple induction. In these later forms of scientism the reference to God drops out—a fact which inspired Sartre to say that though God is dead man wants to go on living as though nothing had changed. If there is no God to guarantee the pattern behind observable events or to endow man with a mind suited to discovering that pattern, what reason is there to believe either that the pattern exists or that we can know it? Einstein, who realized better than Descartes and the nineteenth-century materialists how beastly complicated the order of things is, again invoked the deity to justify his faith that the order exists. "God may be sophisticated," Einstein said, "but he is not evil." The pattern behind the scenes is there and with enough patience man can discover it.

The true empiricist, by contrast, holds that the real world is the world presented to the senses and that the unobservable entities of the scientist are merely "logical constructs" or useful conceptual tools by which it is possible to calculate more precisely the relationships among observable objects. The technical name for this doctrine is "phenomenalism," and as the name indicates, it is an attempt to reinstate what Kant and the philosophers of scientism call "phenomena" or "appearances" as the ultimate realities.

The empiricist epistemology does not necessarily exclude the *possibility* of there being an orderly mathematical pattern behind observable things; but except by the most nimble sort of mental gymnastic it is difficult to see how an empiricist could consistently affirm either that a pattern behind the scenes does actually exist or that the mind could know it.

For the empiricist the only knowable natural order is the order *in*, not behind, observable events. Natural laws are ultimately nothing but the regular conjunction of observable kinds of things and events. If "faith in reason" is, as White-head says, "the faith that at the basis of things we shall not find mere arbitrary mystery,"[3] then the empiricist is not a rationalist. Things have no basis, no ground, no bottom; but if we persist none the less in talking about a basis or a ground or a bottom of things, let us at least admit that it *is* an absolute mystery.

Furthermore, the empiricist is not logically justified in imputing to nature more order than has actually been observed. William James and his successors have made themselves the special guardians of this tenet of empiricist ontology. James saw the world as a "blooming, buzzing confusion," a disorderly sequence of specific causal patterns without any master plan. He decried "monism," by which he meant the theory that the universe constitutes a single bloc whose unity was guaranteed by a few simple and universally applicable natural laws. To monism he opposed his own doctrine of "pluralism."

So much for empiricist ontology. The next question is what kind of value does empirical knowledge have. The classic statement of the empiricist theory about the value of knowledge is that of Francis Bacon, who declared simply that "knowledge is power." The kind of power in question is largely the power to act upon and to modify the world, but this formula can be understood in two ways. For the ordinary man who takes the rough outlines of his natural and social environment for granted, empirical knowledge is valuable because through it he comes into possession of certain material devices which contribute to his wealth, pleasure, and prestige. Knowledge means television sets, automobiles, automatic washing machines, gray flannel suits, and ranch houses.

As a matter of historical record many of the major empiricist philosophers have been ordinary men, and the empiricists of the present generation are very ordinary indeed. Most philosophers of the present generation in England and America have gravitated to the analytic movement, according to which the practice of philosophy itself is nothing more than an innocent pastime in which a man may take pleasure, by which he may earn a living, and as a result of which he could not conceivably incur animosity from any quarter.

The analysts have taken over from the logical positivists of a few decades back the contention that statements of value are either meaningless or disguised factual claims which in the interests of clarity ought to be reformulated. At the same time they have propounded the view that the major philosophical issues of the past have either been solved or dissolved by linguistic analysis and that nothing remains for the philosopher to do except to clear up a few relatively minor linguistic ambiguities. Accordingly, they do not take up an official position with respect to any question of value, not even the value of empirical knowledge. It is only by observing their practice that one can place them on the side of the ordinary man who finds knowledge valuable only in so far as it contributes to personal comfort and security.

The second interpretation of Bacon's dictum is that of the eighteenth-century Enlightenment thinkers, of nineteenth-century utilitarian liberals such as John Stuart Mill, and of twentieth-century pragmatists such as John Dewey. For them empirical knowledge is valuable because it represents man's only hope of progressively mastering nature and rationally reorganizing society. Knowing for them means human progress, not merely individual well-being.

Common to both the conservative and the liberal wing of the empiricist movements, however, is the view that empirical methods may be applied to the understanding of social institutions and of human nature. Just as the earlier stages of empiricism coincided with the rise of the modern physical sciences, so its later stages coincided with the rise of the behavioral sciences.

Also common to both wings of the empiricist movement is the view that happiness or contentment, not existential intensity, is the ultimate goal of human endeavor. Pragmatism is often rightly regarded as a movement favoring the active life, but it is most often a smooth, unimpeded form of activity that pragmatists favor. According to James, the whole "intellectual apparatus" of mankind has as its sole purpose the resolution of conflicts between the individual's instincts or between the individual and his environment. It is simply an instrument by which the organism is restored to a state of internal and external equilibrium.

The chief difference between the two wings is that the conservative empiricist either does not believe that an understanding of social institutions and human nature can be used to benefit mankind or does not much care. The liberal empiricist for his part both believes and cares.

Also involved, however, is a difference of opinion about the status of value judgments. The conservative wing argues that value judgments are obviously neither statements about a regular conjunction of natural events nor a priori statements such as are found in logic and mathematics, from which it follows that value judgments must be meaningless. The liberal wing, on the other hand, argues that most value judgments are obviously meaningful and obviously not a priori statements, concluding that value judgments must be a special kind of empirical proposition which the behavioral sciences could conceivably confirm or disconfirm.

The distance between the two wings has been narrowed somewhat by admissions from the conservative side that value judgments are often disguised empirical propositions, asserting implicitly that something is a useful means to an end. If, for instance, someone says that democracy is the best form of government, he may mean simply that democracy is the form of government which best conduces to universal well-being. And this is, in principle at least, an empirical proposition. None the less, the vast majority of present-day empiricists remain highly dubious both about the meaningfulness of value judgments and also about the propriety of philosophers' making value judgments. If, they say, value judgments are empirical propositions, then the behavioral scientist rather than the philosopher is the man to deal with them.

The Existentialist Alternative

The existentialists answer the question "What can man know?" by saying that man can know the human condition. To the question "How can man know?" their answer is: by intuitive insight resulting from affective experiences such as anguish. To the question "What is the value of knowledge?" they answer that a proper understanding of the human condition is essential to the experience of existentialist values, the only values genuinely available to mankind.

The answer to the first of these questions is overly simplified and could be misleading. The rationalists say that man can know nothing but the eternal and the universal. The empiricists say that man can know nothing but matters of empirical fact and man-made a priori truths. The existentialists do not, however, say that man can know *nothing but* the human condition. Their position is rather that nothing but the human condition is ultimately worth knowing. They often deny that an alleged object of knowledge exists, and they often deny that the object could be known if it did exist. But the essence of their position is much more likely to be that even if the object existed and even if it could be known, the knowledge of this object would be without human significance. Existentialism is first and foremost an axiology, or theory of value.

Sartre, for instance, does not believe in the existence of God, and if he did he would certainly agree with Christian existentialists, who say that man cannot have an adequate knowledge of the divine nature. Yet, as he has repeatedly declared, emphasis should be placed upon the fact that even if God did exist and even if man could know God, nothing would be changed. Since man is free, he must choose his own values and take upon himself the responsibility for his choice. He cannot shift this responsibility to God. The rationalist who says that knowledge of eternal objects is valuable because the good life in the world of becoming should be modeled upon the eternal objects has simply forgotten that finitude means freedom and that freedom means man must choose for himself.

Similarly, few existentialists have shown much interest in determining whether abstract ideas have any ontological status, and none of them has hailed the empiricist attempt to reduce Platonic Ideas or Aristotelian essences to linguistic conventions. Most often they simply ignore the problem, apparently allowing that abstract ideas do have some sort of being. Heidegger goes so far by way of concession to the rationalists as to house abstract ideas in a special region of being. The principal existentialist argument is that whether abstract ideas exist or not they are uninteresting and unimportant to the existing individual who has to make concrete decisions.

Again, the existentialists agree with the anti-scientism of the empiricists; even more than the empiricists they are prone to insist that the totality of being has no ground and that there is no pattern or system of order lying beyond what we directly observe which explains the visible sequence of events. But even on this point there are exceptions. Kierkegaard, for instance, declared that nature does exist as a unitary system, adding simply that the system exists for God alone, not for man who is tied to the here and now. And of the majority, who wholeheartedly reject monism and scientism, few show any great interest in tracing the implications of this stand so far as it concerns the status and knowability of laws of nature. Are laws of nature merely observed regularities among different kinds of things in the world? Or are they, Kantian-fashion, forms imposed upon a nameless and shapeless matter? Sartre and Heidegger lean strongly toward a Kantian interpretation, but it would be hazardous to say much more on the subject. All existentialists agree, however, that knowledge of the laws of nature has no human value. Television and automobiles have not made man happy, and the chief accomplishment of medical science has been to prolong senility. Countries such as Switzerland, Sweden, and the United States with their high level of material prosperity and long average life span are also countries with an extremely high incidence of suicide, mental illness, alcoholism, and dope addiction.

The existentialist arguments against the behavioral sciences have a similar focus. The value of psychoanalysis has yet to be proved; no satisfactory study has yet been made showing that the rate of recovery for persons treated on the couch is higher than the rate of recovery among persons with similar ailments who have received no treatment at all. Experimental psychologists have successfully predicted the behavior of rats and of certain types of human behavior closely resembling that of rats. Sociologists have successfully predicted which segments of the population are most likely to buy striped toothpaste or powdered coffee. But neither the experimental psychologists nor the sociologists have much else to show for their efforts. And so on down the line of the behavioral sciences.

To be sure, the existentialists explain the failure of the behavioral sciences by asserting the necessary unpredictability of human behavior in so far as it depends upon choices of vital concern to the individual. If a sociologist can successfully predict the proper time and place to market striped toothpaste, this is only because the choice of a dentifrice is a matter of little importance and most persons are quite willing to allow that choice to be made for them. None the less, even here axiological considerations predominate over ontological considerations. The existentialist does not say simply that since man is free human behavior cannot be predicted. The existentialist also says that since man is free he ought to take consciousness of the fact and act in a manner appropriate to a free man. Specifically, this means that although freedom is inalienable, it is still possible for the individual to *choose* that his behavior be dictated by others, thus permitting himself to become a manipulable and predictable object for the social engineer. This kind of behavior is what the existentialists call "flight from freedom," an attempt to make life easy which succeeds only in depriving life of existential intensity. And it is their opposition to the flight from freedom, far more than their commitment to the ontological doctrine that freedom is ultimately inalienable, which lies at the source of their attitudes toward the behavioral sciences.

In sum, the proper object of human concern for the existentialists is not God, abstract ideas, laws of nature, or empirical knowledge of human beings. What man should strive to know is the human condition. And by an understanding of the human condition the existentialists do not mean knowledge of human history, of man's natural and social environment, or of the so-called laws of human behavior. An understanding of the human condition is rather a knowledge of certain general traits of human existence which remain the same in all ages: of man's contingency, particularity, and freedom; of man's fundamental aspirations; and of the basic ways in which the individual can relate to the world and to other human beings.

With regard to the means by which man can know what is worth knowing, the existentialists are closer to the rationalists than to the empiricists. It is characteristic of them to assert that the fundamental features of the human condition are "ontological necessities" which can and must be known a priori. Their language itself often smacks of old-fashioned rationalism. In this connection, therefore, two problems arise. How does the method of the existentialists differ from that of the rationalists? And how can the existentialists defend their claim to know a priori certain necessary features of human existence?

Between the existentialists and the rationalists there are two important differences. First, for almost all rationalists intuitive insight is exclusively the function of the intellect; the passions, it was said, obscure the intellect. The existentialist, on the other hand, either denies that any sharp distinction exists between intellect and passion or else regards the latter as a condition for the successful operation of the former. The human condition is revealed to us in anguish. Second, almost all traditional philosophers regarded the acquisition of knowledge as an act of grasping or apprehending some external object. What is known lies outside the knowing subject, and in the act of knowing the individual comes into possession of the known for the first time. The existentialists, on the contrary, maintain that the insights delivered in the experience of anguish are merely a rendering explicit of a state of affairs in which the individual is himself deeply involved and that in some sense the individual already knows what anguish reveals to him.

The historical origins of the existentialist position are not easy to trace. Ironically, however, Plato himself with his doctrine of knowledge by reminiscence must be held partially responsible. A less distant source is St. Augustine, who held not only that God, the true object of human knowledge, is to be discovered in the inmost recesses of the human soul, but also that man can know the truth only if God first grants him the privilege of believing without understanding. Still nearer in time is Pascal, who said "the heart has its reasons which the mind does not know."

Whatever the sources, the logical connection between the view that knowing is an act of making explicit what we already know and the view that passion is a condition of knowing becomes clear when one remembers that for the existentialist what is known is the human condition and that the index of involvement in the human condition is passion or intensity. When the tendency to incorporate into one's very concept of a thing the necessary conditions of its existence is taken into account, one can also readily understand why some existentialists should prefer to say that passion is a mode of knowing rather than merely a condition of knowing. Wealth, for instance, is perhaps most properly regarded as a necessary condition of happiness, happiness itself being a subjective state of enjoyment or contentment. Many persons, however, do not bother to keep the concept of happiness as a subjective state rigidly separate from the concept of wealth. For them, wealth is not simply a condition of happiness; it is a part of happiness.

The sense in which we already know what is explicitly revealed in the experience of anguish is by no means clear. Through Freud the notion of the unconscious has become exceedingly popular in the twentieth century. When, therefore, the existentialists say that anguish merely makes explicit what we have in some sense known prior to the experience, the contemporary reader finds nothing exceptionally puzzling in this and almost irresistibly understands that what was already known was known by a kind of Freudian unconscious. This interpretation could lead to serious misunderstandings. For one thing, Freud's unconscious consists among other things of biological needs or innate drives, in which the existentialists do not believe. In the existentialist view what makes man go is not a set of innate drives or biological needs but free and fully conscious choices. Man is not driven by animal exigencies; he makes himself by his own choices. For another thing, several existentialists have denied the existence of the unconscious as an ontological entity. Sartre even argues that the concept of the unconscious is self-contradictory.

Is it then possible, without invoking the notion of the unconscious, to make sense out of the contention that we know what is revealed through the experience of anguish prior to that experience even though we have no explicit awareness of it? It would seem that we can in either of two ways.

One way in which we may know something without being explicitly aware of it is illustrated by the act of remembering. It frequently happens that one knows another person's name without being able to think of it. A second way is illustrated in certain problem-solving situations. It frequently happens that a person has present to mind all the ideas needed to resolve a problem on which he is working, that the solution is somehow there in his mind the way the conclusion of an argument is in the premises, but that he is unable to articulate the solution. In this case, as in the first, we often say that we know something even though there is no explicit awareness of it.

No doubt, these two kinds of situations have helped to give rise to the concept of the unconscious. Since one of the criteria of knowing is having explicitly present to mind and being able to articulate what is known, we tend to say that we do not know the name or the answer to the problem. But since there are other criteria of knowing which permit us to say that we do know the name or do know the answer to the problem, we introduce the idea of an unconscious. On one level of consciousness we know; on another level we do not.

There is no need, however, to invoke the idea of the unconscious to explain these situations. There is no more reason to believe that the solution to a problem is literally in the mind so long as we are unable to articulate it than there is to believe that the conclusion of an argument is literally in the premises. And the same remark applies to the name we have forgotten. The mind is not a box, and to say that something is "in" the mind could be a purely metaphorical mode of speech.

Since, therefore, many existentialists do not believe in the unconscious as an ontological reality, it would probably be best to interpret their doctrine that anguish merely makes explicit or fully conscious what we already know in the light of the above remarks. Their probable intent is to suggest that in the experience of anguish either facts which we have always known in the noncontroversial sense of "to know" take on a new significance and we draw from them their full logical conclusions, or else facts which we had known before are recalled. An example of drawing the logical implications of what we already know would be the anguish before the here and now. We all know that we are tied to a limited region of space and time; but how many of us have drawn from this simple item of knowledge the logical implications which the existentialists claim to have drawn from it? An example of recall might be the anguish of freedom. All of the existentialists insist that man can and frequently does conceal from himself fundamental facts about his being. We "flee" from freedom by refusing to focus attention upon it, by deliberately diverting the mind to other things. The anguish of freedom could therefore be produced by a simple act of recall.

How does the existentialist support his claim to have an a priori intuition of necessary features of human existence? According to the empiricist we can know nothing about mankind except by induction from particular instances of human behavior in determinate natural and social conditions. If in the past men have always behaved in a certain way in a certain type of situation, then one can infer with a high degree of probability that they will continue to behave that way in similar situations in the future. But no empiricist would admit that a universal pattern of behavior is an "ontological necessity" or that any pattern of human behavior can be known a priori.

It would be possible to present the existentialist argument by taking any one of the features of the human condition revealed in the three basic types of anguish as a basis of discussion. The issues will emerge most clearly, however, by considering the fact of freedom. The existentialist cannot and does not pretend to prove that man is free by logical argument or by empirical observation. Freedom, he insists, is a directly and immediately intuited fact of human existence, and the person who does not intuit it cannot be made to accept it by a process of reasoning. The existentialist, therefore, limits himself to showing that the empiricist contention according to which man is not free is itself incapable of rational demonstration, that if it can be known that man is not free this will have to be known by an intuitive insight of exactly the same character as the one by which the existentialist claims to establish human freedom.

Belief in determinism is closely associated in empiricist thinking with belief in the validity of the principle of induction. If, says the empiricist, two kinds of events have been uniformly conjoined in the past, then we have good reason to believe that they will continue to be conjoined in the future. If human beings have behaved in certain ways in the past, then they will continue to behave in the same way under similar conditions in the future. They are not free to do otherwise. What, then, asks the existentialist, is the status of these statements? What reason has the empiricist for believing them to be true? If he cannot present an argument for these statements he is in no position to criticize the existentialist for maintaining their contraries.

Since the time of Hume, of course, empiricists have recognized that the principle of induction and along with it the belief in determinism cannot be established by rational argument unless one invokes God to guarantee that the course of nature will

remain uniform. And since they are unwilling to do this,
they have usually admitted that there is no argument by which
their position can be confirmed.

Hume's view was that man believes in the principle of induction and in determinism because he cannot help doing so,
because it is psychologically impossible for him to do otherwise.
To this the existentialist retorts by saying that if it were psychologically impossible for man not to believe in determinism then
he would not be subject to the anguish of freedom, which in
fact he is. Hume conceded that in the quiet of his study a
man could imagine the course of nature not remaining uniform,
but added that his doubts on this subject would be merely hypo-
thetical and could not be maintained over any period of time.
To this the existentialists reply that the anguish of freedom is a
concrete fact of life from which no man ever really escapes.

The logical positivists and pragmatists have typically taken a
different position. They claim, not that men are psychologically
compelled to believe in determinism, but rather that men ought
to act as if determinism were a fact. When they say that the
course of nature will remain uniform or that men will behave in
the future as they have behaved in the past, they are not asserting
the truth of a factual proposition. They are rather exhorting
us to persist in the search for undiscovered uniformities and to
utilize the results of past scientific inquiry for the purpose of
predicting and controlling future behavior. The grounds for
so exhorting us are purely pragmatic: it is only by acting in this
way that we may hope to contribute to human progress. Here,
too, however, the existentialist has a retort. How can the
logical positivist or the pragmatist support his contention that
by acting as if the course of nature would remain constant we
advance the cause of human progress, without presupposing
that the course of nature will remain uniform? If the course
of nature does not remain uniform, then the results of past
scientific inquiry will be utterly useless for the purpose of prediction and control and faith in the principle of induction will
not lead to future discoveries.

Still a third position has been taken by members of the analytic
movement. Many of them argue that the statement "These
two types of events have always been conjoined in the past" is
logically substitutable for the statement "We have good reason
to believe that these two types of events will probably be

conjoined in the future," in much the same way that "10" and "X" are substitutable. Rules governing linguistic usage decree that the person who asserts the former must also assert the latter, and vice versa. In effect, this is to make the principle of induction an a priori truth. "If two types of events have always been conjoined in the past, then we have good reason to believe that these two types of events will probably be conjoined in the future" becomes a statement very similar to "All bachelors are unmarried men." Most existentialists have never heard of this argument and would probably consider it beneath their dignity to answer it if they had. But, no doubt, if they did answer it they would point out that linguistic rules require a justification, and that the only possible justification for making the principle of induction an a priori truth in the sense in which empiricists have analyzed a priori truths is that one first accept it as a statement of fact and that one believe in its truth in so far as it is taken as a simple statement of fact.

The upshot of all this is that the existentialist refuses to accept criticism from the empiricist, since he believes that ultimately the empiricist uses the very same method of intuitive insight he uses himself. And once the indispensability of intuitive insight in order to found a philosophical position is admitted, there is no reason to accept as correct only those insights required to found an empiricist theory of knowledge.

As remarked above, the case for the indispensability of intuitive insight could also be made out with respect to traits such as the contingency of being and the particularity of human existence. On the face of it, it seems absurd to claim that man's being limited to the here and now is a fact known by induction. On the contrary, this appears to be a fact which each of us knows immediately and directly; it is a condition of our making any empirical observations at all, not a fact established by empirical observation. At the same time, it would not be difficult for the existentialist to argue that the empiricist proof for the contingency of being based on their theory of knowledge is circular. If the empiricist did not know by intuitive insight that the whole of things is contingent, he would never have been led to adopt a theory of knowledge according to which only particulars and the relationships between particulars can be known. Since, however, empiricists and existentialists agree about the contingency of being and about human particularity, there is no compelling reason to go into these matters.

There is, however, one further point which does require consideration. If the empiricists' fundamental "intuitions" are correct, then any trait of human existence which could be established by induction can only be established by induction. Heidegger, for instance, claims that death is an ontological necessity, but since there is no reason to say that mortality as a fact of human existence could only be established by intuitive insight, the empiricist will have to deny Heidegger's claim. The empiricist does not, of course, believe that someday man will become immortal; there are very good inductive grounds for asserting the contrary. Nor does he object strongly, if at all, to listing mortality among the defining properties of man. The issue is how and with what degree of certainty we can know that the objective property of mortality characterizing the beings presently denoted by the word "man" will continue to characterize these or similar beings in the future. Heidegger claims to know this with absolute certainty by intuitive insight. The empiricist asserts that we know it by induction from particular instances and that our knowledge of this fact, as of all matters of fact, is probable. The degree of probability is so high that for all practical purposes no harm is done by claiming complete certainty. Still we cannot exclude a priori the possibility of man's becoming immortal unless we choose to define man as mortal. And if we define man as mortal, we are no longer asserting that man is mortal; we are simply resolving not to use the word "man" to denote immortal things. According to the empiricist, Heidegger has surreptitiously defined man as mortal and has illegitimately attributed to an objective state of affairs the subjective impossibility of imagining a being without the property of mortality whom he would be prepared to call man. A confusion of this kind would not be difficult to make, especially by philosophers who have little sympathy with Anglo-American philosophy and who have often not kept up with its latest developments.

Moreover, whether one accepts or rejects the empiricistic theory of knowledge, one must distinguish between the contention that certain issues must and consequently should be decided by intuitive insight and the contention that one may and should use intuitive insight to establish facts which could be established by other methods. Unfortunately, it is very common for a person who believes himself to have proved the indispensability of intuition in deciding certain issues, to feel himself justified without further reason to use intuition in order to decide any and all issues.

After this unavoidably long review of the major answers to the three questions raised at the beginning of this chapter, it is now possible to ask " Are the existentialists irrationalists or are they not?" Like the word "happiness" and its synonyms, the word "rationalist" and its synonyms have both a general and several more specific meanings. In the widest and most general sense of the term, a rationalist is one who believes that there exists some method by which those things which it is humanly desirable to know may be known. Now, if the existentialist ontology, epistemology, and axiology are acceptable, the existentialists have almost as much right to call themselves rationalists as either the philosophical rationalists or the empiricists. To the extent that they do not do so, it is largely because they wish to avoid misunderstandings due to the crowd of associations which have accrued to the term "rationalist" in the course of Western history.

The qualification "almost as much right" is owed to the fact that most of the existentialists, especially Kierkegaard and the religious existentialists, do not fully believe that a method exists for knowing what it is humanly desirable to know. The anguish of the religious existentialists stems in good part from their belief that God cannot be known. But even this qualification may be unwarranted; for if the universal existentialist conviction that life is fundamentally tragic is accepted, it would make as much sense to qualify the definition of rationalism as to qualify the existentialists' claim to the term. Why not define a rationalist as one who believes that it is possible for man to know whatever it is desirable for a being irrevocably condemned to incompleteness and tragedy to know?

The pragmatists have actually done something similar. To take a specific example, Dewey believed that rationality consists in the ability to adjust oneself to the circumstances of one's life, where by "adjustment" is meant either "accommodation," i.e., a kind of Stoic renunciation of impossible desires, or "adaptation," i.e., a transformation of the physical and social environment permitting the realization of desire. Where possible we transform the environment; where this is not possible, we accommodate ourselves to it. But according to Dewey, perfect adjustment is an impossible ideal both for the individual and for the race. The rational being does not attempt to create a paradise on earth, nor does he deceive himself into believing that he can be happy even on the rack. The rational man is one who attempts by a gradual and piece-meal process to eliminate the hardships of life which it is within his power to eliminate and to accommodate to those hardships which he cannot eliminate—but bearing always in mind that total adjustment is impossible.

Some persons, of course, would argue that the essence of rationality is a willingness to accept the elementary principles of logic and would refuse existentialists the title of rationalists on the grounds that they disdain these principles. In fact, however, the existentialists do not disdain the principles of logic. The existentialists do have a penchant for paradox, but almost all of their paradoxes are purely verbal. When Jaspers says that he who loves everybody loves nobody or when Sartre says that man is not the being which he is, neither of them is betraying the logical principle of contradiction. They are merely expressing themselves in a rhetorically arresting manner.

The closest one comes to genuine logical paradoxes in the whole of existentialist literature is in the elaboration of the Christian existentialist doctrine of faith. For the empiricists faith means a willingness to act on the basis of probable knowledge. If one has good but not conclusive evidence that a friend is trustworthy, one nevertheless reposes faith in him. This kind of faith is in no sense irrational. For the traditional Christians faith meant belief in a proposition for which there is no evidence one way or the other, but which might so far as logic is concerned be true. St. Augustine and St. Thomas speak of Christian mysteries, but they emphatically deny that any article of faith contradicts reason. Faith is nonrational, but not irrational. Faith surpasses reason, but it does not cancel it out. The Christian existentialists, however, strenuously insist that Christian dogma, notably the dogma of creation, of the Man-God, and of the Trinity, do contradict reason. It is logically impossible that God be a creator, that he be both wholly divine and wholly human, that he be simultaneously one and three persons. Thus faith becomes belief in the logically impossible—or so it would seem.

In fact, Kierkegaard did occasionally define faith in this manner. But so long as he did, he insisted that he was not a Christian—that he was arguing for honesty, not Christianity. Nobody believes in the logically impossible. The logically impossible cannot be conceived, much less believed in. That was Kierkegaard's despair. He was a man who wanted to be a Christian, who wanted to believe in the absurd, but who could not succeed. He was merely the "poet of Christianity." The source of his despair, it should be observed, was nothing other than his extreme respect for the principles of logic. The irrationality is all on the side of the traditional Christian who either ignored the essentials of Christian doctrine or refused to recognize the evident logical contradictions in those essentials.

Since, however, faith defined as belief in the logically impossible is a human impossibility, Kierkegaard more frequently used a different definition of faith. Faith became simply the desire to believe, intense care or concern for one's fate. "Faith," he says, "is precisely the contradiction between the infinite passion of the individual's inwardness and the objective uncertainty." At the same time Kierkegaard redefined religious truth. Religious truth, he declared, was not objective belief, but subjective passion. The savage who worshipped an idol with passion was in the truth, whereas the civilized man who worshipped the "true God" without passion was false. Nothing would be more illogical, however, than to take the Christian existentialists' redefinitions of faith and religious truth as evidence of illogicality. These existentialist redefinitions are a tribute to logic of the very highest order. They may also be a *reductio ad absurdum* of Christianity, but in this case Christianity, not logic, is the loser.

IV. Freedom

Non-existentialist Theories

To judge by the use to which the word "freedom" is most often put in ordinary discourse, a man is free in the measure that he can achieve chosen goals with a minimum of effort. Conversely, in the measure that he discovers obstacles in his way he is not free.   If one has chosen to become a doctor, then one is free to do so on condition that one has been accepted by a medical school, has the money to pay the tuition, possesses the native endowment required to pass the courses, and so on. If, however, one does not have the mental equipment to pass the courses, cannot pay the tuition, or cannot find a medical school that will accept one, then one is not free to become a doctor.

In political discussion this sense of the term "freedom" is also the one which most often comes to the fore.   If a man has freedom of speech or freedom of assembly, this means that if he chooses to speak or to assemble with others for political purposes he will encounter no legal obstacles.   He will not be clubbed by the police or thrown in jail.   When the socialist criticizes capitalistic societies by declaring that in these societies the rich man is as free as the poor man since both could starve to death in a public park if they so chose, he is at one and the same time implying that the laws of capitalistic societies place no obstacles in the way of the person who chooses to starve to death and that in a truly free society no one would ever encounter serious obstacles in the effort to acquire a decent subsistence.

Despite the fact that the most common meaning of freedom both in ordinary discourse and in political discussion is ability to achieve chosen goals, traditional philosophers rarely used the term that way.   The most common meanings of the term in traditional philosophizing are known technically as "freedom of self-realization" and "freedom of indeterminism" or "freedom of the will." The common source of both of these concepts of freedom is Christian doctrine. And although they are apparently antithetical it is not uncommon to find them linked together in a single philosophical system. It would not be wholly correct to say that ancient philosophers knew no problem of freedom, but the problem of freedom which most Western philosophers claim to have discovered among the ancients is undoubtedly their own.

One arrived at the notion of freedom of self-realization in roughly the following way. Since God is both omniscient and omnipotent, God both foreknew and foreordained that whatever happens would happen. What a man does may thus have as its immediate cause the man's own individual choice, but its ultimate and only true cause is the will of God. It is as if a man's individual history were originally an idea in God's mind, to which God gave physical reality by an act of creation. Man, of course, cannot and ought not attempt to tinker with God's handiwork. Freedom, therefore, cannot in fact and ought not by right consist in an active effort to achieve individually chosen goals. This is impossible and impious. True freedom can only exist for the man who humbly acknowledges the individual history or nature which God gave him and who observes with wholehearted approval the temporal realization of God's eternal idea of him.

The theory of freedom of self-realization has many different versions, some of them secular. The existentialists would probably argue that the secular versions, most of which were developed in the late eighteenth and nineteenth centuries, are merely hangovers from an earlier day, a result of the fact that after God's death men tried to go on living as if nothing had happened. Be that as it may, only one specific version of the theory need be considered here. It is that of Leibniz.

First, however, it should be noted that when with the birth of the Christian God Platonic Ideas and Aristotelian essences were absorbed in the divine intellect, the concept of essence was gradually enlarged. For the ancient world essences were always and only of universals; individuals could not be known in the strict sense of the term precisely because there were no individual essences. Christian philosophers, however, were bit by bit led to the concept of individual essences. The Christian God is after all a personal god who supposedly sees into each individual's mind and heart.

Let us then assume that at the moment of creation God has present to mind a complete catalogue of all possible individual essences, and let us further assume that of the many possible individual essences only certain combinations can logically coexist. Which of these combinations will God allow to pass into concrete existence? Obviously the best of all possible combinations! This, in brief, is Leibniz's doctrine that the physically existing world is the "best of all possible worlds." But of interest in connection with the problem of freedom is the fact that the individual essences which God chose for physical incarnation must have that history and only that history which God foresaw for them. If after creation individuals decided to alter the course of their divinely appointed history, they would completely upset God's calculations. God has to know down to the last detail what each of these individuals will do in order to be sure that they are logically "compossible" and also to be sure that he has chosen the best possible combination of compossibles. God knew in advance, to use two of Leibniz's own examples, that Adam would eat the apple and that Caesar would cross the Rubicon. He even knew the exact moment at which these events would occur.

It follows that the serf who complains he is unfree because he cannot realize his personally chosen goal of enjoying privileges reserved by his master is simply attempting to upset God's plan. It is for him to accept his status by recognizing that there is no other logically possible role for him than that of a serf and that he is a part of the best of all possible worlds. His individual history, harsh though it may be, is merely a temporal unfolding or historical realization of his very own individual essence. To wish that his life had a different pattern would be like wishing for the logically impossible. It would be as if Adam wanted to be Eve without ceasing to be Adam.

Some philosophers have argued that if God had to choose for creation from a limited set of uncreated individual essences and that if furthermore God was limited to choosing one or another set of compossibles from within the larger set, he would not be omnipotent. The answer was in part that a limitation upon any being's power is by definition an external obstacle and that since uncreated essences are ideas in God's own mind he cannot be limited by them. The other part of the answer is that so-called logical limitations are not genuine limitations. Who, for instance, would lament the impossibility of believing that the product of one plus one is three or feel that his power had thereby been diminished? God's power is no more limited by the fact that he must observe the principles of logic than by the fact that he cannot through an arbitrary act of will make virtues out of wanton murder and incest. If God's will were not subordinate to his intellect, he would not be God. He would be a monster.

One arrived at the notion of freedom of indeterminism or freedom of the will by arguing from the premise that if God foreordained that we would sin then we are not responsible for our sin and that if we are not responsible for our sin, then it is unjust of God to punish us eternally in hell. God, however, does punish many of us with eternal torment in hell, and God is not unjust. Our sin cannot, therefore, have been foreordained. Our sin must be the result of individual volition. It is we as individuals who by our own undetermined choices sin.

The problem for Christian defenders of the freedom of inde-terminism was to explain how free will is compatible with God's omniscience or foreknowledge. The answer is owed to St. Augustine, who declared that God does not literally foreknow. God is outside time; for him there is only one ever-present moment. He sees all things—past, present, and future—non-discursively and *sub specie aeternitatis* in a single glance. To foreknow he need not therefore foreordain. That St. Augustine should have argued in this way is somewhat surprising, since he is the most famous of all defenders of the dogma of pre-destination, which seems to imply complete foreordination. But as remarked at the outset, it is not unusual for a philosopher to hold both to a doctrine of freedom through self-realization and a doctrine of free will. Christian philosophers like St. Augustine who wish simultaneously to uphold the omnipotence of God through the doctrine of predestination and to uphold the justice of God by regarding man as the true cause of his sin are almost compelled to adopt some version of both theories of freedom.

Despite the enormous importance which they attribute to

human freedom, Sartre alone among the existentialists has elaborated a systematic and detailed theory of freedom. Fortunately, the brilliance and originality of his theory compensates for the relative neglect of the problem by others. There is some question as to whether other existentialists would accept Sartre's views on freedom. This much, however, can be said with certainty. There is little in Sartre's theory which contradicts anything said on the subject by other existentialists, and there is nothing in it incompatible with the major premises of existentialist thinking. Moreover, as with all existentialists, Sartre's position is closer to that upheld by defenders of freedom of indeterminism than to either the common-sense position or the position of those who uphold freedom of self-realization, and it is doubtful whether any contemporary philosopher who took the pains to develop a detailed theory of freedom based on the idea of undetermined choice could come up with anything better.

The term "freedom" is as ambiguous as the term "happiness" and the term "rationality." It does not, however, have a single generic meaning from which the others have been derived, even though the several specific meanings of the term are loosely associated. Nor have the existentialists decided to abandon the word because of its popular and historical connotations. All of them use it, and all of them use it to refer to something which they consider to be a genuinely existing and valuable feature of the human condition. In this respect the existentialists are like the rest of us, who consciously or unconsciously select from the several meanings of the term the one which we believe to stand for a reality of great human importance. If we believe that one of the established meanings of the term either does not stand for a reality or does not stand for a reality of great value, we reject that meaning as improper. The best introduction to the existentialist theory will, therefore, be a consideration of the reasons which induced the existentialists to reject non-existentialist concepts of freedom.

The existentialists do not deny that man has the power to achieve chosen goals by his own efforts. Underprivileged workers do sometimes achieve better working conditions, prisoners do sometimes escape from prison, would-be doctors do sometimes become doctors, and so on. What Sartre calls "the coefficient of adversity," i.e., the resistance presented by the external environment, is not always insuperable. What leads the existentialists to reject or ignore the common-sense conception of freedom is their belief that the power to achieve particular goals is not itself a great value. And that belief rests upon three others.

First, man is a being who exists only by projecting himself beyond the present into the future. To exist is to posit goals and to pursue them. There is no escape from our condition as flight or pursuit toward projected values. This means that if one empirical desire is fulfilled, we will and must replace that desire with another. A state of complete desire fulfillment would be equivalent to death. A part of the tragedy of the human condition is that man is a desiring being and that desire is a state of lack or incompletion. "That the human reality is lack," says Sartre, "the existence of desire as a human fact could suffice as proof."[2] This argument derives, of course, from traditional Platonic and Aristotelian metaphysics. The gods, it will be recalled, cannot desire, because desire is lack, and the gods lack nothing. A state of lack is incompatible with a state of perfection. According to the existentialists the common man has defined freedom on the basis of a mistaken notion that there is a state of happiness, satisfied desire, or absence of frustration which can be achieved by fulfilling empirical desires. But in so far as human consciousness is always characterized by lack, there can be no suspension of the unhappy consciousness. Man must desire in order to exist, and in the act of desiring he constitutes himself as incomplete and unfulfilled.

Moreover, this incompleteness or unfulfillment is necessary if man is to be free even in the sense of being able to overcome obstacles. This point was made effectively by Nietzsche, who asked: "How is freedom measured?—By the resistance which has to be overcome, by the effort it takes to maintain oneself on top." Sartre expresses the same point in his own language. Freedom, he says, "itself creates the obstacles from which we suffer." An insignificant public official in Mont-de-Marsan without means may not have the opportunity to go to New York if that be his ambition. But the obstacles which stand in his way would not exist as obstacles were it not for his free choice of values: in this case, his desire to go to New York. It is freedom itself

> which in posing its ends—in choosing them as inaccessible or difficult of access—causes our location to appear as a . . . restriction upon our projects. . . . It is therefore of no avail to say that I am not free to go to New York because of the fact that I am an unimportant functionary in Mont-de-Marsan. It is on the contrary with respect to my project to go to New York that I situate myself at Mont-de-Marsan.[2]

Sartre makes the same point in still another way:

> In order for the act to be able to allow a realization, the simple projection of a possible end must be distinguished a priori from the realization of this end. If conceiving is enough for realizing, then I am plunged in a world like that of a dream in which the possible is no longer in any way distinguished from the real. . . . If the object appears as soon as it is simply conceived, it will no longer be chosen or even wished for. Once the distinction between the simple wish, the representation which I choose, and the choice is abolished, freedom disappears too.[3]

Second, even if man could succeed in fulfilling all his particular, empirical desires, he would still not achieve happiness; for the desire of particular, empirical objects in the world is always suspended from and merely a specification of an over-arching desire for the impossible. This point was developed in the chapter on the human condition. Man's fundamental project to be God, to be an in-itself-for-itself without any duality between the two aspects of his being, can no more be satisfied through empirical desire than a man's Oedipus complex can be resolved by dreaming that a soldier kills a czar. The argument here is not simply that the satisfaction of one empirical desire requires us to take up a new goal or that we are necessarily committed to a "round of desire." The argument here is that a satisfied desire in the sense of an achieved desire does not bring satisfaction in the sense of pleasure or happiness.

Third, even if man could escape from the round of desire and could find pleasure or happiness in a state of total desire fulfillment, this could only be at the cost of intensity and the existentialist values. And, of course, the intense life with the existentialist values would be superior to a state of contentment or happiness.

The existentialist argument against freedom through self-realization rests primarily upon the belief that man has no ready-made or prehuman nature, no divine essence which is to be automatically realized. Sartre has even defined existentialism as the view that "existence precedes essence." In Leibniz's view, says Sartre, "Adam's essence is for Adam himself a given; Adam has not chosen it; he could not choose to be Adam. Consequently he does not support the responsibility for his being. . . . For us, on the contrary, Adam is not defined by an essence since for human reality essences come after existence."[4] In other words, man makes his own history by his own choices, and his true life history or individual essence could not conceivably be known or defined until after his death.

Here, too, however, questions of value as well as questions of fact are involved. Believers in freedom of self-realization belong to the Platonic tradition. Their chief interest is in an eternal object—in the case of Leibniz, God. One of the things they hope to achieve by their theory of freedom is to preserve the dignity of the eternal object: in Leibniz's case, it was a matter of exalting God by demonstrating his omnipotence. The existentialists, on the contrary, are perfectly willing to let God and other eternal objects take care of themselves. They are interested in the dignity of the individual person; and according to them a being who does not personally support the responsibility for his individual history, who does not choose himself, is without dignity.

The existentialist elaboration of the theory of freedom of indeterminism is and has to be very different from classical versions. But it will be helpful at this point before discussing the differences to indicate how the existentialists meet the chief common-sense objection to any theory of freedom of indeterminism. That objection was stated with great literary skill by Voltaire in *Candide*. Voltaire maneuvers his hero Candide into a position such that he must choose between thirty-six series of lashings or a dozen bullets in his brain. At this point Voltaire writes: "Although he protested that man's will is free and that he wanted neither one nor the other, he had to make a choice; by virtue of that gift of God which is called liberty he determined to run the gauntlet thirty-six times."

Voltaire wrote *Candide* as a satire on Leibniz's doctrine that this is the best of all possible worlds, and since Leibniz is well known as an advocate of freedom of self-realization it might be thought that this particular attack is misdirected. In fact, however, Leibniz shares with St. Augustine a general theory of freedom in which freedom as self-realization and freedom as undetermined choice both figure. It was, therefore, entirely appropriate that Voltaire ridicule the latter concept of freedom in a satire on Leibniz.

The whole point of the quoted passage is to emphasize that what man most wants is, not the power to choose, but rather the power to accomplish chosen goals, and that a theory of freedom which fails to take this into account rests upon a faulty sense of values. The privilege of choosing is as nothing compared to relief from the necessity of choosing between unpalatable options imposed by the environment. The secure and tranquil life is one in which the individual faces no extreme situations requiring that a difficult choice be made.

Although Voltaire himself does not go this far, it could even be argued that in so far as one must choose between various courses of action, it is better that the choice be compelled than free. If every time one tried to figure the sum of two plus two one had to choose an answer, it would be impossible to get anywhere; we should be grateful that we are compelled by the laws of logic to accept four and only four as the correct answer to the problem. Similarly in more important matters of human concern. There is a story of a Greek mother who was obliged to choose which one of three sons held as hostages was to be executed. It would, perhaps, be better for her if she did not have to choose at all. But she must. What makes her problem of choice so terrifying is that nothing apparently compels or determines her to choose one son over the others. Presumably she loves all three sons equally well. If one of them were a black sheep whom she hated with all her heart, the choice would be less terrifying. In fact, given hatred of one and love for the others, it is a nice question in what sense she could be said to choose at all. She would probably "have no choice." It would be impossible for her to select any but the son she hated.

Of course, Voltaire was an Enlightenment thinker, and like the ordinary man, he believed that the route to happiness lies in the elimination of external obstacles to the accomplishment of human desires. If, however, one is an existentialist, if one believes that life is ineradicably tragic, if one believes that the external environment poses nothing but difficult options and that whatever option one chooses one is still unhappy, if one believes that the fundamental problems of life are like those of Candide or the Greek mother, then almost the only value which can be salvaged is dignified choice. And the more difficult the choice, the greater is the opportunity to demonstrate one's dignity.

It will be remembered that for the existentialists man is free by ontological necessity and that any attempt to escape from freedom is necessarily self-defeating. In one sense, then, freedom is a universal human phenomenon which does not permit of degrees. At the same time, however, the existentialists have an axiological doctrine of freedom. According to this doctrine, one is more or less free depending upon the extent to which one is aware of freedom as an ontological necessity and ceases to project escape from freedom. An individual exposed to a situation which obliges him to become conscious of his freedom is thus more free than the individual not so obliged.

A rather famous Sartrean text, often regarded as incomprehensible or stupid, is merely a logical extension of these ideas. Writing of life in France during the war years, Sartre says:

> We were never more free than during the German occupation. We had lost all our rights, beginning with the right to talk. Every day we were insulted to our faces and had to take it in silence. Under one pretext or another, as workers, Jews, or political prisoners, we were deported *en masse*. . . . And because of all this we were free. Because the Nazi venom seeped even into our thoughts, every accurate thought was a conquest. . . . At every instant we lived up to the full sense of this commonplace little phrase: "Man is mortal." And the choice that each of us made of his life and his being was an authentic choice because it was made face to face with death, because it could always have been expressed in these terms: "Rather death than. . . ." All those among us who knew any details concerning the Resistance asked themselves anxiously, "If they torture me, shall I be able to keep silent?" Thus the basic question of liberty itself was posed, and we were brought to the verge of the deepest knowledge that man can have of himself. For the secret of man is not his Oedipus complex or his inferiority complex : it is this limit of his own liberty, his capacity for resisting torture and death.[5]

The existentialist is thus at the opposite pole from the ordinary man. The ordinary man believes he is most free when he is not obliged to choose or when circumstances clearly

dictate which choice is best.   The existentialist believes that
man is most free when he recognizes that he is obliged to choose.
The ordinary man says that freedom is valuable because it
leads to happiness, security, contentment.   The existentialist
says that freedom is valuable because through it man may
realize his own dignity, and triumph over the unhappiness to
which he is irrevocably condemned.   The ordinary man tries
to ignore the unpleasant facts of life, and if he is exposed to an
"impossible situation" where no choice could conceivably be
a choice of happiness, he is without recourse.   The existentialist
refuses to ignore the unpleasant facts of life, and he spends most
of his time trying to find some technique by which to triumph
over them.

Modern Versions of Determinism

One difference between existentialists and classical exponents
of freedom of indeterminism parallels a difference between
existentialists and exponents of freedom of self-determination.
Both of these classical positions were inspired by a desire to
justify the ways of God to man and to buoy up the authors' faith
in God.   In order to accomplish their goals Leibniz and those
who adopted his solution tended to reduce the individual to
hardly more than a figment in God's imagination.   The
exponents of freedom of indeterminism, on the other hand,
accomplished the same goals by making man responsible for his
sins.   Logic, of course, requires that a being responsible for
his sins be also responsible for his virtues.   But this logical
consequence of the theory was rarely drawn.   Calvinists
expatiate at great length about the individual's personal responsibility for his sinfulness while at the same time stressing that the
good a man does is done by the grace of God.   The intent of
exalting God and humbling man is as apparent in classical
statements of the freedom of indeterminism as in classical
statements of freedom of self-realization.   No such intent will
be discovered among the existentialists.

This difference between existentialists and their predecessors in theory of freedom is, however, of little importance so long as the problem at hand is that of determining whether undetermined choice is a genuine feature of the human reality. The differences relative to this problem are of a different order. Since these differences derive from an attempt to revamp the classical theory in order to meet modern objections, they will be most easily grasped after a brief restatement of the classical theory and of the objections to it.

The first thing to observe is that in the classical theory not all of an individual's choices are free. Ordinarily the individual's choices are determined by an objective situation together with a subjective motive. To take a prosaic example, if a person chooses one apple over another, it is usually because there are ready at hand a certain number of apples one of which is redder and juicier than the others (objective situation) and because the person likes or enjoys red and juicy apples (subjective motive). The question of free choice arises only when the objective situation and a subjective motive determine or dispose one to act in a manner which one apprehends in some way to be wrong or injurious to one's own best long-range interests. If, for instance, a starving beggar came along or if the doctor had ordered one not to eat apples, then one might decide to resist the determining influences of the empirical situation and the subjective motive; and it is at this point alone that the question of undetermined choice arises.

How, then, can one resist the determining influences? The apprehension that an envisaged act is wrong or injurious cannot by itself do the job. This mental apprehension is an item of knowledge; it belongs to the rational faculty of man which in some way participates in the immutability and imperturbability of the eternal objects. Knowledge, being eternal, cannot move us to act in the finite world. Besides, there are cases in which people know that something is bad for them and decide not to do it without having any success at all in executing their decision. Alcoholics and dope addicts know this; and so does anybody who has tried unsuccessfully to quit smoking. Neither can the passions or emotions do the job; these are among the very determining influences which we are trying to resist. There must, then, be a third faculty, which like the passions can move us to act but which unlike the passions is in the service of reason. This faculty is called the will.

An individual's choice is then free when it is in accordance with a decision by reason and has been executed by the will. It should be noted that the term "choice" as used here denotes, not the decision of the rational faculty, but the act of the reasoning being. Moreover, the choice or act is free only in the sense that it is not determined by external circumstance or by passion; for it *is* determined by a decision of reason and a movement of the will. This would seem to destroy the case being argued for. But the reasoning is that since man is by definition a rational being with free will, an act determined by reason and will is determined by the actor and is free in the sense that the individual is the author of it. By contrast, an act inspired by external environment or by passion, the latter being merely an accidental feature of the human personality, is not free because the determining factors are not properly parts of the individual's own person. Since the aim of the classical theory was simply to show that the individual may legitimately be held responsible for his behavior and since an individual was assumed to be responsible for behavior of which he is or could be the author, exponents of the theory usually rested their case here.

It is not necessary for an understanding of the existentialist theory to review all the many objections raised against the classical view. Those urged by medieval and early modern thinkers have almost no interest for us, in so far as they are based upon much the same premises as those of the thinkers against whom the criticisms were directed. The so-called faculty psychology or tripartite division of the human psyche into reason, will, and passion was one of these. So was the assumption that reason or the knowing faculty of man is sharply opposed to the passions and could not move man to act without the aid of the will. So, too, was the assumption that man is essentially a reasoning being and that the function of reason is to keep the passions under control.

Since Hume it has become customary to regard reason as "the slave of passion," its function being to satisfy human desires, not to keep them in check. Since the time of the Romantic movement it has become customary to regard passion as an essential and perhaps even more important attribute of the person than reason. And since the time of Freud the tripartite division of the soul into reason, will, and passion has been replaced by a tripartite division of the psyche into id, ego, and superego. Furthermore, throughout this whole period there has been relatively little interest in proving that man is the ultimate author of his actions, but a great deal of interest in proving that the methods of modern science which presuppose determinism can be applied to the area of human behavior.

One popular modern position, closely associated with scientism and epiphenomenalism, may be called the theory of determinism by the passions. On this view there is no free will. The classical argument for freedom of the will was based on the apparently observable fact that decisions of reason do often lead man to resist the solicitation of passion plus the classical premise that reason, the immortal and eternal faculty of mankind, is incapable of participating directly in the finite world of everyday affairs. Those who hold to the theory of determinism by the passions retain the classical philosophical premise involved but deny that decisions of reason influence conduct in any way. The actual causal determinant of behavior is passion. For instance, a man may have a passionate interest in being a doctor and at the same time a passionate interest in being a lawyer. After long deliberation the man may decide to become a doctor and subsequently actually become one. But the decision was not the cause of his behavior. At the very most it will be regarded as a link in a causal chain going back to the passions and ultimately to external circumstances. But more usually it is regarded as an epiphenomenon, that is to say, a reflection or ratification in consciousness of a causal process to which it does not belong at all. What happened according to the theory of determinism by the passions is that the passionate desire to become a doctor was stronger or weightier than the passionate desire to become a lawyer, with the result that the desire to become a doctor finally triumphed. Leibniz once spoke of the uncreated individual essences as if they had certain weights and as if they were all trying to push themselves into existence. Those with the greatest weight were physically incarnated. Similarly, the desires or passions have relative weights, and when an individual acts on one rather than another it is because the one adopted has more weight than the one rejected.

In arguing against the classical theory persons who hold to

the doctrine of determinism by the passions will often point out that the concept of the will is vague and useless. If reason cannot move man to act by itself and if reason does none the less in some way determine man to act, then the concept is indispensable. But what direct empirical or scientific reason is there for believing that the will exists? Frequently, rational decisions do not result in overt behavior. Frequently, a man decides to do something but finds that he is unable to act on his decision. Consider again the case of the man who decides to quit smoking but fails to do so. Various names exist for such cases: compulsion, incontinence, weakness of the will. Now, the argument is that if the will were an observable or knowable entity, there ought to be some reasonable criterion by which one can decide whether the person who decides to quit smoking but fails is a victim of passion or is simply weak-willed. But no such criterion exists. There is no way of knowing whether a person who fails to execute a rational decision has failed to do so because he is compelled by the passions or because he has not tried hard enough. The concept of the will cannot, therefore, stand for an observable entity or serve any useful purpose in the analysis of human motivation.

Sartre accepts this argument against the classical theory of freedom of the will, pointing out that neither the Stoics nor Descartes nor anyone else who has preached control of the passions by the will has ever explained how this control was to be achieved. But Sartre uses a similar argument against the doctrine of determinism by the passions. What, asks Sartre, can possibly be meant by saying that one passion is stronger or has more weight than another? Passions are not physical objects, and physical objects alone can be weighed. The only conceivable reason for saying that one passion is stronger than another in any given individual is that the individual actually chooses to act on one rather than the other. If the passions had observable weights, then the individual would know in advance what choices he would make by simple introspection of his passions. The fact, however, is that he does not know what choice he will make by any such method. It is a mistake to talk about passions as having weights in the first place, but if one must use this language then it should be recognized that "passions have only as much weight as we give to them."6

Freudianism is another modern position which arose as a

reaction against the classical theory of indeterminism and with respect to which Sartre defines his own views. According to Freud, the human psyche has three parts. The id consists of congenital drives or instincts such as the libido or love impulse, the instinct of aggression, and the death wish plus repressed desires, i.e., once fully conscious but now forgotten desires. The superego is that dimension of the self which internalizes parental commands and social precepts. The ego is the rational and deliberative level of the human psyche. The id and superego belong to the unconscious; the ego alone is conscious.

The Freudian theory may be called the theory of determinism by the unconscious, since according to it the primary determinants of human behavior are the drives, instincts, or desires residing in the id. Freud does, however, attribute some efficacy to the ego, i.e., the conscious and deliberative side of the human personality. In view of the knowledge it possesses about the physical and social environment, the ego, usually with the cooperation of the superego, does often prevent impulses of the id from expressing themselves in overt behavior. In the normal personality the ego acts on the unconscious whenever unconscious desires would lead to the performance of an act which the ego recognizes to be destructive or injurious to the total personality. It is, for instance, the ego which restrains an individual from acting out aggressive impulses against his father in Oedipus-complex rivalry. It does so because it knows that overt expression of that impulse could lead to his own destruction or to some damaging deprivation.

The restraint placed upon damaging unconscious impulses does not, however, result in their disappearance. Either the unconscious impulse is sublimated, that is, directed toward a different object from which the individual has less to fear, as when love for the mother is converted into a love of poetry, or else the unconscious impulse is repressed, in which case the impulse will find expression in dreams or some form of neurotic behavior. Furthermore, Freud was very dubious about the extent to which techniques of sublimation may be employed and also about the degree of satisfaction which the individual could derive from the sublimation of unconscious drives. Like the existentialists, Freud is a part of the anti-Enlightenment.

The major disagreement between Freud and the existentialists has to do with the role of choice as opposed to unconscious impulse in determining human behavior. Despite the qualifications discussed above, unconscious impulse is for Freud the original and major determinant of human behavior. For the existentialists the original and ultimately the only determinant of human behavior is free and conscious choice.

Sartre uses two principal arguments against Freudianism. The first of these has to do with the phenomenon of patient resistance. It often happens, according to Freud, that the patient resists the analyst, often even refusing to continue therapy, just as the analyst is on the verge of discovering the true cause of the patient's neurosis. Sartre does not deny that this phenomenon occurs; on the contrary, he accepts psychoanalytic reports to this effect implicitly. He says, however, that if the human personality were constituted in the manner Freud claims it is, this phenomenon could not occur.

Which part of the self, he asks, does the resisting? It cannot be the unconscious complex or impulse in the id. "The complex as such is rather the collaborator of the psychoanalyst since it aims at expressing itself in clear consciousness."[7] Neither can it be the ego which "by a conscious decision is in pursuit of psychoanalytic therapy."[8] Finally, it cannot be the unconscious superego or, as Freud also calls it, the censor. "The censor in order to apply its activity with discernment must know what it is repressing. . . . The resistance of the patient implies on the level of the censor an awareness of the thing repressed as such, a comprehension of the end toward which the questions of the psychoanalyst are leading, and an act . . . by which it compares the truth of the repressed complex to the psychoanalytic hypothesis which aims at it. These various operations . . . imply that the censor is conscious."[9]

The second argument has to do with the fact that psychoanalysts frequently offer as evidence of their analysis an intuitive sense of its correctness on the part of the patient. Again, Sartre does not deny the reality of this phenomenon or the evidential value of the patient's intuitive grasp of his own problem. What Sartre contends is that so long as one holds to the Freudian concept of the human personality one can explain neither the phenomenon itself nor its evidential value. At a certain state in treatment, says Sartre:

the resistance of the subject suddenly collapses and he recognizes the image of himself which is presented to him as if he were seeing himself in a mirror. This involuntary testimony of the subject is precious for the psychoanalyst; he sees there the sign that he has reached his goal; he can pass on from the investigation proper to the cure. But nothing in his principles or in his initial postulates permits him to understand or to utilize this testimony. Where could he get any such right? If the complex is really unconscious—that is, if there is a barrier separating the sign from the thing signified—how could the subject recognize it? Does the unconscious complex recognize itself? But haven't we been told that it lacks understanding? . . . Shall we say on the other hand that it is the subject as conscious who recognizes the image presented? But how could he compare it with his true state since that is out of reach . . . ? At most he will be able to judge that the psychoanalytic explanation of his case is a probable hypothesis, which derives its probability from the number of behavior patterns which it explains. His relation to this interpretation is that of a third party, that of the psychoanalyst himself; he has no privileged position.[10]

In sum, "the psychoanalyst doubtless has some obscure picture of an abrupt coincidence of conscious and unconscious. But he has removed all methods of conceiving of this coincidence in any positive sense."[11]

Still a third position with respect to the issues under consideration has made its appearance since the Western world rejected the fundamental premises in terms of which the classical doctrine of freedom of indeterminism was formulated. Since, however, Sartre has not explicitly dealt with this third position, it will be best to reserve discussion of it until after Sartre's own theory has been presented.

The Existentialist Theory

The chief difference between Sartre's and classical theories of free choice can be summarized in a single sentence: "Man," says Sartre, "cannot be sometimes slave and sometimes free; he is wholly and forever free, or he is not free at all."[12] According to classical theories, human behavior is most often determined by an objective situation and a subjective motive; it is only when reason indicates that behavior so determined is morally wrong or injurious to one's best long-range interests that free choice comes into play. Sartre, on the contrary, denies that either objective situations or subjective motives ever really move us to act. The objective situation moves us to act only in so far as we apprehend it, and our apprehension of an objective situation is itself determined by a free choice of goals. Similarly, passions or subjective motives can be said to move us only in a derivative sense, since passions have only the weight we give them. We are not playthings of our passions; it is we who choose them.

No great harm is done at the level of popular discourse if we say that the conversion of Clovis is to be explained in terms of his subjective passion, that is, his ambition for fame and power, together with an objective situation, that is, the existence of the Church as a powerful political ally. In the same way no great harm is done if we explain that a man joined a socialist party because he believed that in the years to come socialism "will become the principal historical force" (objective situation) and also because he has certain subjective motives such as "a feeling of pity or charity for certain classes of the oppressed, a feeling of shame at being on the 'good side of the barricade,' . . . or again an inferiority complex, a desire to shock his relatives."[13]

It is obvious that passions or subjective motives do in some sense exist. The mistake consists in regarding them as "little psychical entities inhabiting consciousness"[14] and exercising an original causal influence rather than as manifestations of a prior choice. It is also obvious that there are objective, environmental situations. The mistake consists in believing either that these objective situations can move us to act independently of the way in which the reflective or deliberative consciousness apprehends them or that consciousness simply mirrors an already structured reality. It would be nearer the truth to say that the world mirrors consciousness than that consciousness mirrors the world; and it is of course our personal apprehension of the world, not the world itself, which effectively determines behavior.

Deliberation, says Sartre, is merely "an evaluation of means in relation to already existing ends."[15] Clovis no doubt had an objective appreciation of the political and religious state of

Gaul, the relative strength of the episcopate, the great land-owners, the common people, and so forth.

> Nevertheless this objective appreciation can be made only in the light of a presupposed end and within the limits of a project of the for-itself towards this end. . . . In a word the world gives counsel only if one questions it, and one can question it only for a well-determined end.   Therefore, the objective apprecia-tion, far from determining the action, appears only in and through the project of an action.   It is in and through the project of imposing his rule on all of Gaul that the state of the Western Church appears objectively to Clovis as a cause of conversion.   In other words the consciousness which carves out the cause in the ensemble of the world has already its own structure; it has given its own ends to itself.[16]

The true cause, the real motive of human behavior is thus an original project of being freely chosen at the moment one wrenches oneself away from the in-itself to create one's own world.   And it is in terms of this original project of being and it alone that human behavior receives its ultimate explanation. "Heredity, education, environment, physiological constitu-tion" are "the great explanatory idols of our time,"[17] but they explain nothing.   The only genuine cause of human behavior is the individual's fundamental project of being.   And that project is a "choice, not a state";[18] it is not buried in "the shadows of the subconscious."   It is rather a "free and conscious determination"[19] of oneself.

Great care must be taken to avoid misinterpretation.   Free-dom, for Sartre, does not consist, as it did for Dostoyevsky, in mere caprice.   The individual's fundamental and freely chosen project of being expresses the "totality of his movement toward being, his original relationship to himself, the world, and others."   Man, Sartre says, "is a totality, not a collection."[20] An act of caprice by which the individual belies his original choice and renders his behavior inexplicable is totally impossible. On the contrary, given knowledge of an individual's fundamental project of being, it is possible to understand "the most insig-nificant and the most superficial aspects of his conduct."[21]

For Sartre, as for Leibniz, "the problem of freedom is placed on the level of Adam's choice of himself,"[22] not on the level of Adam's choosing or not choosing to eat the apple.   Given Adam's choice of himself, he could not but eat the apple.

Furthermore, for Sartre, as for Leibniz, a different subsidiary choice of Adam would imply another Adam, which in turn would imply another world. "But by 'another world' we do not mean a particular organization of compossibles such that the other possible Adam finds his place there, but rather that the revelation of another face of the world will correspond to another being-in-the-world of Adam."[23] The individual's choice of himself is, of course, subject to change in moments of anguish. None the less Sartre agrees with Leibniz in rejecting a conception of freedom as mere caprice.

Another misinterpretation to be avoided consists in confusing the consciousness which makes the choice of an initial or fundamental project of being with the reflective or deliberative consciousness, which is subsequent to that choice. Sartre does not accept the Freudian division of the self into conscious and unconscious. He does, however, himself distinguish between what he calls the "reflective" and what he calls the "nonreflective" consciousness; and he insists that it is at the level of the nonreflective consciousness that we make our fundamental choice of ourselves. "It is necessary to stress the fact that this [man's original choice] is in no way a deliberate choice. This is not because it would be less conscious or less explicit than a deliberation, but on the contrary because it is the foundation of all deliberation and because . . . a deliberation requires an interpretation in terms of an original choice."[24]

It follows that "a voluntary deliberation is always a deception." When I deliberate, "the die is already cast." If I find myself deliberating, "it is simply because one of the features of my original project is to make myself aware of the motives of my conduct by deliberation rather than by some other form of discovery (by passion, for example, or quite simply by action)."[25] It will readily be seen that Sartre goes even farther than Freud with respect to the ultimate inefficacy of the reflective consciousness.

Sartre recognizes, however, that the reflective consciousness can decide to set itself up in opposition to the nonreflective consciousness and that sometimes it can succeed in thwarting the aims of the nonreflective consciousness, just as Freud recognized that the ego can oppose the id and by so doing alter the individual's behavior. To explain these facts without compromising his belief in the ultimate inefficacy of reflective consciousness, Sartre reasons as follows: A man, he says,

> can make voluntary decisions which are opposed to the fundamental ends which he has chosen. These decisions can be only voluntary—that is, reflective. . . . Thus, for example, . . . I can . . . decide to cure myself of stuttering. I can even succeed in it. . . . In fact I can obtain a result by using merely technical methods. . . . But these results will only displace the infirmity from which I suffer; another will arise in its place and will in its own way express the total end which I pursue. . . . It is the same with these cures as it is with the cure of hysteria by electric shock treatment. We know that this therapy can effect the disappearance of an hysterical contraction of the leg, but as one will see some time later the contraction will appear in the arm. This is because the hysteria can be cured only as a totality, for it is a total project of the for-itself.[26]

Sartre's ultimate proof that an individual's behavior is fully determined by a free, prereflective or nonreflective choice of himself is, of course, the experience of anguish in which the individual finds himself compelled to reconstitute his being in utter isolation and without external help. But he offers three additional arguments. One of these is contained in the statement: "A deliberation requires an interpretation in terms of an original choice." The point is that if an individual is trying to decide whether to be a doctor or a lawyer, his final decision can be explained only on the assumption that there was an overarching value or desire which guided the process of deliberation. In the pamphlet "Existentialism Is a Humanism" Sartre tells of a young man who came to him during the war for advice. He wanted to know whether he should stay in France with his mother who had no other means of support or to leave France to join Free French forces abroad. Sartre says that he did not advise the man because one person can no more decide for another than the individual can decide for himself at the purely reflective level of consciousness. The man, he says, had already made up his mind; it was in terms of his original choice that he chose an adviser.

The second argument is based upon "the frequent upsurge of 'conversions' which cause me totally to metamorphose my original project. These conversions, which have not been studied by philosophers, have often inspired novelists. One may recall the instant at which Gide's Philoctetes casts off his hate, his fundamental project, his reason for being, and his being. One may recall the instant when Raskolnikoff decides to give himself up."[27] The point of this argument appears to be, as an American philosopher who on this score holds a position similar to Sartre's has put it, that "when we repudiate our constitutive values altogether and forge an entirely new personality, a naked, empty self must do the choosing."[28] In other words, radical conversions do exist and cannot be explained as a product of rational deliberation, passion, or environmental circumstances.

The third argument is based upon "the twofold 'feeling' of anguish and of responsibility." For most persons "consciousness" means what Sartre calls "reflective consciousness," and they might very well argue that if we are not aware of having made a choice of ourselves on the level of the reflective consciousness, we could not be aware of it at all. Moreover, we are not aware of choosing ourselves on the level of the reflective consciousness. To the reflective consciousness our behavior appears to be determined largely by passion and environmental circumstance. Sartre is aware of this possible line of attack. "We are fully conscious of the choice which we are," he says. "And if someone objects that . . . it would be necessary to be conscious not of *our-being-chosen* but of *choosing* ourselves, we reply that this consciousness is expressed by the twofold 'feeling' of anguish and responsibility."[29]

By the sense of responsibility Sartre means the sense of being "the incontestable author" of one's being.[30] The feeling of anguish is an awareness either "muted or full-strength" that "an abrupt metamorphosis of my initial project is always possible."[31] Now, for the person who has known the full-strength experience of anguish there can be no question, according to Sartre, that one is the free author of one's actual behavior or that one could by a subsequent free choice totally change one's initial project. Sartre comes close to defining the experience of anguish as one which brings a realization of these facts to the very surface of consciousness. But how is the person who has not personally had the full-strength experience of anguish to know that it is possible? Sartre's answer is not as clear as might be wished; but it appears to be as follows. The prereflective or nonreflective awareness of anguish and responsibility is manifested on the surface of consciousness in the sense of pride or shame; and it is perfectly clear even to the reflective consciousness that we are often proud or ashamed of features of our behavior which we have not chosen at that level of consciousness.

The homosexual, for instance, often insists that he is compelled to behave as he does, that he is not the author of his homosexuality. On the reflective level of consciousness there is no awareness of having chosen this behavior, and often the reflective consciousness is actively engaged in resisting the homosexual inclinations. At the same time, however, the homosexual experiences a strong and fully conscious sense of shame. Why, however, should he feel ashamed of his behavior if he has not chosen it? And if he has not chosen it on the reflective level of consciousness, must he not have chosen it on the nonreflective level of consciousness? What is his shame but a muted consciousness of anguish and responsibility? Is it not an implicit awareness that he is the incontestable author of his behavior and that it is possible for him, if he so chooses, to abandon his homosexuality? Shame under these circumstances is an indisputable fact; and once the inescapable logical consequences have been made explicit, it is no longer possible to deny the facts which the existentialists claim to be revealed in the full-strength experience of anguish. Speaking of the person subjected to torture, Sartre writes: "No matter how long he has waited before begging for mercy, he would have been able despite all to wait ten minutes, one minute, one second longer. He has determined the moment at which the pain becomes unbearable. The proof of this is the fact that he will later live out his abjuration in remorse and shame. Thus he is entirely responsible for it."[32]

Criticism

The third non-existentialist position on the problems under discussion is widely held by Anglo-American philosophers. Most of the theory underlying this position was worked out by the pragmatists, and for lack of a more precise or convenient label it will be referred to here as the pragmatic position.

For the pragmatists, as for the ordinary man, freedom consists in the power to achieve chosen goals. The pragmatists do not deny that there may be *some* undetermined choices, but this question does not much interest them. What matters is that man be able to achieve the goals he has actually set for himself, regardless of whether his decision to pursue these goals was determined or undetermined. The pragmatists are not interested in God or sin. And, as they see it, human dignity consists not in the anguished sense of total responsibility for one's being but rather in the full exercise of those faculties by which the individual can hope to achieve well-being for himself and his fellow men. The question of determinism arises in this connection only because in order to achieve general well-being human behavior must be at least partially determined. If it were not, prediction and consequently control over the future course of events would be impossible.

The pragmatists are not the least bit disturbed by the existentialist contention that happiness is impossible of achievement and that freedom even in the sense of power to achieve goals has as its logical condition the existence of external obstacles. If by happiness one means a state of complete desire fulfillment and if by freedom one means a state of being such that the external environment offers not the slightest resistance to human effort, then happiness and freedom are impossible of achievement. The existentialist arguments are unassailable. But the pragmatists do not believe in either the desirability or the possibility of happiness and freedom so conceived.

Happiness for the pragmatists is not a state of sated desire. It is a state of being such that a man can look forward to the realization of his desires with *relative* ease. The existentialists have taken over from the classical tradition the idea that desire as such is a state of lack or imperfection. Perhaps so, say the pragmatists; it depends upon what you mean by lack or imperfection. But it is certain that a state of desire is not necessarily a state of unhappiness, misery, or psychic distress. A man who is only moderately hungry and who can look forward to eating a good meal at no great sacrifice to purse or health is not unhappy. Some people enjoy the anticipation of a good meal more than the actual eating. Similarly, the student who is working for a college degree need not be unhappy because the goal is as yet unachieved; some students deliberately prolong their student days because they find student activities pleasant. Moreover, there is no reason to define happiness so narrowly as to bar the pleasures of pursuit and risk. Some people find happiness in danger; that is their privilege. But it is clear that most men's well-being would be promoted if the number of obstacles presented by their social and natural environment was considerably reduced.

Dewey was so displeased with the traditional associations of the word "happiness" that he abandoned it altogether. He agrees, none the less, with other pragmatists in holding that the object of human striving is a state of being which permits the satisfaction of desire with relative ease, "relative ease" being defined differently for each individual according to the nature of his desires, the nature of his environment, and his own temperamental bias.

The mistake of the existentialists is similar to that of philosophers in the classical tradition. They pushed a concept to its very limits and found themselves with nothing but a meaningless and self-contradictory concept on their hands. Had the existentialists, however, exercised a little more care and had they taken seriously their own strictures against empty abstractions, they would not have found themselves with a concept requiring to be rejected.

On the question of freedom the pragmatists make out a similar case. By freedom they do not mean the possibility of doing anything at all that comes to mind. As Justus Buchler, the most profound of contemporary American thinkers in the pragmatic tradition, has pointed out, the degree of freedom and the degree of restraint are roughly equivalent. To be able to achieve chosen goals, one must first be able to choose. But if the environment is not well structured, i.e., if the range of choice is not limited and determined by external circumstances, then one hardly knows what one wants. One can, of course, wish for anything at all, as a child may wish to jump over the moon. But a wish does not become a want until one has determined that and how the goal may be achieved. In a state of complete anarchy or disorder the environment would be so complex and the result of one's behavior so unpredictable that one could have little adequate knowledge of means to ends, consequently

few well-defined wants, and consequently only a small degree
of freedom.

The mistake of the existentialists was once again to push the
concept of freedom as ability to achieve chosen goals to its
furthest limits, only to discover that it was empty. Had they
remembered the elementary fact of both private and political
life that the desirable state of affairs is one with a maximum of
order and a maximum of freedom and were they less disposed
to think in terms of rigid antitheses, they would have taken care
not to empty the word "freedom" of its concreteness. We are
not less but more free because there are laws against murder
and because there are police around to enforce them. If we
want to kill someone, laws and police are obstacles which limit
our freedom. But if, as is more often the case, we want to walk
without fear down the streets, these "obstacles" liberate us.
Freedom to achieve chosen goals thus implies, not the absence
of obstacles, but the existence of the right kinds of obstacles in
the right amounts.

The most important pragmatic tenet, however, concerns the
role of what Freud called the ego and what Sartre called the
reflective consciousness. The pragmatists agree with almost
all modern thinkers in regarding man as fundamentally a
desiring or passionate being. It would be impossible to understand any major human pursuits or even to define them without
taking human affectivity into account. Happiness and freedom
are not just abstract concepts, they are states of being toward
which men passionately strive; and it is as such that they must
be defined. None the less, the pragmatists differ from the
existentialists, the Freudians, and the proponents of determinism
by the passions in attributing substantial efficacy to rational
reflection.

It is not that the pragmatists are under any illusion as to the
extent to which men do in fact employ their intelligence; nor are
the pragmatists excessively optimistic about the possibility of
humankind ever making full use of intelligence. Their position is simply that the exercise of intelligence is almost always a
necessary condition of general human well-being and that,
barring unfavorable environmental conditions it would also
be a sufficient condition. If men have not utilized their
intelligence to create a substantially better world, it is largely
because so few men believe in it. Either in the manner of

traditional philosophers and the world's major religions they seek a short cut to happiness through eternal objects; or else like the Roman plebs and America's Beats they settle for cheap sensations and kicks rather than more solid satisfactions requiring an expenditure of mental effort; or else again they wallow in the sense of their own helplessness, calling it the tragic sense of life, like the existentialists. It is the flight from intelligence, not the human condition, which is truly tragic.

The first major argument against the efficacy of the reflective consciousness was that the only proper objects of human thinking are eternal and immutable objects and that since like alone knows like, the mind itself must be eternal and immutable, consequently unable to act in the finite world of everyday affairs. This argument has little cogency for twentieth-century man and need not detain us.

The second major argument was based on the fact of compulsion or incontinence. Here the problem is not to explain how man the thinker can relate to the nonthinking world but rather how man the thinker can act upon his passions. It is clear that often he cannot. According to the theory of determinism by the passions he never does. If, however, the classical philosophical premise that the mind cannot move us to act is squarely rejected, what grounds are there for maintaining that conscious human decisions never act upon the passions? The empirical fact that they sometimes do not do so proves only that. And if we admit as evidence of a noncausal relationship between conscious decision and passion the fact that a decision to stop smoking is sometimes not successful, then one must also admit as evidence of a causal relationship between conscious decision and passion the fact that a decision to stop smoking *is* sometimes successful.

To say that *A* is the cause of *B* is to assert simply that *A* and *B* are two natural types of events which have been observed to be correlated in certain types of circumstances. The only problem then is to find out what types of decisions correlate with what types of affective experience and under what circumstances. There can be no empirical, much less philosophical, barrier to construing the reflective or deliberative consciousness as a genuine cause of human behavior.

Empirically we have nothing to go on but what we actually observe either through introspection or through the physical senses. And what we actually observe, says the pragmatist, is that just as a decision to lift one's arm is followed by the lifting of the arm except in cases of physical paralysis, so a decision to stop drinking is followed by the execution of the decision unless we are paralyzed by habit or some other empirically describable obstacle. The nonalcoholic who decides not to drink does not drink; it is only the man who has been drinking heavily for a long time and under very special circumstances who cannot act on a decision to stop drinking. Moreover, there is good reason to believe that most actual limits of rational decision have been produced by a past failure to exercise reason and that these limits may someday be removed by the future exercise of reason. Had the alcoholic fully reflected upon the possible consequences of his drinking when he first noted the symptoms of alcoholism, he might never have found himself so hopelessly in the grip of the habit. And if modern research into the problem of alcoholism is successful, it may one day be possible to cure even the confirmed alcoholic.

Of course, limits to the power of rational decision are many and varied; habit is only one of them. But if the limits have actually been observed, they are in every case empirical, not a priori. And if it is reasonable on pragmatic grounds to believe that the course of nature will remain constant, it is also reasonable on pragmatic grounds to believe that man can triumph over empirically observed limits of reason by a more persistent application of reason. Both assumptions are required to promote scientific inquiry, and there is not the slightest shred of evidence to the contrary. In fact, the belief that man can triumph over empirically observed limits of reason is not simply an assumption; it is an empirically founded generalization. By the use of reason man has obviously overcome many limits imposed upon him by the natural environment; no less obviously he has learned to control some aspects of human behavior.

It can be plausibly argued that these past triumphs of reason have not brought man happiness; but the pragmatist can plausibly argue that this is not because of an intrinsic defect in reason. On the contrary, there is nothing reasonable about using scientific knowledge to build atomic bombs instead of hospitals or to sell toothpaste instead of books. If reason has failed to benefit us, it is simply because men have misused it.

No extensive criticism of existentialism from the pragmatic point of view exists, but it is not difficult to see what form that criticism would take. Consider the three arguments for a fundamental choice of oneself which Sartre offers to the person who has not known the full-strength experience of anguish. The first was to the effect that the process of rational deliberation in which the individual attempts to choose between two or more envisaged lines of conduct cannot have a successful issue unless there be an antecedently given overarching desire in the light of which he can evaluate the envisaged lines of conduct. Why, however, the pragmatists would ask, should it not happen that the process of deliberation itself be a means by which the individual shapes his desires? If, for instance, in the process of deliberation the person who is trying to choose between a career as a doctor or a career as a lawyer discovers that there is a third profession which combines most of the advantages he had hoped for in the first two professions, one might be tempted to say that this third profession is the one he had always really wanted to pursue from the beginning. Would it not, however, be more correct to say simply that a new desire had emerged as a result of rational reflection?

In *Being and Nothingness* Sartre made a concession to the pragmatic point of view. In discussing existential psychoanalysis, the method for discovering an individual's fundamental project of being, Sartre declared that the "principle of this psychoanalysis is that man is a totality and not a collection; he therefore expresses himself in his totality in the most insignificant and the most superficial aspects of his conduct." It obviously follows from this principle that all reflective choices as well as all overt acts are rigidly determined by the fundamental choice. Later, however, Sartre qualified this principle. There are, he says, certain voluntary choices which he calls "indifferents." If, for instance, I become fatigued on a camping trip, this is because of my original project of being, but "to relieve my fatigue it is indifferent whether I sit down on the side of the road or whether I take a hundred steps more in order to stop at the inn which I see from a distance. This means that the apprehension of the complex, global form which I have chosen as my ultimate possible does not suffice to account for the choice of one possible rather than another."[33] The example Sartre gives, as also his use of the term "indifferents" to describe choices of this kind, would indicate that the concession is not an important one.

The passage quoted, however, concludes as follows: "There is not here an act deprived of motives and causes but rather a spontaneous invention of motives and causes, which placed within the compass of my fundamental choice thereby enriches it."[34] Now, if one grants that a reflective decision can enrich one's fundamental project, there is no reason to deny that it can also alter it. The example of the young man who had to choose between remaining in France or joining the French forces abroad was introduced earlier to illustrate Sartre's contention that when one begins to deliberate the die is already cast. The man could not, said Sartre, even decide whom to consult for advice unless he had already made his choice. Significantly, however, Sartre also uses this example to illustrate the necessity we are under to "invent." And indeed why not? If the man had already decided, why was it so difficult for him to decide? If there was an overarching choice which demanded that he choose one possibility rather than another, why did he not know it? And certainly in this case the choice is not aptly described as an "indifferent."

The second argument was based on radical conversions. But are there radical conversions? Does it ever happen that an individual rejects all of the values and desires which had hitherto constituted his being? Unless this can be shown, conversion phenomena can always be explained as the end products of a long struggle between competing scales of value or competing desire systems. Moreover, a choice of oneself made by a naked and empty nothingness in the face of a massive, undifferentiated, meaningless in-itself would appear to be as impossible as lifting oneself up by one's own bootstraps.

Sartre seems to have come around to this view himself. In the *Critique of Dialectical Reason*, where he attempts to reconcile his doctrine of total freedom with his Marxism, Sartre introduces the expression "field of possibilities" and tells us that freedom must operate within this field. "The field of possibilities," he says, "is the end toward which the agent surpasses his objective situation. And this field, in its turn, is closely linked to historical and social reality. ... We ought not to regard it as a zone of indetermination but, on the contrary, as a highly structured region, which depends upon the entire historical situation."[35]

The third argument was based on the experience of shame, guilt, and pride. The homosexual and the person who yields to torture have no reflective awareness of having chosen their behavior; yet they experience shame because of it. Must it not, therefore, be assumed that they have chosen their behavior on the nonreflective level of consciousness? There is, however, another explanation of feelings of shame. One could say with great plausibility that the homosexual and the person who has yielded to torture feel ashamed not because they have a pre-reflective awareness of being the authors of their behavior, but rather because they are aware that others do or may despise them for it. And the fact of their being an object of contempt for others may very well be something for which they are in no way responsible. Sartre himself offers this alternative explanation of shame. "It is," he writes, "before the Other that I am guilty. . . . But this guilt is accompanied by helplessness without this helplessness ever succeeding in cleansing me of my guilt."[36]

There remains, then, only the most basic of Sartre's arguments, that founded on the full-strength experience of anguish. On the pragmatic view the ultimate external realities are individual beings presented to the physical senses: mountains, trees, houses, airplanes, dogs, human beings, and so forth. These objects are related to one another in a variety of ways, and although there is much confusion in the external world a number of regularities may be discovered. Man comes into this world as one being among others, but during the course of his existence he discerns causal patterns among natural events and gradually becomes an active, desiring being. These things the pragmatist claims to know by simple observation or common sense. For Sartre, on the other hand, the ultimate external reality is an undifferentiated mass, the in-itself, and man comes into the world as a pure nothingness face to face with the in-itself. This Sartre claims to know through the experience of anguish.

What, then, is the validity of anguish as opposed to daily, common-sense observation? Why should anguish be said to be revelatory of the nature of things? Christian mystics often claim to have had a direct experience of the divine presence in much the same way that other people have a direct experience of physical objects. As a rule, pragmatists have not denied the reality of the mystic experience. They have simply denied that the experience had revelatory value. The feeling of a divine presence does not prove the existence of God. It often happens that we have an almost palpable sense of the presence of another person in the same room with us even though that person left unobserved several minutes earlier. Why should the feeling of a divine presence not be a phenomenon of the same order? In like manner, the pragmatists would probably not deny that Sartre and others have had an experience in which the world of ordinary objects and the personal values which they say sustain that world are dissolved. What they would deny is that this experience has weight as evidence of the true nature of man and external reality.

Because it is impossible to observe colors at night, it does not follow that colors have no real existence. Because a person with jaundice sees an object as yellow, it does not follow that the object is in fact yellow. Similarly, because in the experience of anguish the world disappears from view, it does not follow that the world is merely a thin crust of meaning imposed upon an in-itself or that the ultimate external reality is really an undifferentiated mass. When in ordinary discourse we say that something appears to be *A* but is really *B*, we confirm our statement by recourse to one of two criteria. A thing, we say, is really what it appears to be to the normal or standard observer under normal or standard conditions. The real color of an object, for instance, is the color the object has for a person with ordinary vision who observes it in ordinary light. Here the criterion is the democratic one of how a thing usually appears to the majority of human beings. Other times we have recourse to a second criterion. We say that the real color of an object is the color it has for the person with exceptionally good vision who observes it under a strong, pure white light. Here the criterion of reality is that of the specialist, who wishes to make the maximum number of possible discriminations. By either of these criteria the experience of anguish must be rejected as a means of discovering the nature of reality.

The existentialist would point out in answer that the criteria of reality employed by the pragmatist presuppose his own system of values and his own ontological commitments. It is because pragmatism is essentially a philosophy for the ordinary man that the democratic criterion is employed; and it is because the ordinary man believes in the value of science and has in the modern age entrusted himself to the experts that pragmatism also uses the specialists' criterion. At the same time, it is because the pragmatist has already decided that physically observable objects are the ultimate realities that he frames his criteria of reality with respect to individual physical objects. His criteria of reality are, therefore, no better than his system of values and his ontology; and to employ these criteria to refute a rival system of values and a rival ontology is merely to beg the question.

One could, as many members of the analytic movement have done, attempt to show that the pragmatic criteria of reality are among the rules governing the usage of terms such as "real" and "reality," and that it is therefore an abuse of language to employ these terms in any other sense. But again the existentialists would retort that the rules governing ordinary discourse are merely reflections of the ordinary man's values and unconscious ontological commitments. The person who rejects the ordinary man's values and ontology is, therefore, under no obligation to observe them.

If, of course, the pragmatist must presuppose his own axiology and ontology in order to argue against the existentialists, then the existentialist will have to presuppose his axiology and ontology to argue against the pragmatist. It would appear that we have at this point reached an ultimate impasse. What is certainly clear is that no simple arguments of either a logical or an empirical character will provide an exit. As Buchler has shown, an escape from an impasse of this kind between rival philosophical schemes can only be effected by providing a philosophical framework sufficiently broad and generous to permit thinkers in both schools to incorporate whatever they still consider to be true and valuable after they have traced the full implications of their initial beliefs and value orientations.

V. Authenticity

Heidegger on Authenticity

The term "authenticity" was introduced by Heidegger and was later taken over by Sartre. The term does not, however, have precisely the same meaning for the two authors. In the widest sense an authentic life is one based upon an accurate appraisal of the human condition. Sartre's and Heidegger's concepts of authenticity therefore reflect not only the similarities but also the differences in their views about the human condition.

The first and most important of the similarities is insistence upon the radical duality between the human and the nonhuman, which both authors express by reserving the term "existence" for man alone. Heidegger writes: "The being that exists is man. Man alone exists. Rocks are, but they do not exist. Trees are, but they do not exist. Horses are, but they do not exist. Angels are, but they do not exist. God is, but he does not exist."[1] And, of course, for both Heidegger and Sartre it is the fact of consciousness which radically distinguishes man from other beings. "The existential nature of man is the reason why man can represent beings as such, and why he can be conscious of them."[2]

Aristotle had listed a set of basic categories; among them were quantity, quality, space, and cause. Now, according to Heidegger, categories of this kind are suitable enough for the scientific study of material objects, but are totally unsuitable for the study of man. Human beings do not exist in space and they do not have quantities or qualities. Neither are they to be understood as links in some causal chain of events. If Heidegger is right, however, traditional philosophers from Socrates on down all made the mistake of attributing to man properties which properly belong only to material objects. To correct this mistake Heidegger lists what he calls existentialia, i.e., basic categories of human existence. There are three of them: feeling or affectivity, understanding, and speech. Sartre did not take over Heidegger's doctrine of existentialia, but he is of course sympathetic to Heidegger's rejection of traditional categories in so far as these were believed to apply to human beings.

The second major similarity is the view that man, though radically distinct from physical objects, is directly present to the world. Heidegger's technical expression for man is *Dasein*, which means literally "being-there." Man is the being who is immediately present to the world and who must live out his life in and through his inescapable relationship to the world.

Thirdly, both Sartre and Heidegger distinguish between man's being-in-the-world and his being-in-the-midst-of-the-world, between what they also call the ontological and the ontic dimension of his being. The purpose of drawing this distinction is to make clear that although man is necessarily present to the world and cannot withdraw from it into some sheltered or self-contained region of being which is purely his, he need not for this reason get lost in the world and sink to the level of brute material objects. Man is present to or next to the world, but not in the way that two chairs may be present to or next to one another. Physical objects are literally in the world; they are spatial beings. But man is not literally "in" the world; his being-in-the-world is merely a presence to the world.

For both Sartre and Heidegger, then, an authentic man is one who recognizes the radical duality between the human and the nonhuman, who recognizes that man must live in the world, and who also recognizes that being-in-the-world does not imply being-in-the-midst-of-the-world. It is in the light of these themes that Heidegger formulates his theory of inauthenticity.

To the state of being-in-the-midst-of-the-world Heidegger also gives the name of "fallenness" (*Verfallenheit*). The choice of this term is a bit curious, since Heidegger regards this condition as the one in which all of us find ourselves upon the dawning of consciousness. There is no primitive paradise or original condition of being from which we have fallen; there is only a superior mode of being to which we must rise. Be that as it may, fallenness, being-in-the-midst-of-the-world, and inauthenticity are three names for the same thing.

This inauthentic state of fallenness or being-in-the-midst-of-the-world has a subjective and an objective pole. The subjective pole is what Heidegger calls *das Man*, a term which has been variously translated as "the One," "the Public," and "the Anonymous They." The most literal translation is "the One." What Heidegger had in mind in choosing this term was the German expression *Man sagt*, which means in English "One says" or "They say." In the state of fallenness it is the public or an anonymous and amorphous third party—a kind of degraded or pseudo-subjectivity—which commands the individual's consciousness. If he refrains from acting, it is because "that isn't done." When he acts, it is because it is "the thing to do." Fallenness is a state in which the individual constantly obeys commands and prohibitions whose source is unknown and unidentifiable and whose justification he does not bother to inquire into.

The objective pole of fallenness is the artificial, man-made world, the world as transformed by human technology. It is also, of course, the public world or world which groups of human beings share in common. This world has its own time; for clock time bears little or no resemblance to time as it is subjectively experienced. It also has its own space; for subjectively it is by an act of care or attention that we decide what will be present to us and in what degree, whereas in the public world distances between objects are precisely determinable by mathematical measurement, and the standard of reference by which these determinations are made is wholly impersonal. Subjectively, the distant mountains which we look at are nearer to us than the spectacles on our nose, but objectively the reverse is true. Most important of all, the public world or world of *das Man* is a world in which objects exist almost entirely as instruments to be manipulated for the advantage of the public.

The artificial human milieu of the factory best illustrates this last point, since it consists almost wholly of machines designed to produce a product for sale to a public. The worker himself becomes hardly more than a machine. His every act is determined by a group of managers whom he does not know and who do not know him. His work is completely routinized; almost anybody could replace him. And he has not the slightest interest in the product which is ultimately turned out. He is simply an object serving the needs of a voracious public. He is not present to the world as a painter or poet is present to the world; he is *in* that world as one physical object is in the world with other physical objects.

In a region of being whose one pole is the pseudo-subjectivity of *das Man* and whose other pole is a pseudo-objectivity or artificial human environment, we become forgetful of the ontological roots of our being. The existentialia are, according to Heidegger, ontological necessities of the human condition from which no one can possibly escape, but in the state of fallenness or inauthenticity they become degraded. In this mode of being we have no deep feelings, only petty fears and neurotic anxieties. We do not attempt to understand what we are doing; our behavior is determined by habit, custom, or a vague sense of what is required of us by *das Man*. We do not talk seriously about matters of any importance; it is bad taste to discuss religion, politics, or philosophy. Instead we talk shop or gossip about friends. Perhaps, if we have intellectual pretensions, we try to prove that we are *au courant*: that we have read all the latest books and attended all the current art exhibits. But we do not seriously discuss the content of the books we read, and in all likelihood when we go to the museum we take care to bring someone along to distract our attention from the exhibits.

How can we escape from this condition of being-in-the-midst-of-the-world, from fallenness, from inauthenticity, from *das Man* and the machine culture which is its correlate? The obvious answer is by becoming conscious through anguish of the radical duality between the human and the nonhuman and by recognizing the difference between being-in-the-world and being-in-the-midst-of-the-world. This answer does not, however, take us far enough. Like Sartre, Heidegger distinguishes between the everyday world of instrumental complexes and a world which lies behind it; and, like Sartre, Heidegger distinguishes between a level of consciousness which is engaged in the everyday world and another level of consciousness which lies beyond it. Despite these similarities, Sartre and Heidegger begin to part company at this point.

For Heidegger the ultimately real world is not a massive, undifferentiated in-itself which inspires nausea; it is rather the world of the artist and the poet—a richer and more luminous world than the skeletal world of steel and glass which man has invented; a world of fleshy elements such as air, fire, water, and earth; a world which speaks to man, imperiously perhaps and obscurely, but also inspiringly. On the other hand, the level of consciousness by which man has access to the real world is not a pure nothingness which creates its own meanings out of whole cloth. It is rather a level of consciousness which hearkens to the voice of Being and which consents to be "the shepherd of Being."

This last point is one of the most puzzling and difficult in Heidegger's system. Heidegger has several times said that he is not an existentialist, that he is interested in Being rather than man. His major work, *Being and Time*, was to consist of two parts, the first being an analysis of human existence and the second an analysis of Being. Only the first has appeared, and critics almost unanimously declare that the second never will appear. None the less, Heidegger declared already in the preface to the published half of *Being and Time* that he undertook the analysis of human existence only because it was a necessary preliminary to the analysis of Being. And it is clear from *Being and Time* no less than from Heidegger's later writings that he does not believe man invents meaning and truth. Man can invent only pragmatic truths, and these do not deserve the title. Truth itself, the real truth, man can know only to the extent that he agrees to be illuminated by Being.

For Heidegger, Being is neither a particular being nor the whole of all particular beings, not even a particular being or the whole of particular beings revealed to the consciousness which lies beyond the everyday world of instrumental complexes and *das Man*. Being is rather that which makes or causes the world to be and which at the same time illuminates or makes appear to man the world which it also causes to be. Unfortunately, Heidegger has not given us a sufficiently adequate description of Being or explained in sufficient detail how Being accomplishes the functions attributed to it to warrant further exposition. In fact, Heidegger's theory up to this point resembles so closely a theory developed by Plato in the *Republic* that, given Heidegger's insistence upon his own originality, one cannot even be sure that the exposition so far as it has gone is wholly correct. The chief difference between Plato's theory in the *Republic* and Heidegger's is that what Heidegger calls "Being" Plato called the One. Suffice it to say that for Heidegger the authentic man is ultimately a person who has been illuminated by Being and who has made himself the shepherd of Being.

The qualification "ultimately" in the last sentence is important because the Heideggerian theory of authenticity just presented is drawn largely from later writings. In *Being and Time* Heidegger tended to define the authentic man exclusively in terms of his attitude toward death, the authentic man being one who escaped from the banality of everyday existence by recognizing his finitude and courageously facing up to the fact of death. This more limited Heideggerian concept of authenticity will be dealt with in the last chapter.

Sartre on Authenticity

The authentic man for Sartre is the person who undergoes a radical conversion through anguish and who assumes his freedom. He recognizes himself, not as a shepherd of Being, but as the cause of there being a world and as the unique source of the world's values and intelligibility. In the working out of this fundamental conception Sartre is led to distinguish between three forms of inauthenticity. One, which will be discussed in the following chapter, arises from a failure to recognize the duality between our being-for-ourselves and our being-for-others. Another is based upon the confusion between our being-in-the-world and our being-in-the-midst-of-the-world; but this form of inauthenticity is analyzed somewhat differently from the similar form in Heidegger and receives relatively little attention. The third form of inauthenticity arises from a failure to recognize our ambiguous status as a detotalized in-itself-for-itself, or a confusion between our being as in-itself and our being as for-itself. In this chapter attention will be focused largely upon this third form of inauthenticity.

Consider the following two cases:

Mr. A is a liar. He repeatedly tells untruths, sometimes with malicious intent, sometimes for the purpose of dramatizing himself. Although he is perfectly aware of telling these untruths, he none the less ardently proclaims to himself and to others his complete honesty. In doing so it is no part of his intention to deny or to overlook the facts of the case. On the contrary he confesses his misdeeds with an embarrassing frankness. Mr. A's intention is to explain and to excuse these misdeeds. He says that each of his lies has been required by some accidental or unusual external circumstance, that his true inner self is in no way responsible for them and in no way affected by them. By nature, in his essence, he claims to be absolutely honest.

Mr. B is also a liar, repeatedly telling untruths for much the same reasons as Mr. A. Like Mr. A he does not deny that he tells these untruths; he, too, frankly admits the facts of the case. And like Mr. A he has an excuse. The difference between the two men lies in the character of the excuses they offer. Mr. B does not contrast his true inner self with his outer self. On the contrary, he vigorously denies that he has a true inner self. He claims to be a product of strict causal determinism. He is a liar and that is all there is to it. That is the way God or Nature made him. He claims credit for honestly facing up to the fact that he is a liar and humbly accepting his place in the scheme of things.

In each of these cases not only a general theory of selfhood but a total metaphysics is implicit. Mr. A appeals to the doctrine of substantial souls, the view that man's true nature is concealed in an inner spirituality only imperfectly manifested or perhaps not manifested at all in his observable behavior. Mr. B, on the other hand, appeals to the doctrine of universal determinism, the view that the individual human personality is a total zero, a kind of mathematical point or infinitesimal quantity at which a series of impersonal causal laws intersect.

For want of more convenient labels, Mr. A will be called a subjectivist; Mr. B, an objectivist. Subjectivism had its origins in the Augustinian theory of predestination and was most elaborately developed by Leibniz. The view was that every individual human personality comes into the world with a god-given soul, a nature or essence which determines its every action and from a knowledge of which its entire life history might be predicted. In the Romantic movement of the nineteenth century subjectivism was considerably transformed, the accent falling not so much on the determinism of psychic events as on the independence of the human psyche from the restraints of external circumstance. In the twentieth century we have offshoots of subjectivism in the theory of man as a bundle of innate drives or instincts and in the Freudian theory of man as largely a plaything of the unconscious. Objectivism, on the other hand, consists in the view that everything in the universe is causally related to everything else in such a way that nothing can be said to have independent existence, or alternatively that a complete understanding of any one event necessarily involves a thorough knowledge of the whole of things. This view had its origins in Stoicism and has been developed most consistently by. Spinoza, Hegel, and certain post-Hegelian idealists. Its greatest popular triumph was nineteenth-century mechanistic determinism.

Consistently with its premises, objectivism allows no place for the human personality. There is no possibility; everything is necessity. Freedom can consist only in a release from finitude, either by overcoming the illusion of selfhood or by somehow identifying the self with the totality of what is. The highest goal of life is a mystical vision of eternal necessity and a merging with the infinite or some other largely aesthetic experience. Our moral responsibility, in so far as we can be said to have one, is to understand the world, not to alter it. The subjectivist, by contrast, immortalizes the individual human personality. Each individual is a live center of spirituality or a substantial, enduring soul. His world is but the face of his soul seen as in a mirror; or, changing the metaphor, but the hollow husk of his inner self, the inner self being the only true reality. For the subjectivist freedom lies in the realization or unfolding of already existing subjective potentialities. And as for the objectivist, our moral responsibility, in so far as we can be said to have one, is to *understand* and to *accept* our already existing nature, not to *change* it.

The existentialists in general have launched a crushing attack upon these two concepts of the human self. According to the existentialists, both Mr. A, the subjectivist, and Mr. B, the objectivist, have failed to understand the true nature of the human personality and its real relationship to the external world. Mr. A has failed to realize that human beings must by their nature live out of doors in the world, that man *is* wholly what he does. Mr. B has failed to realize that human beings must by their nature transcend their being in the world, that man *exists* beyond all causal determinism. For the existentialist both objectivism and subjectivism are philosophies of despair. The despair of the objectivist is what Kierkegaard calls the "despair of necessity." "The loss of possibility," he writes, "signifies . . . that everything has become necessary to man. . . . The determinist or the fatalist is in despair, and in despair he has lost his self, because for him everything is necessary. . . . The self of the determinist cannot breathe, for it is impossible to breathe necessity alone, which taken pure and simple suffocates the human self."[3] The despair of the subjectivist, however—and here Kierkegaard has especially in mind subjectivism in its romanticized nineteenth-century version—is the despair of possibility. When the self turns too far inward and chases the pale shadows of subjective potentiality, "it runs away from itself, so that it has no necessity whereto it is bound to return. . . . This is the despair of possibility. Possibility then appears to the self ever greater and greater, more and more things become possible, because nothing becomes actual. At last it is as if everything were possible."[4] In other words, man is rooted to the brute necessities of the external world and he must live in that world if he is to attain true spirituality. This is the profound source of Kierkegaard's, as of all existentialists', antipathy to romanticism and aestheticism.

The objectivist recognizes that man lives in the external world, but he denies that man transcends it. The subjectivist recognizes that man transcends the world, but denies that he lives in it. Curiously, it is the existentialist whose position is nearest to common sense. It is the existentialist who refuses to deny that there are selves, that there is a world which they inhabit, and that there is an uneasy but inevitable commerce between them. The existentialist will not allow either the universe or the self to be conjured away. For him the self is present to but not literally in the world. It is equally mistaken to isolate the self from the world or to allow it to be absorbed in the world, for in either case true selfhood is lost. The subjectivist is no less guilty than the objectivist. The self cannot breathe pure necessity, but neither can it survive in pure possibility. In the one case it is suffocated; in the other it is vaporized. When everything becomes possible and nothing actual, then once again, to use the words of Kierkegaard, "the abyss has swallowed up the self."[5] The man who loses his capacity to distinguish between image and reality soon loses his anchor in the world. By living in a world of reverie he becomes himself as unreal as a dream.

It was Sartre, however, not Kierkegaard, who most brilliantly and succinctly developed these themes. Consider again Sartre's definition of man as a being who is not what he is and who is what he is not. This definition is intended to point up the fact that in the act of *ex*isting man transcends his past self by making it into an object of his regard. Just as by looking at an external object I posit it as "not-me" and thus in Sartrean language "nihilate" it, so by making my past self an object of scrutiny I posit it as "not-me" and "nihilate" it. However, whereas I am usually content to say simply and without further ado that I am not an inkwell, I am not usually content to say simply and without further ado that I am not my past self. There is some sense in which I still am the man I was ten years ago even though I place myself at a distance from him in the mere act of existing.

Sartre calls the relationship which my present self supports to my past self an "internal relationship" and contrasts it with purely external relationships between physical objects. Two beings are related to one another internally when each affects the other in its being; two things are related externally when neither affects the other in its being. Put somewhat differently two things are related internally when to understand one it is necessary to take the other into account; they are related externally when this is not the case. Now, obviously if I want a full and adequate understanding of either my past or my present self I must take the other into account, whereas to understand the nature of two chairs standing alongside each other I will examine each separately. In still other language, things which are related to one another externally are "not" one another in the full logical sense of the term. But things which are related to one another internally are not one another in a very special sense of the term "not." It would be plainly self-contradictory to say that the chair is the table. But it would not be self-contradictory to say either that I *am* my past self or that I *am not* my past self.

Abstractly considered, the relationship of past self to present self may be a kind of logical puzzle.   The concrete awareness of this relationship, however, is one source of anguish.   Sartre illustrates by citing the example of a gambler who has "freely and sincerely decided not to gamble any more and who when he approaches the gaming table, suddenly sees all his resolutions melt away. . . ."   He then apprehends in anguish

> the total inefficacy of the past resolution.   It is there doubtless, but fixed, ineffectual, surpassed by the very fact that I am conscious *of* it.   The resolution is still *me* to the extent that I realize constantly my identity with myself across the temporal flux, but it is no longer *me*—due to the fact that it has become an object *for* my consciousness.   I am not subject to it, it fails in the mission which I have given it.   The resolution is there still, I *am* it in the mode of not-being.   What the gambler apprehends at this instant is . . . the permanent rupture in determinism; it is nothingness which separates him from himself. . . . By the very fact of taking my position in existence as consciousness of being, I make myself *not to be* the past of good resolutions *which I am.*[6]

Sartre's definition of man also points to the parallel fact that man both is and is not his future, or alternatively, that man is his future in the same peculiar way that he is his past: in the mode of not being it.   Just as my past self is powerless to influence my present self without the consent of my present self, so my present self is powerless to influence my future self without the consent of my future self.   The anguish which we experience when we stand on a high cliff is taken as an illustration of this fact.   In the experience of vertigo we realize that we cannot guarantee to our present self that our future self will not jump. Between our present and our future self there is a gap or a void; and to exist we must give ourselves a rendezvous the other side of that gap.   But we have no guarantee of what we shall find or even that we will be there; for "nothing compels me to save my life, nothing prevents me from precipitating myself into the abyss."[7]

Thus we both are and are not our past selves; we both are and are not our future selves.   Absolutely nothing stands between past and present or between present and future.   We should, however, guard against the temptation to push too far the analogy between the relationship of present to past and the relationship of present to future.   Our past history is what it is; we cannot alter it.   It is there irrevocably.   It constitutes a part of what Sartre calls our "facticity" and has, once it has been lived through, the same ontological status as material objects. Our past is a part of our facticity, our being as an in-itself. Our future, however, is absolutely open, absolutely undetermined either by our past self or by the external world. This supposedly follows from the fact that it is only through the for-itself or consciousness that the future comes into being.

It is from this analysis of selfhood that Sartre derives his theory of freedom and authenticity. To be free is to be under the necessity of transcending one's past. On the other hand authenticity, or, if you prefer, moral responsibility, consists in an unwavering recognition of the necessity one is under to be free. Only the morally responsible or authentic man recognizes his past for what it is, recognizes that it is *his* past and assumes responsibility for it, while at the same time recognizing that his future is free and that at every moment he is called upon to transcend his past and to make himself anew, for the future, too, is *his*.

One may accordingly be inauthentic in either of two ways. One may attempt to deny one's facticity or being as in-itself. This was the mistake of Mr. A who claimed that he was not a liar while admitting that he had repeatedly told lies. Or one may attempt to deny one's subjectivity, i.e., one's being as for-itself. This was the mistake of Mr. B who took comfort in insisting that he *was* a liar and that was the whole of the matter. Although Sartre sometimes uses the term "bad faith" in a wide sense as a synonym for inauthenticity, he also uses it in a narrow sense to indicate the specific form of inauthenticity adopted by Mr. A. In this narrow sense of the term the opposite of bad faith is what Sartre calls "the project of sincerity."

Sartre illustrates the two forms of inauthenticity with the examples of a homosexual and his critic. The homosexual, he points out,

> frequently has an intolerable feeling of guilt, and his whole existence is determined in relation to this feeling. One will readily see that he is in bad faith. In fact, it frequently happens that this man, while recognizing his homosexual inclination, while avowing each and every particular misdeed which he has committed, refuses with all his strength to consider himself a "homosexual." His case is always "different," peculiar; there enters into it something of a game, of chance, of bad luck. . . . The critic asks only one thing . . . : that the guilty one recognize himself as guilty, that the homosexual

declare frankly . . . : "I am a homosexual." We ask here who is
in bad faith. The homosexual or the champion of sincerity?
   The homosexual recognizes his faults, but he struggles with
all his strength against the crushing view that his weakness
constitutes for him a *destiny*. He has an obscure but strong
feeling that a homosexual is not a homosexual as this table
is a table or as this red-haired man is red-haired. . . . Does he
not recognize in himself the peculiar, irreducible character of
human reality ? . . . He would be right actually if he understood
the phrase "I am not a homosexual" in the sense of "I am not
what I am." That is, if he declared to himself, "To the extent
that a pattern of conduct is defined as the conduct of a homosexual and to the extent that I have adopted this conduct, I
am a homosexual. But to the extent that human reality cannot
be finally defined by patterns of conduct, I am not one." But
instead of this he slides surreptitiously toward "not being"
in the sense of "not-being-in-itself." He lays claim to "not
being a homosexual" in the sense in which this table *is not*
an inkwell. He is in bad faith.

The champion of sincerity, however, makes the opposite
mistake.

   The critic demands of the guilty one that he constitute himself
   as a thing. . . . Who cannot see how offensive to the other and
   how reassuring for me is a statement such as "He's just a
   homosexual," which removes a disturbing freedom from a
   trait and which aims at henceforth constituting all the acts of
   the Other as consequences following strictly from his essence.
   That is actually what the critic is demanding of his victim—
   that he constitute himself as a thing.[8]

   Although in this particular passage the champion of sincerity is seen exercising his inauthenticity upon another person,
it is evident that the project of sincerity is also an attitude one
may and frequently does adopt toward oneself. In *The
Reprieve* Sartre has the homosexual Daniel say: "Why can't I
be what I am, be a pederast, villain, coward, a loathsome
object. . . . If I had been an insensible stone figure, a fantastic
white-eyed statue, devoid of purpose, impervious to pain, I
might then have coincided with myself. . . . Just *to be*. In the
dark, at random. To be a homosexual just as the oak is an
oak. To extinguish myself. Extinguish the inner eye."[9]
   Although the project of bad faith and the project of sincerity
differ in their structure, they do not differ in their goal. The
underlying motive is always the same: namely, to unburden
oneself of one's freedom and moral responsibility by denying

the essential ambiguity of human existence. Objectivist and subjectivist alike fail to realize that man both is and exists. The one denies that he must choose his future; the other, that his past is his. They are haunted by the primitive notion of substance. They cannot bear to envision the possibility of genuine freedom. An *ens causa sui,* whether it be a self sufficient unto itself and isolated from the world or a world sufficient unto itself and without persons, is for them a psychological necessity. A past that is irremediably gone or a future which is of their own making is as frightening to them as the infinite spaces were to Pascal.

Moreover, the two projects do not differ as much in structure as at first sight appears, and they tend constantly to pass into the other. In bad faith one denies one's facticity. But at the same time one tends to invest one's subjectivity with the weight of being which belongs only to the in-itself, the soul or nature or essence being regarded as a thing, ultimately not too much unlike an in-itself. In the project of sincerity one denies one's subjectivity as such; one forgets that one *exists* and that in the act of existing one necessarily transcends what one is. But in this case there is a strong tendency to invest one's past or being as in-itself with properties which belong exclusively to the for-itself. The obscure awareness of the duality of our being is too strong to permit us wholly to forget either facticity or subjectivity. The true mark of inauthenticity is less a forgetfulness of one or the other aspect of our being than a confused attempt to disguise the ambiguity of the human situation by positing the existence of entities to which one illogically attributes properties derived from two wholly distinct dimensions of being.

Inauthenticity and Philosophical Error

It is not surprising that Sartre should analyze a large number of philosophical concepts as instances of inauthenticity. Chief among the philosophical concepts so analyzed are passion or emotion, the unconscious, the ego, and sensation. The first three of these Sartre declares to be impossible attempts to invest our subjectivity with properties of material objects and thereby escape consciousness of freedom.   The fourth results from a form of inauthenticity similar to that analyzed by Heidegger and based upon a confusion of our being-in-the-world with our being-in-the-midst-of-the-world.

It will be recalled from the previous chapter that one of Sartre's arguments against the theory of determinism by the passions was that passions have no weight.   Weight is strictly a property of physical objects.   Sartre maintains that passions or emotions are not entities at all, much less entities inhabiting consciousness and compelling us to act in certain ways.   Passions or emotions are merely ways of apprehending the world and modes of conduct in the world.   Anger, for instance,is not a psychic force which compels us to punch someone in the nose. Anger is rather the apprehension of someone as deserving to be punched in the nose and the act of hitting him, the cause of this apprehension and this conduct being my own free choice of an ultimate project of being.   If human beings find it congenial to interpret passions as things with weights which compel us to act, it is only because they do not want to recognize their freedom.   The concept of passion is simply a "deterministic excuse" for freely chosen behavior we do not wish to acknowledge as ours.

Sartre uses a similar argument against the concept of the unconscious.   He calls Freud's division of the human personality into id, ego, and superego a case of "materialistic mythology."   The id, for instance, is conceived primarily as a thing, a something to which I am related only externally, which acts upon me in the way that bodies other than my own might act upon my body.   I am compelled by the id and I am not responsible for the behavior it determines.   The id is given to me prior to my existence as a free and conscious being.

> By the distinction between the "id" and the "ego," Freud has cut the psychic whole into two.   I *am* the ego but *I am not the id*.   I hold no privileged position in relation to my unconscious psyche.   I *am* my own psychic phenonema in so far as I establish them in their conscious reality.   For example, I am the impulse to steal this or that book from this bookstall. I am an integral part of the impulse; I bring it to light and I determine myself hand-in-hand with it to commit the theft. But I *am* not these psychic facts in so far as I receive them

passively and am obliged to resort to hypotheses about their origin and true meaning, just as the scholar makes conjectures about the nature and essence of an external phenomenon. The theft, for example, which I interpret as an immediate impulse determined by the rarity, the interest, or the price of the volume which I am going to steal—it is in truth a process derived from self-punishment, which is attached more or less directly to an Oedipus complex.[10]

That this concept of the id as an independent external force which acts upon us was formed in bad faith is shown by the fact that Freud cannot consistently hold to it. Freud is finally compelled to recognize that the id and the ego interact not in the way of physical objects but by an internal relationship which affects both ego and id in their very nature. The concept of the unconscious, like the concept of passion or emotion as psychic objects, is a bastard concept in which properties such as spontaneity and consciousness which belong only to human subjectivity are surreptitiously read into an entity conceived in the first instance as having only the properties of physical objects.

> Considered more closely the psychoanalytic theory is not as simple as it first appears. It is not accurate to hold that the "id" is presented as a thing in relation to the hypothesis of the psychoanalyst, for a thing is indifferent to the conjectures we make concerning it, while the "id" on the contrary is sensitive to them when we approach the truth. Freud in fact reports resistance when at the end of the first period the doctor is approaching the truth.[11]

The point, of course, is that two things which are related to one another only externally and have to be studied by the impersonal methods of modern science could not possibly resist one another. In resisting one another they affect one another in their being and cease to be two distinct and independently definable entities. If the id were an entity external to me as a conscious agent, then it would be as indifferent to my conjectures about it as a table or an inkwell. Upon analysis, therefore, the theory of determinism by the unconscious breaks down as completely as the theory of determinism by the passions, and for the same reasons. The only question is why one should be so enamored of it, and the only answer to this question is that one wishes to escape responsibility for one's being.

What about the concept of the ego? As will be seen in the following chapter, Sartre himself in one sense accepts the concept of the ego, i.e., of an individual essence or nature. But for Sartre the individual's ego, in so far as he can properly be said to have one, comes into existence only through the mediation of other persons. This contention has to be understood in terms of Leibnizian theory. For Leibniz the individual's essence or nature was his life history as seen by God. Sartre has secularized this theory. Since God does not exist, the individual essence or life history can exist only as an object for other persons.

When, however, Sartre is attacking the doctrine of the ego and declaring its nonexistence, what he usually has in mind is the concept of the ego as conceived in the theory of determinism by the passions or the theory of determinism by the unconscious. According to Sartre, as a detotalized in-itself-for-itself (abstraction made of his being for others) the individual has no nature, essence, or ego. He is a pure field of consciousness, a point of view upon the world, nothing more. He can try to take a point of view upon himself as a point of view upon the world. But he will never succeed. Just as man is the foundation without foundation of his values, so he is a point of view upon the world without any possible point of view upon himself. The theories of determinism by the passions and determinism by the unconscious are, he says, nothing but impossible attempts to take a view upon the individual by construing him as a thing rather than a pure point of view upon things. And what greater evidence could there be that these theories are formed in bad faith than the fact that they cannot be consistently developed?

The doctrine of determinism by the passions will have it that man is essentially a passionate being and that his apparently free and conscious determinations of himself are wholly illusory. Yet does not that doctrine invariably and almost imperceptibly pass into another according to which a proper understanding of ourselves as an ensemble of passions will permit us to make free and conscious determinations of ourselves? Similarly, the doctrine of determinism by the unconscious declares that man is essentially an ensemble of unconscious drives, but the intent of so construing man is to restore to him his freedom by giving him power over those unconscious drives. In the first instance the passions and the unconscious are conceived as objects. They are to be studied by the impersonal methods of science; they are assigned weights; they are links in some sort of deterministic scheme. But what is left of the notions of passion and the unconscious as *psychic* entities if properties drawn from the realm of consciousness are wholly excluded from them? Surreptitiously such properties are always restored to them. And in the last analysis they turn out to be hybrid concepts whose only practical function is to permit us to deny man's radical duality as a detotalized in-itself-for-itself.

In order to understand Sartre's position with respect to the concept of sensation, it will be necessary to reintroduce the concepts of being-in-the-world and being-in-the-midst-of-the-world. So far, in the discussion of man's direct presence to the world the accent has fallen upon the fact that man has no inner nature or hard core of selfhood into which he can retreat. It is quite conceivable, however, that a philosopher would be willing to accept the Heideggerian and Sartrean view that man is a pure point of view (a substanceless transcendental field of awareness or activity) and none the less deny that man is directly or immediately present to the world. He might do so by taking the position that consciousness relates to the world through the intermediary of sensations conceived less as parts of human subjectivity or ideas in the human mind than as objects for the knowing consciousness. Man, the pure transcendental field of awareness, would thus be separated from the world because he knows it only through the veil of sensations.

According to Sartre, this position arises only through a confusion between our being-in-the-world or pure presence to the world and the inauthentic mode of existence called being-in-the-midst-of-the-world. By definition the person who exists in the midst of the world is also existing in the domain of *das Man* and of instrumental complexes. He is an ordinary man, and he will take as his criterion of reality or objectivity either the democratic criterion of how things normally appear to most people or else the specialist's criterion of how things appear under conditions which permit a maximum number of discriminations. If he is wearing yellow glasses, objects in the world will appear yellow, but he will say that they are not really yellow because this is not the way they appear to most men or even to himself under normal conditions. Similarly, if he first plunges his hand into a bucket of hot water and then into a bucket of warm water, the warm water will appear cold to him;

but he will say that the water is really warm, because he knows that a thermometer reading would reveal it to be warm.

Up to a point Sartre regards this as right and proper. In the discussion of sensation he is not concerned to prove the existence of an in-itself behind the world. And he recognizes that if one lives, as all of us must during a good part of our lives, in the realm of *das Man*, it will be necessary to communicate with others in the appropriate vocabulary. Moreover, so long as one attributes to expressions of the form "*A* is really *B*" no meaning other than that "*A* appears to be *B* to *das Man*," no harm is done. The ordinary man and the philosopher of the ordinary man do not, however, interpret such statements in this harmless way. From the fact that they do not always perceive the "real" color or the "real" temperature of an object, they conclude that what they immediately and directly perceive is an ontological entity to which they give the name "sensation," and that opposed to the ontological entity called sensation stands an ontological entity to which they give the name "real object."

According to Sartre, this inference is not only unwarranted but patently illogical. Sartre's reasoning is that in order to make a meaningful distinction between a thing as it appears to an individual and a thing as it appears to *das Man*, one must already assume that individuals are immediately present to the world without the intermediary of sensation. If, for instance, we say that a thing is really what it appears to be to most people, this presupposes that the thing appears in person to the majority. It is because most people do not apprehend all objects with a yellow tint that we say the vision of the individual who does is distorted, but in saying this we are assuming that the vision of most people is not distorted, that they are not seeing things through a veil of sensations. If, on the other hand, we say that a thing is really what it appears to be to the expert, this is because we assume that the expert directly perceives it as it really is. It is because we accept the objectivity and reality of the perception which shows a temperature reading of warm that we declare the bucket of water to be really warm.

According to Sartre, all objects of perceptual experience exist on the same ontological plane, and all perceptions are equally objective in the sense that there is no veil of sensation which distorts or disguises them. Moreover, he says that since all of us assume that this is the case in order to make the distinction between sensation and real object, we are not entitled to draw any ontological conclusions from the fact that this distinction is popularly made.   All that we are entitled to say is that out of a mass of equally objective and equally real perceptual experiences, certain ones may be chosen as having a greater value. To those which we regard as having the greater value we give the name "objective" or "real."   To those which we regard as possessing lesser value we give the name "subjective" or "illusory."   But these words in this context reveal absolutely nothing except a value decision.

On occasion I have served as a subject for the research work of physiologists or psychologists. If I volunteered for some experiment of this kind I found myself suddenly in a laboratory where I perceived a more or less illuminated screen, or else felt tiny electric shocks, or I was brushed by an object which I could not exactly determine. . . . Not for an instant was I isolated from the world; all these events happened for me in a laboratory in the middle of Paris, in the south building of the Sorbonne. . . . Sometimes an inept experimenter asked me if "my sensation of light was stronger or weaker, more or less intense."   Since I was in the midst of objects and in the process of observing these objects, his phrase would have had no meaning for me if I had not long since learned to use the expression "sensation of light" for objective light as it appeared to me in the world at a given instant.   I replied therefore that the sensation of light was, for example, less intense, but I meant by this that the screen was *in my opinion* less illuminated. Since I *actually* apprehended the screen as less illuminated, the phrase "in my opinion" corresponded to nothing real except to an attempt not to confuse the objectivity of the world-for-me with a stricter objectivity, which is the result of experimental measures and of the agreement of minds with each other. . . . Why indeed should we use the term "subjectivity" for the ensemble of luminous or heavy or odorous objects such as they appeared to me *in this laboratory at Paris on a day in February, etc.?* And if despite all we are to consider this ensemble as subjective, then why should we recognize objectivity in the system of objects which were revealed simultaneously to the experimenter, in this laboratory, this same day in February. . . . Of course these comparisons can give certain objective results: for example, I can establish that the warm water appears cold to me when I put my hand in it after having first plunged my hand in hot water. But this establishment which we pompously call "the law of relativity of sensations" has nothing to do with sensations. Actually we are dealing with a quality of the object which is revealed to me: the warm water *is* cold when I submerge my heated hand in it.   A comparison of this objective quality of the water to equally objective information which the thermometer gives me simply ... motivates on my part a free choice of true objectivity.   I shall give the name subjectivity to the objectivity which I have not chosen.[12]

Why, indeed, should we give the name "objectivity" to the perceptual experiences of *das Man* and the name "subjectivity" to our own individual perceptual experiences?   The answer is so obvious to Sartre that he does not even bother to state it explicitly.   Either we dò this for the purpose of communicating more easily with other human beings, which is perfectly harmless and natural, or else we do so because we wish to reject our individual person as having less value than the nonentity *das Man*.   Our being-in-the-world is an original act by an individual human being, but we are afraid of our individuality. We attempt to submerge it in *das Man* by converting our being-in-the-world into a being-in-the-midst-of-the-world.   And it is not only our own individuality which we fear.   We also fear the individuality of the exceptional person.   The great artist, for instance, who perceives the world differently from the majority is, we say, incapable of revealing reality.   His work has no truth in it; it is *merely* subjective.   The logical error involved in the doctrine of sensations thus has as its foundation a scale of values which diminishes the worth of the individual in favor of the public.   The doctrine is therefore a manifestation of inauthenticity.

Criticism

As is often the case, the ideas of the existentialists can be most instructively compared and contrasted with those of the pragmatists.   There are several areas of agreement on questions of ontology.   The pragmatist accepts the view that consciousness is not a thing.   One of William James' most famous essays was entitled "Does Consciousness Exist?"   The answer to the question was an emphatic "No" so long as by consciousness one understands an ontological entity possessing the properties of material objects. Consciousness, said James, is not a thing; it is a function. Man is not a substantial ego, and he has no soul. He is an active agent in immediate contact with the world. At the same time pragmatists share Sartre's antipathies toward a conception of man as an ensemble of passions or a collection of unconscious drives. And Buchler has developed views with respect to sensation which closely parallel those of Sartre—not by borrowing from Sartre, of course, but simply by tracing the implications of basic pragmatic beliefs.

On moral issues there are also important areas of agreement. The pragmatists regret as much as the existentialists the mass culture of the machine age. Dewey was at least as violent as the existentialists in his attack upon work as mere routine and upon the conformist, anti-individualistic bias of technological society. He was also a severe critic of those who attempt to escape their being-in-the-world by a flight into pure subjectivity. Romanticism and mysticism were for him ugly words, no less ugly than conformism.

None the less, the differences are substantial. The existentialists reject the view of a bloc universe in which man is encased, but they continue to regard the nonhuman world as a bloc. The principal characteristic of Sartre's in-itself is its solidity or undifferentiatedness; and even the "world" as opposed to the in-itself is considered to be a fissureless unit or totality. The pragmatists, on the other hand, are thoroughgoing pluralists. For the pragmatists the universe is a congeries of loosely integrated and relatively isolable but overlapping causal systems. If, they say, the nonhuman or material world were a bloc, there could be no scientific knowledge. This contention can best be understood if it is recalled that for the objectivist or the person who holds to the view of a bloc universe a full understanding of any one event in the world involves a thorough understanding of the whole of things. To understand any one event nothing may be left out of account, since we are entitled to no judgments of relevance or irrelevance. Everything is equally relevant to everything else. But this strikes the pragmatist as ridiculous. To use an example from the American pragmatist Peirce, many events may be thoroughly understood without our knowing that the mayor of Hong Kong has just had a sneezing fit. Or to use an example which often appears in the literature of the logical positivists, in determining the correct weight of an object one need not necessarily take into account the color of the pans which one uses to weigh it.   Since scientific knowledge exists and since it depends upon our being able to declare that some things are irrelevant to other things, the world cannot but be pluralistic.

At the same time the pragmatist differs from the existentialist in regarding the human personality pluralistically.   The unity of the human personality is never complete.   On this point Sartre and many other existentialists have simply fallen back into subjectivism.   The subjectivists make a claim similar to that of the objectivists, except that the subjectivists' bloc is the self-contained world of each individual human self.   But if this view were correct, then, say the pragmatists, there could be no genuine knowledge of the human person.   If one person says that the significant causal factor accounting for Mr. A's telling lies is that he had the measles at age three, if another person says that the significant causal factor is his having been weaned too early, and if still a third person says that it is his having failed early in life to establish habits of rational self-control, there is no way that the issue could be resolved.   All three persons would be talking nonsense.   The only significant factor would be the total history of the self, and it makes no difference whether that history be the result of a divine decision or of a fundamental choice of oneself.

As for the relationship between man and the world, the differences are also impressive.   The pragmatists grant that man is a conscious being, but for them consciousness is simply a natural trait among others—infinitely more interesting and important to us than the distinguishing traits of other beings in the world, but no more miraculous.   An ontological dualism between man and the world is no more warranted than an ontological dualism between birds and nonbirds.   Man is in the world in so far as he shares traits with inanimate objects or the lower animals and in so far as he causally interacts with them; he is not in the world only in the sense that he has natural traits which do not belong to inanimate objects or the lower animals and in the sense that he can, if he so chooses, remain wholly or partially aloof from many natural complexes.   Since man *is* relatively independent of the external world, our common-sense conviction that some natural events are irrelevant to an understanding of human behavior finds its justification. But since man is *only* relatively independent of the external world, so does our common-sense conviction that we genuinely interact with the world.

Similarly, since the individual is relatively independent of other human beings, he can exist as a true individual, and to understand his behavior one need not take into account the fact that his mother once painted her apartment beige or that Adam covered himself with a fig leaf. But since the individual is only relatively independent of others, one can also understand why he must often take others into account in order to understand his behavior and why his mother's having weaned him too early might have an influence upon his adult conduct.

Differences on questions of value follow naturally from these differences in ontology. With respect to the form of inauthenticity which turns on the duality between man's being-in-the-world and man's being-in-the-midst-of-the-world, the pragmatist will readily grant that conformist, machine-age culture is deplorable. But he will argue against the existentialists in two ways. First, to the extent that a conformist, machine-age culture is an indispensable condition of securing physical and social well-being for all men, it must be tolerated. The ordinary man's and the scientist's concept of reality and truth is purely pragmatic; but in the measure that a person wishes to improve his standard of living or to extend the benefits of science to others it would be foolish to use another. Moreover, so long as an individual takes full cognizance of what he is doing in adopting this concept of truth and reality, he is in no way prejudicing the rights or the dignity of the creative artist and the exceptional person. It is because the pragmatists want material and social well-being for all, not because they are afraid of individuality, that they respect the "objectivity" of the scientist. Second, violently to assert oneself against the historical conditions of the time is no more a solution to the evils of mass culture than withdrawal into an ineffable subjectivity. The only viable solution is the transformation of our natural and social environment through a more persistent and intelligent application of technology. Through automation, to take a single example, the machine-man may eventually be replaced by a real machine and restored to his humanity.

Consider now the form of inauthenticity which turns on the confusion of man's being as in-itself and his being as for-itself. To be sure, the pragmatist will say, man is and is not his past and his future self—but not at the same time and in the same respects. A past or future act is mine or not mine according as it belongs or fails to belong to the more or less tightly knit and relatively isolable series of acts of which my present consciousness is focus. I am my past and future self in the sense that there is a genuine causal continuity between most of my past and future acts, on the one hand, and my present desires and intentions, on the other. I am not my past or future self only in the sense that the causal connections between some of my past or future acts and my present desires and intentions are either nonexistent or so tenuous that for all practical purposes they may be counted as nonexistent.

A man, for instance, might be much more willing to say that he is not the man he was during a three-year period he spent in the Army than to say that he is not the man he was in the period immediately following or immediately preceding his military service. The reason would be that the activities and projects of the period immediately before and immediately after his military service are far more intimately related causally to his present activities and projects than those of his wartime experiences. In explaining his present attitudes and conduct to himself or others he must make frequent reference to what happened before and after military service, but he rarely needs to make reference to the wartime experiences. It is this fact of causal relevance or causal irrelevance, not the fact of self-transcendence or facticity, which is implicitly recognized in locutions such as "I am the man I was ten years ago" or "I am not the man I was ten years ago."

This is particularly obvious if you consider the conditions under which such claims are made and the manner in which they are falsified. It is usually when someone contends that we have acted from a disreputable motive and cites earlier behavior as evidence, that we deny identity with our past selves. And it is by piling up evidence for the causal relevance of our past activities to our present misbehavior that our denial of identity is falsified. Exactly the same analysis applies to denials or assertions of identity with our future selves. The man about to be tortured for information begs those whose secrets he may betray to realize that if information is extracted it will not be extracted from him but rather from another man who has been brutalized and deprived of selfhood, meaning thereby that the causally relevant factors in terms of which his behavior is to be understood do not include his present choices and intentions. It would be nonsensical for him either to affirm or to deny his identity with his future self on the grounds that he is by virtue of his humanity an essentially ambiguous for-itself-in-itself whose destiny it is to live in the world without being a part of it. This, being true of everybody, cannot be used as an excuse for him as an individual.

The pragmatist may accordingly accommodate Sartre's insights with respect to authenticity, but without accepting his definition of man. In concrete and commonsensical terms the requirement of authenticity is that man assume responsibility for his past while simultaneously recognizing his responsibility to surpass it toward a future. It forbids us to be ourselves only in so far as being oneself means a slavish and supine acceptance of one's past history and the world as presently constituted. It forbids us to refuse to be ourselves only in so far as refusing to be one's self means a quixotic rejection of one's past history and the world as one finds it. Nothing, however, could better preserve us against these opposite extremes of bourgeois conformism and romantic idealism than what Dewey calls "natural piety," i.e., a view of life resting upon a "just sense of nature as the whole of which we are parts, while it also recognizes that we are parts that are marked by intelligence and purpose, having the capacity to strive by their aid to bring conditions into greater consonance with what is humanly possible."[13]

It could even be argued that the pragmatic ontology provides a safer berth for the concept of authenticity than the existentialist ontology. From the premise that man *is* his past and future self, Sartre concludes that man is totally responsible, while from the premise that man is *not* his past and future self, Sartre concludes that man is totally free. But one could with equal justice draw the opposite conclusions. From the premise that man is his past and future self, one could legitimately infer that he is totally determined, and from the premise that man is not his past and future self, one could conclude that he has no moral responsibility whatsoever. By a turn of the screw the intricate dialectical machine reverses gear: what started out as a doctrine of total responsibility and total freedom becomes a doctrine of total irresponsibility and total slavery.

The pragmatist for his part will have nothing to do with the doctrines of total responsibility and total freedom. As he sees it, no one is totally free or totally responsible. To be free is to be able to do what one chooses to do, and this ability is obviously limited. To act morally is to do what one can to promote the happiness or well-being of oneself and others; and since our ability to promote human happiness is at least as limited as our ability to do what we choose to do, our moral responsibility will be at least as limited as our freedom. We cannot and ought not to drag the dead weight of our past with us throughout all eternity. We cannot and ought not assume responsibility for every cruel blow which a future we have never made may bring. The reformed criminal, if he has truly reformed, has simply ceased to be a criminal. And the man who reveals a secret under the influence of a truth serum is not betraying his comrades; he is simply an unhappy victim of circumstances beyond his control.

But above all, the pragmatist rejects the doctrine of freedom as undetermined choice. Not only the possibility of making undetermined choices but the relevance of such choices to moral responsibility is open to doubt. Freedom as the capacity of implementing choices, however, is an undisputed fact of human experience whose relevance to moral responsibility may be easily demonstrated.

Consider, for instance, Sartre's example of the gambler. Sartre says that a present decision not to gamble provides no guarantee of one's future behavior. In this, say the pragmatists, he is right. But Sartre concludes that at every moment man is free of past commitments and must therefore choose himself anew. In this he is wrong. To be sure, no one's present decision not to gamble commits him irrevocably and no one can predict his future behavior with absolute assurance. But there are degrees of commitment just as there are degrees of moral responsibility and degrees of accuracy in our predictions of the future.

In ordinary life the measure of a man's freedom and moral responsibility is very nicely equated with the degree of causal relevance which his present decision is believed to have upon his future conduct. The man whose decision not to gamble would have little or no effect upon his future behavior is to that extent neither free nor morally responsible. We may pity him or we may ridicule him; but his capacity for rational self-control is not sufficiently developed that we will praise or blame him. A free and morally responsible agent is primarily one who understands the world in which he lives and who has sufficient mastery over it and over himself to accomplish his chosen goals. What separates a man from his future is not the nothingness of his being but rather ignorance, lack of self-control, or the cruelty of an as yet untamed natural and social environment.

If the existentialist objects that the pragmatic outlook fails to do justice to the tragedy of the human condition, the pragmatist will probably retort that the existentialist has simply not yet learned to distinguish between tragedy and melodrama.

VI. The Other

The Historical Setting

One of the most notable characteristics of twentieth-century man is his growing preoccupation with the problem of human relationships. In the measure that men have abandoned God they have turned to one another. The behavioral sciences are still in their infancy, but they have already assumed a more prominent place in the curriculum of Western educational institutions than theology. A person who considers himself educated may regret being totally ignorant of St. Augustine or St. Thomas, but he is not usually ashamed of it. The person who is totally ignorant of Marx or Freud, however, belongs clearly in the ranks of the illiterate.

Many thinkers long before the twentieth century stressed human relationships. Aristotle, for instance, declared that man is by nature a social animal, and the nineteenth-century humanists said the same thing even more emphatically. But in general, philosophers were less interested in man than in eternal objects; this was true even of Aristotle. Furthermore, they rarely saw a *problem* of human relationships. Traditional philosophers almost invariably regarded ideal human relationships as harmonious in nature and almost always displayed relatively great faith in the possibility of realizing harmonious interpersonal relationships.

Twentieth-century thinkers, by contrast, either do not conceive of ideal human relationships as harmonious or do not share Aristotle's and the humanists' faith in the possibility of realizing them. D. H. Lawrence is fairly typical in this respect. He wrote:

> Each soul is alone and the aloneness of each soul is a double barrier to perfect relationships between two beings. Each soul should be alone. And in the end the desire for a "perfect

relationship" is just a vicious, unmanly craving. . . . The world
ought not to be a harmonious, loving place. It ought to be a
place of fierce discord and intermittent harmonies; which it is.
Love ought not to be perfect. It ought to have perfect
moments, and wildernesses of thorn bushes. Which it has.
A "perfect" relationship ought not to be possible. Every
relationship should have its absolute limits, its absolute
reserves, essential to the singleness of the soul in each person.[1]

In *Civilization and Its Discontents*, one of his most influential
books, Freud began by pointing out that the individual must
face three types of danger: disease of the body, natural calamities from the external physical environment, and the hostility
of other persons. Through the advance of medical science and
the development of modern technology the first two dangers
have lost much of their terror; but danger from the hostility of
other persons has not decreased. The question then arises:
Has this danger not diminished because men have as yet been
unsuccessful in finding a way of reducing it, or because the
nature of man is such that the danger cannot conceivably be
reduced?

Freud's answer to this question is qualified, but he strongly
tended to regard substantial interpersonal hostility as a permanent and unavoidable fact of life. The aggressive or destructive impulses in the unconscious are so deeply rooted that they
cannot be extirpated. Attempts to prevent their passing into
overt acts of hostility against their original objects will either
result in repression and neurosis or else lead to their being
rechanneled against other objects. Carnal impulses, such as
the incestuous love of the mother at the root of the Oedipus
complex, may be more or less successfully sublimated in artistic,
intellectual, or religious activity; but aggressive impulses, such
as hostility toward the father, apparently cannot be sublimated.
The man who suppresses hatred of his father will have to divert
his hatred to other persons or direct it against himself through
the superego or conscience.

Not all twentieth-century thinkers are equally pessimistic.
William James wrote an essay entitled "The Moral Equivalent
of War," in which he tried to show that the aggressive instincts
of mankind could be rechanneled in socially harmless ways
through sport and organized efforts to master the external
physical environment. Dewey, after James, argued again and

again that original human impulses are highly plastic, that there is even now almost an infinity of socially satisfactory outlets for them, and that given proper social and economic conditions many undesirable aggressive impulses as we know them today could be wholly eradicated. The modern temper is, however, more Freudian than pragmatic. And the pragmatists themselves are considerably less optimistic than the humanists. The humanists typically *predicted* the coming of a day when all men would be united by ties of brotherhood. The pragmatists make no such predictions; many of them foresee a mounting of tension rather than a decrease of tension. They say, not that men *will*, but that they *may* achieve relatively harmonious personal relationships—if they use their intelligence. Pragmatism is less an optimism than an appeal.

The existentialists are, of course, not much interested in the economic and social conditions which the pragmatists believe to breed personal hostilities and social tension. Their interest is in discovering techniques by which the individual can salvage from the human condition the values which it presently permits. To this extent there is a difference of emphasis rather than a logical incompatibility between the pragmatic and the existentialist outlook. It has always been a part of the pragmatic position that adjustment has two dimensions: manipulation of the environment and psychological accommodation to the environment. Nothing prevents the individual from looking ahead and trying to better the world while at the same time seeking some means of reconciling himself to the world as it is at the moment. The open conflict between the two positions arises from the fact that existentialists exalt their own values to the point where pragmatic values appear insignificant by comparison and claim that their own values cannot coexist with the latter.

Compassion is not usually an existentialist value. Most existentialists follow Nietzsche, who considered compassion an insult to human dignity. Dostoyevsky and Gabriel Marcel are exceptional in this regard. None the less, the pattern of the existentialist argument can be clearly illustrated by the use of this example. Since compassion is by definition a form of love or sympathy for those who suffer, compassion would be logically impossible in a world without suffering. One cannot, therefore, attempt to eliminate suffering without at the same time attempting to eliminate compassion. Most people would probably say that a world with no suffering and no compassion is better than a world with suffering and compassion, since the disvalue of suffering is greater than the value of compassion. Some persons, however, would prefer a world with suffering and compassion. Marcel and Dostoyevsky are among them. So is the French Catholic playwright Georges Bernanos, who has stated this position in its most extreme form. In common with the Christian existentialists, Bernanos is acutely conscious of the voluntary poverty and suffering of Christ and the Christian saints, and he sees in this the clue to Christian love and compassion. At the same time he finds Christ's declaration that the poor will always be with us fraught with meaning. There is, he says

> a mystery in poverty, and I am not coward enough to pretend to believe that it is merely an economic problem to be resolved by political methods. . . . I am not afraid to say that a society without poor men could not conceivably be Christian. . . . The voluntary victims of poverty . . . maintain among us this smoldering fire beneath the ashes where from generation to generation the high flame of pure love suddenly leaps up. . . . Eliminate a single poor man and you will have a hundred monsters; eliminate one saint, and you will have a hundred thousand.[2]

To further deepen the disagreement between themselves and the pragmatists, the existentialists argue not only for the incompatibility of existentialist and pragmatic values but also for the necessity of *recognizing* the total impossibility of achieving pragmatic values. To illustrate again with the example of compassion, if the Christian permitted himself to hope that suffering and poverty could be eliminated at some future date, that fact alone would prevent him from experiencing true Christian compassion. For one thing, to the extent that evils are believed to be eliminable, they cease to be evils. For another, the person who has compassion for the poor and who also believes that poverty can be eradicated becomes a social reformer rather than a saint, and to function effectively as a social reformer he dare not permit himself the exquisite pain-pleasure of compassion. This admirable force of compassion when joined to the hope of eliminating its cause drives a man into revolutionary political activity, and unless he withdraws soon afterwards his compassion dries up. He becomes a ruthless party whip or a bloated bureaucrat. The reader of Dostoyevsky may compare the saintly hero of *The Idiot* with the diabolical social reformer hero in *The Possessed* for a literary illustration of this point.

The existentialist, then, agrees with Freud that harmonious interpersonal relationships are impossible because of the very nature of the human condition, but he goes much further than Freud in two respects. First, Freud regretted the impossibility of establishing harmonious personal relationships; for him this was a source of deep distress. The existentialist, on the contrary, almost rejoices in this impossibility since it secures the possibility of realizing other and more important values than harmony. Secondly, Freud himself took no comfort in the "comforting illusions" by which people disguise to themselves the impossibility of achieving interpersonal harmony, and he exposed many of these "illusions" as neurotic or damaging to human well-being. He did not, however, categorically deny that some of these illusions might bring genuine comfort to some people, nor did he positively assert that to take satisfaction in major human values one must reject these illusions. On this point, as on the first, the existentialists have left Freud far behind and widened the gulf between the largely pragmatic Anglo-American world and the increasingly existentialist Continental world.

The nature of the values which interpersonal disharmony promotes and the arguments by which the existentialists support their position will be presented shortly. It will be best, however, to approach these questions obliquely. There can be no doubt that existentialists have greatly emphasized human relationships. Sartre says that our being-for-others is every bit as fundamental as our being-for-ourselves, that the one dimension of our being has "equal dignity" with the other. The concept of being-with (*Mitsein*) is one of the most crucial in Heidegger's *Being and Time*. Jaspers writes: "The individual cannot become human by himself. Self-being is only real in communication with another self-being. Alone, I sink into gloomy isolation—only in communication with others can I be revealed."[3] It is unnecessary to multiply instances. The existentialists have stressed the fundamental significance of interpersonal relationships for the individual more than the members of any other philosophical movement with the single exception of humanism.

Many critics of existentialism, however, have found this fact puzzling. Why, they ask, should a movement which is intensely individualistic devote so much space to the analysis of human relationships? And is there not an inconsistency in maintaining the importance of other persons in our lives while at the same time vigorously asserting that in the last analysis each of us stands alone and must himself as an individual bear full responsibility for his being?

Actually, there should be no puzzle, and there is no inconsistency. In the first place, individuality does not usually consist in living alone or isolating oneself from others. The individualist has to be defined by the manner in which he relates to others. Socrates and Kierkegaard were both intense individualists in that they had nothing but contempt for herd mentality. Kierkegaard despised the plebs; and Socrates was executed because of his open contempt for "the opinion of the many," which he believed a true philosopher or lover of wisdom ought totally to ignore. Their dress and behavior was nonconformist to the point of eccentricity; and even their physical appearance set them apart from others. Yet in the range of their social contacts and in the intensity of their personal relationships few men are able to match them. Kierkegaard's relationship to his father and to his fiancée were crucial factors in his life, and much of his philosophy is hardly more than an attempt to explain these relationships. Socrates was a street philosopher, who made it his business to talk with anybody who would spare the time. Sartre's much-talked-about café life is as nothing compared to it.

In the second place, even the man who does live in seclusion, as Nietzsche did a good part of his life, is not thereby cut off from others spiritually. Physical isolation does not mean indifference to others. The man who deliberately cuts himself off from others does so, not because he is indifferent, but on the contrary because his consciousness of others is so acute that he cannot bear their physical presence. Physical isolation is simply one way in which men relate to others and thereby define their own being. If there were but one man in the world it would be impossible for him to withdraw or retreat from other human beings. Robinson Crusoe was no recluse. The very concept of a recluse is a social concept; one could not be or be defined as such except in a social world. After the death of Camus, Sartre wrote a tribute to him. In it he mentioned that they had quarreled and ceased to see much of one another. But, Sartre adds, this was of no importance. They were still close in the sense that they read what each other wrote and reacted strongly to it. Even after the quarrel each figured prominently in the life of the other.

In the third place, there is absolutely no logical reason for assuming the impossibility of retaining one's aloneness in the sense of not allowing others to dictate one's choices while simultaneously maintaining valuable physical or spiritual contact with others. Persons who feel that there is some sort of logical inconsistency in stressing at one and the same time the uniqueness of the individual and his dependence upon others are merely betraying the fact that they themselves do not share the existentialists' beliefs about the nature and value of personal relationships. In all likelihood they belong to one of three often related but distinguishable groups whom the existentialists have bitterly attacked.

The first of these groups is comprised of romantic lovers who wish to merge their individual personalities and be as one, of humanists who wish to immerse themselves in the sea of humanity, and of extreme nationalists who desire union through ties of blood with the race. If God is regarded as a person, religious mystics who wish to be as one with God may also be included in this list. All of these persons desire to put an end to conflict and strife by merging with the Other.

The existentialist argument against this group is already familiar. The individual is tied to the here and now; he cannot extend the boundaries of his being either by absorbing others or by being absorbed by them. The desire to merge with others is unwholesome and can never be satisfied. Its satisfaction would mean the end of human existence. It is well known that in the heyday of Romanticism love and death became interlocking themes and the suicide pact a fairly common event. In mystic literature one is told to die to this life—for the existentialists the only humanly possible life—in order to live in God. The extreme humanist or nationalist presumably finds his greatest satisfaction in dying for the group. The explanation is not far to seek. In its essence the appetite for being which is demonstrated by these persons is nothing but a desire to kill oneself as an existing individual.

The second group is best exemplified by the conformist American who always does and says "the right thing" because he never does or says anything without first anticipating the reaction of others and acting in a manner designed to please or at least not to offend them. These persons are trying to escape from the responsibility of individual choice by living according to the dictates of Heidegger's *das Man*, the public at large, or some other nameless and impersonal nonentity. The existentialist argument against this group is also familiar to the reader by now. The individual cannot escape individual responsibility since it is he who has decided to entrust himself to *das Man*. Moreover, the attempt to do so only impoverishes the individual by converting authentic anguish into banal anxiety and petty fear.

The third group is best exemplified by the social engineer, the state planner, the advertising man, and the behavioral scientist. Their fundamental relationship to the other is one in which the other figures almost exclusively as a thing or object to be manipulated. These persons are trying to avoid conflict and tension by depriving the other of his humanity, i.e., his power of independent choice and action. The other is treated as if he were wholly passive.

The first formulation of this inauthentic attitude toward the other was by Kierkegaard in his analysis of the relationship between God and man. God, said Kierkegaard, was a free person, but the philosopher and theologian tried to deprive the relationship between God and man of its dread by pigeon-holing God as an element in a system of ideas, by treating Him as if he were an abstraction which would fit neatly into a purely formal scheme of concepts. Martin Buber has developed this Kierkegaardian thesis with the greatest thoroughness and extended it to human relationships in the minor existentialist classic *I and Thou*. But the fundamental notion will be discovered in the writings of all existentialists.

The argument against this mode of personal relationship is that it cannot succeed, since no matter how hard one tries, the awareness of the other as a free agent cannot be wholly dissipated. Moreover, even if it were successful, it would not bring satisfaction to the individual. In the measure that the individual succeeded in reducing other human beings to mere digits, he would heighten his own sense of insecurity and isolation.   It is almost a commonplace that the price of power over other men is insecurity and loneliness for oneself.   In one sense, the existentialist argument is as old as Plato, who pointed out that the tyrant has no friends, though he is surrounded by flatterers, and that, though exercising enormous power, he cannot rejoice in it because of an ever-present fear that his subjects will rise against him.

The existentialist criticism of the first group is merely an extension of their contention that the individual is tied to a limited portion of space and time; of the second, an application of their contention that the individual must choose for himself; of the third, an application of their contention that the individual lives in a world of other free agents and that his relationships with others must be reciprocal.   These are irreducible and unavoidable facts of the human condition.

What then are the values in human relationships which the human condition permits, and how does an explicit recognition of the facts of the human condition help us to realize these values?   One value, of course, is intensity.   Since human relationships involve a reciprocity between free human agents, there is an uneliminable element of threat and danger, and the awareness of danger is the source of all intense states of consciousness.

Another value is dignity.   Since there is a necessary reciprocity in human relationships, one's freedom can always be pitted against the freedom of the other.   No matter how adverse the circumstances there is always a possibility of triumph, so long as one maintains the consciousness of one's own freedom. Sartre quotes from Faulkner's *Light in August*.   The Negro hero has been castrated by a group of whites:

> He just lay there, with his eyes open and empty of everything save consciousness. . . . For a long moment he looked up at them with peaceful and unfathomable and unbearable eyes. . . . The man seemed to rise soaring into their memories forever and ever.   They are not to lose it, in whatever peaceful valleys, beside whatever placid and reassuring streams of old age, in the mirroring face of whatever children they will contemplate old disasters and newer hopes.   It will be there, musing, quiet, steadfast, not fading and not particularly threatful, but of itself alone serene, of itself alone triumphant.[4]

Finally, according to some existentialists, the human condition permits personal love. For love is not a merging of personalities or a quiet habit. Love is an intense relationship between two persons, i.e., two free human agents. And the mutual recognition of one's own and of the other's freedom is not only its necessary but also its sufficient condition. Two people who mutually recognize the irreducible human reality of the other cannot not love one another. They may, of course, quarrel, and they may separate or be separated physically; but each will necessarily remain for the other a live presence and a being of inestimable worth. Mutual recognition of the other's freedom separates two persons and guarantees their uniqueness, but at the same time it reveals them to one another as individuals and guarantees the possibility of genuine communication or exchange.

The Existence of the Other

Although pessimism about the possibility of establishing harmonious personal relationships is a hallmark of the twentieth century, philosophers long before the twentieth century did raise a problem concerning the Other. The problem was: How do we know that others exist? This problem was first stated by some sophists in Plato's day, but not until after Descartes did any large number of philosophers pick it up.

Descartes himself did not make much of this problem. He was more interested in proving the existence of the external world. But the kind of thinking which led Descartes to construct a proof for the existence of the external world is very much like that which led subsequent philosophers to construct proofs for the existence of other persons. Descartes' entire philosophy was based on two fundamental and closely linked premises. One premise was that men may know nothing directly and immediately except their own "ideas," under which term Descartes also included images, sensations, and feelings. We have sensations of externally existing physical objects, but we do not know directly either what they are really like or even that they exist. In fact, our sensations are highly deceptive. Sensations lead us to believe that external objects have colors, but in fact they are colorless. What man directly and immediately knows must therefore be in his own mind, and if the external world exists, this will have to be proved by inference from what is directly and immediately known. The other premise was that man and the external world constitute two radically different types of being whose inter-relationships cannot be understood by the mathematical or scientific understanding.

Descartes did, of course, believe that he could prove the existence of things outside the mind. He attempted to do so by a priori arguments. The idea of God in his mind became the basis of a proof of God's existence and benevolence, and this in turn became the basis of a proof of the existence of the external world. Since God existed and wished well to man, Descartes argued, He would not deceive man about the nature or existence of that which he could clearly and distinctly conceive. And since man can clearly and distinctly conceive of an extended substance or external world, the external world must exist and must have the properties we clearly and distinctly conceive it to have.

Almost all subsequent philosophers accepted Descartes' two premises, but they observed that the difficulty of conceiving a positive relationship between the individual mind and the physical world was matched by a difficulty in conceiving a positive relationship between individual minds. If all that I can know is my own ideas, then I cannot know the ideas of others. Consequently, I cannot know that they exist.

The position according to which nothing exists, neither the things I call other people nor the things I call physical objects, except as ideas in my own mind is known as "solipsism." And although no one has actually declared himself a solipsist, many philosophers have declared that solipsism is logically irrefutable. The Spanish-American philosopher Santayana said this and argued that our belief in the existence of the external world and of other persons rests purely on "animal faith."

Many post-Cartesian philosophers, however, tried to argue their way out of the dilemma, either by a priori proofs as did Descartes or by probable arguments based on sense experience. Among empiricists the most popular argument for the existence of other persons is analogical. Let us assume, those who use this argument say, that all I directly know are my own ideas, sensations, feelings, etc. It is none the less clear that I have ideas or sensations or emotions which I call mine in some narrower sense than that used when I say everything immediately present to my mind is "mine." Anger, jealousy, fear, pride, shame, pain, etc., are examples of entities I call mine in this narrow and restricted sense. It is also clear that I have ideas or sensations of two arms, two legs, a head, a torso, etc., which are also mine in the narrow sense and which correlate in a unique way with "my" ideas or sensations of anger, jealousy, pain and the like. When *I* feel anger and look in a mirror I see *my* flushed face. When I smash *my* finger *I* feel a pain. And so on. Finally, it is clear that I have sensations of bodies which do not correlate with the sensations constituting me as a psychic being. That is to say, I see flushed faces and smashed fingers without feeling anger or pain. Since, however, there is a unique correlation between "my" psychic sensations and the sensations of "my" body, is it not reasonable to assume that the sensations of other bodies correlate with a series of psychic sensations other than my own? My psychic sensations are private to me. Why should there not be another series of private psychic sensations behind the sensations of other bodies which I experience? Analogy permits and even encourages me to assume that when I have the sensation of another body with a flushed face and other physical signs of anger there is actually another mind or consciousness which is angry and which accounts for my sensations.

The existentialists have reversed the terms of the problem as it has been posed since Descartes. Nobody, they say, has ever really doubted the existence of others; we are as certain of the existence of others as we are of our own existence. The true problem, therefore, is not how, given a certain set of epistemological or ontological premises, the existence of others can be proved, but rather what kind of epistemology or ontology is required in order to explain the fact that we are incapable of doubting the existence of others. Any theory which fails to explain our intuitive, nonreflective certainty of the existence of others is for that very reason inadequate. "My resistance to solipsism," says Sartre, ". . . proves that I have always known that the Other existed, that I have always had a total though implicit comprehension of his existence, that this preontological comprehension comprises a surer and deeper understanding of the nature of the Other and the relation of his being to my being than all the theories which have been built around it."[5]

If, therefore, solipsism is irrefutable by the reflective consciousness, so much the worse for the reflective consciousness. If the empiricist can only explain the existence of the Other as a probable hypothesis, then so much the worse for empiricism. The Other exists and we know with certainty that he exists. These are the facts.

Sartre calls the position according to which the existence of other minds is merely a probable hypothesis introduced to explain the behavior of bodies other than my own,"realism." His criticism of realism will be the best introduction to his own theory. At the origin of the realists' problem, says Sartre:

> there is a fundamental presupposition: others are *the Other*, that is the self which *is not* myself. Therefore we grasp here a negation as the constitutive structure of the being-of-others. The presupposition . . . is that the constituting negation is an external negation. The Other is the one who is not me and the one who I am not . . . . The realist who believes that he apprehends the Other through his body considers . . . that he is separated from the Other as one body from another body, which means that the ontological meaning of the negation contained in the statement "I am not Paul" is of the same type as that of the negation contained in the judgment "The table is not the chair."[6]

In fact, however, the negation between persons is not an external negation; it is an internal negation. In the same way that I both am and am not my past self, so I both am and am not the Other. The Other constitutes me in my being as surely as my past, but just as in the act of existing I flee my past, so in the act of existing I flee the Other. If the relationship between me and the Other were not an internal negation, my intuitive certainty of the Other's existence would be totally incomprehensible.

The realist was led to make his mistake by posing the problem of the Other on the level of the reflective consciousness. The manner in which the reflective consciousness leads us to make this mistake can best be seen by examining Descartes' problem of the existence of the external world, from which the problem of the existence of the Other derives. Descartes, too, made the mistake of posing his problem on the level of the reflective consciousness. Now, one of the peculiarities of the reflective consciousness is that it is incapable of conceiving any but external relationships. Descartes, for instance, had little difficulty conceiving that two material objects in the world of physical space be related to one another. The reason was that the relationships between physical objects are always external relationships. The one is not the other, and neither affects the other in its being. They are discrete and separate existences which can be related to one another by mathematical or logical reasoning. Descartes could not, however, conceive mathematically or scientifically of a positive relationship between a spiritual being or person and physical objects, precisely because the relationship is not external, and for the reflective consciousness external relationships are the only conceivable kind.

According to Sartre, Descartes turned everything upside down. It is not man and the world, but rather physical objects, which are radically separated from one another. Physical objects are separated by space. But there is nothing, not even space, to separate the person as a conscious being from the world. The relationship between man and the world is internal. The individual comes into existence by an act of nihilating withdrawal from the in-itself and by that very act constitutes both himself and the extended world. One may, if one likes, talk about a psychic distance separating consciousness from physical objects. But psychic distance is a peculiar kind of distance. It is a separation which is also a presence. It is a distance which cannot be measured by any yardstick and which is therefore a nothingness. The distance between my body and the moon can be mathematically measured since my body is radically different from the moon. But the distance between the moon and my mental apprehension of the moon is not of the same type as that which separates my body from the moon. It cannot be measured. To think that it could would be as silly as to say that jealousy is ten feet long. Consciousness is directly and immediately present to the moon without distance. And so is one subjectivity to another.

The originality of the existentialist position can best be seen by contrasting it with that of Leibniz, on the one hand, and with that of Spinoza and Hegel, on the other. For Leibniz each individual was a self-contained essence, and his relationship to others was mediated by God, the individual himself having no "doors or windows" by which he could directly relate to others. Against this Heidegger and other existentialists have argued that indeed man has no doors or windows—not, however, because he is a self-contained essence. The reason is that by his nature he is already out of doors, out in the street. We are immediately and directly present to one another. We are not housed in an opaque shell, not even in a translucent but unbreakable shell which permits us at times to peek out at others.

On this point Spinoza and Hegel are in substantial agreement with the existentialists. Hegel especially insisted that the route to individual selfhood is through the other and that each of us is his own other. Jaspers actually states his views on this issue in Hegelian terminology. For Hegel and Spinoza, however, men are simply parts of Nature or the Absolute Spirit, and as such they tend to lose their individuality. The existentialists do not allow this. The individual must be the Other while simultaneously not being the Other and retaining his uniqueness as an individual.

Sartre refers to the Hegelian position as idealism, and he tries to show that the idealists have made mistakes similar to those of the realists. By placing themselves at the level of the reflective consciousness Spinoza and Hegel were obliged to regard individuals as having purely external relationships to one another. The fact that the relationship is that of part to whole rather than of one discrete thing to another is relatively insignificant. For the concept of part and whole is borrowed from the spatial world, just as is the concept of discrete and unrelated entities. A circle may be sliced up into as many parts as one wishes, but each part will be wholly distinct from the others. Either, therefore, the idealist conceives the individual as literally one with the Absolute, which is nonsense; or else he conceives the individual as a distinct part of the Absolute, in which case idealism reverts to realism.

> For Hegel . . . truth is truth of the Whole. And he places himself at the vantage point of truth—i.e., of the Whole—to consider the problem of the Other. . . . Actually he does not raise the question of the relation between his own consciousness and that of the Other. By effecting completely the abstraction of his own, he studies purely and simply the relation between the consciousnesses of others—i.e., the relation of consciousnesses which are for him already objects.[7]

For the idealist as for the realist one conclusion is imposed: due to the fact that the Other is revealed to us in a spatial world, we are separated from the Other by a real or ideal space.[8]

For Sartre the nonreflective experience which reveals the Other to us and which affects us in our being through an internal negation is the gaze or look of the Other as experienced in pride or shame.

> Let us imagine that moved by jealousy, curiosity, or vice I have just glued my ear to the door and looked through a keyhole. I am alone. . . . Behind the door a spectacle is presented as "to be seen," a conversation "to be heard". . . . No transcending view comes to confer upon my acts the character of a *given* on which a judgment can be brought to bear. . . . My attitude . . . is . . . a pure mode of losing myself in the world, of causing myself to be drunk in by things as ink is by a blotter. . . . But all of a sudden I hear footsteps in the hall. Someone is looking at me! What does this mean? It means that I am suddenly affected in my being and that essential modifications appear in my structure. . . . I now exist as myself for my unreflective consciousness.[9]

That self, of course, is constituted by the look of the Other. For the Other and consequently for myself I am no longer simply a point of view on the world without any possible point of view upon myself. I am now conscious of myself as a spectator of the world before the Other. I now have a nature, a self, an essence, an ego. And although it has been constituted by the Other I experience it myself on the nonreflective level of consciousness. In this case shame is its revelation.

> I am that ego; I do not reject it as a strange image, but it is present to me as a self which I am . . .: for I discover it in shame, and in other instances, in pride. . . . I *am* this being. I do not for an instant think of denying it; my shame is a confession.[10]

If, however, my being-for-myself is constituted by my being-for-others and if in this sense I am what the Other makes me, how can I simultaneously not be the Other? The answer is simple. Just as I am my past but am not my past because my freedom constantly projects me into the future, so I am what others have made me but am not what others have made me because I must always transcend my being-for-others. It is for me to recognize "the being-for-others which I am and . . . give to it a meaning in the light of the ends which I have chosen."[11] "The important thing is not what one makes of us but what we ourselves make of what one makes of us."[12]

My past and my being-for-others, though similar in that both are dimensions of my being which I must assume and yet from which I must perpetually escape, are none the less dissimilar in two important respects. First, my past is part of my facticity and it can be known by the reflective consciousness. My being-for-others, on the other hand, is simultaneous to my being-for-myself and can never be grasped reflectively. I can, of course, on the level of the reflective consciousness gaze or look at the Other and thus know him as a body, but on this level of consciousness I can never know him as a subject. "The Other can exist for us in two forms: If I experience him with self-evidence, I fail to know him; if I know him [reflectively] . . ., I only reach his being-as-object."[13] Similarly, I can experience my own being-for-others nonreflectively in shame or pride, but I cannot know it as I can know my facticity by the impersonal methods of logic and science. Second, my past was founded by my freedom; I chose my past and am responsible for it because I chose it. My being-for-others, however, is not founded by my freedom, and I am responsible for it simply because it *is* a dimension of my being which I have to accept.

Because of these two important differences we are far more radically alienated from our being-for-others than from our facticity. And this, together with the fact that our being-for-others must be lived on the prereflective level in pride or shame, makes of our being-for-others a far more fearful structure of being than facticity. "My original fall," says Sartre, "is the existence of the Other. Shame—like pride—is the apprehension of myself as a nature although that very nature escapes me and is unknowable as such."[14] Or again:

> It is before the Other that *I am guilty*. I am guilty first when beneath the Other's look I experience my alienation and nakedness as a fall from grace which I must assume. This is the meaning of the famous line from Scripture: "They knew they were naked." Again I am guilty when in turn I look at the Other, because by the very fact of my own self-assertion I constitute him as an object which he must assume. Thus original sin is my upsurge in a world where there are others; and whatever may be my further relations with others, these relations will be only variations on the original theme of guilt. But this guilt is accompanied by helplessness without this helplessness ever succeeding in cleansing me of my guilt.[15]

Authenticity and the Other

The duality of my being-for-myself and my being-for-others permits the same possibilities of inauthenticity as does the duality of facticity and freedom.   Like the inauthenticity which results from obscuring the duality of in-itself and for-itself, the inauthenticity which results from obscuring the duality of being-for-oneself and being-for-others has two poles.   One of these corresponds to the project of sincerity, the attempt to read transcendence into facticity, to merge our subjectivity with our past, and to be wholly what we are.   Daniel, the homosexual in *The Reprieve*, wished to be a homosexual as an oak is an oak.   At the same time he attempted to rid himself of his being-for-himself by reducing it to a pure being-for-others. In a letter to the philosopher Mathieu he writes:

> You must have experienced, in the subway, in the foyer of a theater, or in a train, the sudden and irksome sense that you were being looked at from behind. . . . Well, that is what I felt for the first time, on September 26, at three o'clock in the afternoon, in the hotel garden.   I became more compact and concentrated. . . . I existed in the presence of a look. . . . What anguish to discover that look as a universal medium from which I can't escape!   But what a relief as well!   I know at last what I am.   I adapt for my own use . . . your prophet's foolish, wicked words: "I think, therefore I am." . . . I say, "I am seen, therefore I am."   I need no longer bear the responsibility of my turbid and disintegrating self: he who sees me, causes me to be: I am as he sees me. . . . For one instant you were the heaven-sent mediator between me and myself, you perceived that compact and solid entity which I was and wanted to be.[16]

This fundamental pole of the inauthentic attitude in personal relationships has its extreme manifestation in masochism.   It is the desire to be an object for the other, to be manipulated, looked at, and humiliated in order to experience the weight and solidity of being of which freedom necessarily robs us.

The other pole is sadism: the desire to look at others, to

reduce them to objects, to manipulate and humiliate them.   It is comparable to bad faith, the attempt to read facticity into transcendence, to treat our subjective desires or free projects into the future as if they were in-itselfs with the full weight and solidity of being belonging to the past—except that in interpersonal relations it is not our personal subjectivity but rather the subjectivity of the Other which we are trying to capture, to nail down, to invest with the weight of an in-itself.   All of the existentialists recognize this form of inauthenticity in human relationships, but Sartre is alone in having seen that it has an opposite pole which is equally unwholesome and equally common.

Masochism and sadism are, of course, both impossible attempts to escape the duality of our being.   There is an inescapable, implicit comprehension of the Other as a free subjectivity; no one can fool himself into believing that another human being exists only as a thing.   One look from his victim and the sadist's project is foiled.   Moreover, since the sadist wants to capture the other's freedom, it is necessary that the victim voluntarily and of his own free will determine the moment of humiliation at which he will break down and beg for mercy. An animal who has no freedom to surrender would never be a suitable victim for a sadist.   At the same time, however, the sadist wishes to be himself responsible for the moment of humiliation; he wants to achieve his goal by a personal manipulation of instruments since otherwise there would be no victory. His goal is thus "ambiguous, contradictory, without equilibrium since it is both the strict consequence of a technical utilization of determinism and the manifestation of an unconditioned freedom."[17]   The masochist's project is impossible of achievement for similar reasons.   In the case of the masochist it is not the Other's subjectivity but his own which he considers the obstacle to the realization of his goal; but the masochist can no more suppress awareness of his own subjectivity than the sadist can suppress awareness of the Other's subjectivity.   "Even the masochist who pays a woman to whip him is treating her as an instrument and by this very fact posits himself in transcendence in relation to her."[18]   Moreover, the masochist's goal is not simply to be an object for the Other any more than the goal of the sadist is to relate to the Other as a mere object.   The sadist wished to appropriate the freedom of the other and make of it a personal possession. Similarly, the masochist wishes to appropriate the subjectivity of the sadist. Only so can he experience himself as a thing. But this is totally impossible. "It is useless for the masochist to get down on his knees, to show himself in ridiculous positions, to cause himself to be used as a simple lifeless instrument. It is *for the Other* that he will be obscene or simply passive, for the Other that he will undergo these postures; for himself he is forever condemned to give them to himself."[19] It is only by capturing the Other's subjectivity that the masochist could experience himself as object, but this is on principle out of the question.

Sartre's analyses of various other human attitudes such as physical desire, indifference, and love are always subtle and interesting, but all these attitudes reduce in one way or another to some form of sadism or masochism and all are doomed for essentially the same reasons. The exposition, therefore, will be limited to only one further example. To want to be loved is to attempt the assimilation of another's freedom by subjecting it to one's own. "To want to be loved is to want to be placed beyond the whole system of values posited by the Other and to be the condition of all valorization and the objective foundation of all values. . . . The woman in love demands that the beloved in his acts should sacrifice traditional morality for her and is anxious to know whether the beloved would betray his friends for her, 'would steal for her,' 'would kill for her,' etc." To achieve her goal she tries to excite the other's passion; for "who would be content with a love given as pure loyalty to a sworn oath? Who would be satisfied with the words 'I love you because I have freely engaged myself to love you and because I do not want to go back on my word.'" At the same time, however, she does not "want to possess an automaton. . . . If Tristan and Isolde fall madly in love because of a love potion, they are less interesting. . . . Thus the lover . . . wants to possess a freedom as freedom. . . . Thus the lover demands a pledge, yet is irritated by a pledge. He wants to be loved by a freedom but demands that this freedom as freedom should no longer be free. . . . In love it is not a determinism of the passions which we desire in the Other nor a freedom beyond reach; it is a freedom which *plays the role* of a determinism by the passions and which is caught in its own role."[20]

The desire to be loved is thus doomed to perpetual insecurity because of the bad faith required to believe that the Other's valorization of oneself is both free and determined.   But there is still another important reason for the failure of this project. The only possible motive the Other might have for accepting the conditions of the woman who wishes to be loved is that he actually love her.   But if he does actually love her, then he will wish for her love and will want to assimilate her freedom.   At this point a vicious circle begins.   Love is "in essence, a deception and a reference to infinity since to love is to wish to be loved."[21]

There is a widespread misunderstanding to the effect that Sartre does not believe in the possibility of authentic human relationships, that according to him all men are compelled by their nature to assume some form of the inauthentic attitudes just described.   To some extent this is a simple misunderstanding.   In *Being and Nothingness* Sartre explicitly declared his belief in the possibility of authentic human relationships, and he has reaffirmed that belief in the introduction to a book on his philosophy by Francis Jeanson.   Moreover, it is quite clear both that Sartre believes in radical conversions and that the concrete attitudes toward the Other described in *Being and Nothingness* are impossible for the person who has undergone the radical conversion.   The radical conversion consists in an uncompromising assumption of one's own personal freedom; but even sadism, or the attempt to appropriate the freedom of the Other, involves a surrender of one's own freedom.   The sadist cannot achieve his goal without allowing the victim to choose the moment at which the torture stops and thereby renouncing his own right to decide.

There are, however, two things which help to explain how this misunderstanding arose.   First, it is clear that authentic human relationships must be based upon mutual respect for one another's freedom.   But critics of Sartre point to a passage in which Sartre declares that "respect for the Other's freedom is an empty word."   Taken out of context this passage does seem to support the unfriendly critic.   In context, however, it does not.   In this passage Sartre is clearly using the phrase "respect for another's freedom" in the meaning that it has for the liberal democrat, and there is no reason to believe that Sartre could not, if he so chooses, find some other meaning of the phrase suitable to a theory of authentic human relationships as he conceives them.   The paragraph from which the passage in question is taken begins with a reference to "an ethics of 'laisser-faire' and tolerance."   It continues further down as follows:

> To realize tolerance with respect to the Other is to cause the Other to be thrown forcefully into a tolerant world.   It is to remove from him on principle those free possibilities of cour- ageous resistance, of perseverance, of self-assertion which he would have had the opportunity to develop in a world of in- tolerance.   This fact is made still more manifest if we consider the problem of education: a severe education treats the child as an instrument since it tries to bend him by force to values which he has not admitted, but a liberal education in order to make use of other methods nevertheless chooses a priori principles and values in the name of which the child will be trained.   To train the child by persuasion and gentleness is no less to compel him.   Thus respect for the Other's freedom is an empty word; even if we could assume the project of respecting this freedom, each attitude which we adopted with respect to the Other would be a violation of that freedom which we claimed to respect.[22]

Second, there is no reason at all for believing that authentic human attitudes as Sartre might conceive them would involve an absence of conflict.   On the contrary, in view of the general existentialist value orientation it would be most surprising indeed if conflict were not regarded as an essential element in any authentic human relationship.   Conformist Americans may want "to get along with one another" and may consider this to be the supreme value in human relationships, but the existentialists clearly do not.   None the less, many critics of Sartre cannot conceive anyone's using the term "authenticity" for a relationship which involves conflict, and Sartre more than any other existentialist insists upon the inevitability of conflict in personal relations.   Sartre himself criticizes Heidegger for not having fully realized the inevitability of conflict; and Gabriel Marcel criticizes Sartre for having too much insisted upon its inevitability.

The distinctiveness of Sartre's position is that he regards conflict, not merely as a necessary element in human relations, but as the very foundation of human relations.   Heidegger had regarded "being-with" as an original structure of the *Dasein* along with others.   Sartre contends that the "essence of the relations between consciousnesses is not the *Mitsein*; it is conflict."[23]

Sartre calls the consciousness of being a member of a group "we-consciousness," and argues that the we-consciousness can only arise on the ground of the "us-consciousness." "Being-for-others precedes and founds being-with-others." In the same way that I can become conscious of myself only to the extent that the Other intervenes to look at me, so I can adopt the we-consciousness only to the extent that I simultaneously experience an us-consciousness. Whenever there is a we-consciousness there is also consciousness of what Sartre calls a Third, or spectator for whom we exist as an "us."

One form which the Third may take is that of Heidegger's *das Man* or the impersonal public. Consider, for instance, that you are in the subway. You may have a sense of being a part of the crowd pushing toward an exit; but according to Sartre this is possible only because you are obscurely aware of all those anonymous persons who constructed the subway and put up signs marked "Entrance," "Exit," and so forth. "The 'Exit'—considered as pure opening out onto the street—is strictly equivalent to the 'Entrance'; neither its coefficient of adversity nor its visible utility designates it as an exit. I do not submit to the object itself when I use it as an 'Exit'; I adapt myself to the human order. By my very act I recognize the Other's existence."[24] And it should be added: I recognize the Other's existence as a being to whom I submit and who therefore exists as a Third. The we-consciousness, the sense of being part of a group pushing toward an exit, exists only to the extent that we are also conscious of being an object for a Third.

The Third may also be an individual or well-defined human group whom we regard as a free subject and for whom we exist as objects: the teacher to school children, the army officer to enlisted men, the bourgeois to the proletariat, and so on.

Sartre's quarrel with Heidegger derives partly from the fact that Heidegger did not explicitly recognize *das Man* or the Anonymous They as a Third. Heidegger conceived of human groups being united by a common task which they executed in a common world defined by certain instrumental complexes. Workers in a factory, for instance, have a group feeling based on a sense of work to be jointly accomplished in a common human milieu. This implies, of course, an awareness of *das*

Man as the creator of the artificial world, but since Heidegger did not apparently hold that *das Man* constituted a Third for which the workers would be a kind of object, he took the group feeling to be a basic fact.

The other, and more important, source of disagreement between Sartre and Heidegger consists in Sartre's insistence that every group define itself by reference to some specific Other. A group becomes conscious of itself only by reference to another person or group for whom it exists as an object. The workers in the factory are not only united by the necessity they are under to cooperate in producing a certain item of manufacture and by their submission to *das Man*; they are also united by a sense of common opposition to their employers. If through some odd circumstances the employers and workers shared common ends, either the consciousness of solidarity among the workers would be considerably weakened or else their we-consciousness would be broadened to include the employers. But even in the latter case, conflict would continue; for if employees and employers were to develop a sense of solidarity, their we-consciousness would still require an us-consciousness with respect to another group to sustain itself. The other group might be the consumer, a rival producer of the same product, or possibly the government. But another group for whom they existed as an object would have to emerge and the conflict would continue with a new grouping of forces. For a dramatic treatment of this theme the plays of Jean Genet, especially *The Maids* and *The Blacks*, are unsurpassed.

The way in which Sartre uses these themes to attack humanism is of special interest. The humanist, he says, must make some surreptitious appeal to God, i.e., an Absolute Third, a "being-who-looks-at and who can never be looked-at."

Thus the humanistic "Us"—the Us-object—is proposed to each individual consciousness as an ideal impossible to attain although everyone keeps the illusion of being able to succeed by progressively enlarging the circle of communities to which he does belong. This humanistic "Us" remains an empty concept, a pure indication of a possible extension of the ordinary usage of the "Us." Each time that we use the "Us" in this sense (to designate suffering humanity, sinful humanity, to determine an objective historical meaning by considering man as an object which is developing its potentialities) we limit ourselves to indicating a certain concrete experience to be undergone *in the presence of* the Absolute Third; that is, of God. Thus the limiting-concept of humanity (as the totality of the Us-object) and the limiting-concept of God imply one another and are correlative.[25]

Criticism

Whether the existentialist regards conflict as one ineluctable and valuable feature of human relationships among others or whether he regards it as the very foundation of all human relationships is a matter of relatively little importance. No existentialist much believes in the value of group feeling based on a harmony of interests, and none accords any great value to the "spirit of cooperativeness." The core of the existentialist position is that harmony and security in human relationships are impossible of achievement and that the only humanly satisfactory attitude towards others will be based upon an explicit recognition of the fact. Even if man could choose between security and freedom or harmony and conflict, he ought to choose freedom and conflict. The correct choice would mean the difference between boredom and intensity, abjectness and dignity, herd mentality and individualism, routine and creativeness, the Other as object and the Other as subject, oneself as object and oneself as subject, sadism or masochism and authenticity.

What kind of criticism would the pragmatic-oriented Anglo-American offer of this view? There can be no question that the pragmatists tend strongly toward the traditional view that men aspire toward happiness or well-being conceived in terms of harmony and security and that happiness so conceived is an ideal toward which men may make substantial progress. The pages of Dewey and James are full of references to equilibrium, balance, unimpeded activity, adjustment, etc., as the end toward which men strive; and Dewey is without doubt the most influential twentieth-century philosophical heir to Enlightenment attitudes about social progress.

It would, therefore, be tempting to contrast sharply the existentialist and the pragmatist, representing the latter as flatly opposed to the former, point by point. The result would be a picture of the pragmatist as a dull, plodding, naïve, unimaginative ordinary man. To succumb to this temptation, however, would be to misrepresent the pragmatist. The technique of sharply opposing highly abstract concepts such as security and freedom or harmony and conflict, not to mention the in-itself and the for-itself or being-as-object and being-as-subject, is an existentialist device. The pragmatists would regard these concepts as much too abstract and too rigid to serve any useful purpose.

The major pragmatic criticism, therefore, would be that the existentialists have wrongly posed the problem. The pragmatist, for instance, would not for a moment think of denying the existentialist claim that conflict is a necessary feature of the human reality. But neither would he think of denying that conflict is avoidable. The fact is that there are many different types of conflict, some avoidable and some not. Until the types of conflict in question are specified, statements such as that conflict is a necessary feature of the human reality merit neither affirmation nor denial. And until the various forms of concrete conflict have been classified in a sufficiently detailed manner, one cannot even know what conflict means in the generic sense—or, for that matter, whether there is a generic meaning of the term "conflict." It may be that the term "conflict," like the term "freedom," has no single generic meaning.

Clearly, Sartre's "the look" is not a basic ontological fact from which all conflict is derived and in terms of which conflict must be defined. A moment's reflection will reveal that we do not enter into conflict with one another because we look at one another. On the contrary, it is because we conflict with one another that we look. We rarely look at passing strangers on the street, but we do look closely at the man who is competing for a job we want ourselves. Contrariwise, we are not conscious of being looked at by strangers in the street, but we are acutely conscious of being observed by a rival. "The look" is not even a wholly apt metaphor or symbol for conflict. There is nothing particularly upsetting or conflict-generating in, say, the look of an adoring mother or the look of an admiring crowd.

For similar reasons the pragmatist would neither affirm nor deny that conflict is a desirable feature of the human reality. Some forms of conflict are desirable, some not. Friendly rivalry in sport is a desirable form of conflict, and so is the less friendly rivalry between members of opposing philosophical schools in so far as it obliges the interested parties to correct and sharpen their thinking. Atomic warfare, on the other hand, is an undesirable form of conflict. The proper question is not, therefore, whether one ought to prefer security to freedom or harmony to conflict, but rather what kinds and what degree of security or harmony, freedom or conflict, any given group in any given historical situation wants.

Up to a certain point and for certain purposes it is legitimate to classify or to group diverse human needs or desires under a general rubric such as the desire of security or the desire of freedom. But the concrete reality is not a desire of security or a desire of freedom. The concrete reality is rather a multitude of little desires for particular things and specific states of affairs. It is only because certain individuals in certain concrete historical situations have been threatened with arbitrary arrest or lived in fear of war or known physical want that it makes any sense to say that *man* wants *security*. It is only because certain individuals in certain other concrete historical situations have been threatened with boredom or have lost all hope of achieving security that it makes sense to say that *man* wants *intensity*. Men do not come into the world with only two basic aspirations, and these for such vague and generalized goals as freedom and security. Men's original desires are many, and they are invariably desires of particular things and specific states of affairs. Moreover, most human desires are shaped primarily by the social and economic conditions under which they thrive.

There are no overarching, generalized desires which spawn groups of more specific desires. The multitude of specific desires appears first, and what passes by the name of an a priori insight into original and fundamental structures of the human reality is only an abstract and man-made classification of concrete desires made after one has observed these many specific desires emerge in the world. To take the abstract classification for the reality and to pretend that it is the original reality of which specific concrete desires are exemplifications is to mistake a highly artificial logical order of classification for an original, ontological fact.

One of the peculiarities of the reflective consciousness, Sartre and the pragmatists agree, is that the concepts which it generates are mutually exclusive. The reflective consciousness knows only external relations. What has been separated and made distinct by a process of abstract thinking can never be joined together. Is there not, then, a reasonable presumption that the for-itself and the in-itself, whose relationship to one another is by Sartre's own admission abstractly inconceivable, are *merely* abstract concepts? There is no massive and solid bloc of Being lying behind the world. The in-itself is but an abstract, simplified, and falsifying concept of the concrete world. There is no pure act of transcendence, no nothingness. The for-itself is merely an abstract, simplified, and falsifying concept of certain concrete functions of human consciousness. And since the in-itself and the for-itself are Sartre's principal symbols for security and freedom respectively, is there not also a reasonable presumption that similar remarks are in order with regard to security and freedom? Man does not desire security in the abstract or freedom in the abstract. There is no such thing. What man desires is the kind and degree of security and freedom which it is humanly possible to achieve in a given historical epoch.

It follows, of course, that man need make no radical choice between freedom and security. The concrete realities for which the in-itself and the for-itself stand as impoverished symbols are not antithetical. Body and mind are given together in experience. There is no problem about how they coexist. The problem could only arise in so far as one starts from false ontological premises. Similarly, as concrete realities, security and freedom are not antithetical; it is only the existentialists' empty concepts of security and freedom which cannot be joined together.

Of course, many specific desires are incompatible in the sense that they cannot all be simultaneously realized under existing historical conditions. This, however, is not news. And it is utterly ridiculous to dress up this simple fact, which every child learns before the age of two, in an elaborate philosophical terminology and to present it as the philosophy of our times. The dilemmas of our day are more serious and more numerous than in previous ages; but they cannot be deduced, much less resolved, by using a pair of concepts like the for-itself and the in-itself.

There is one other major point with respect to human relationships on which the pragmatists would disagree with Sartre. Sartre says that the concept of mankind has as its necessary correlate the concept of God or the Absolute Third, i.e., a being who can look at us but who cannot be looked at himself. Since, however, the concept of God is a self-contradictory limiting concept, there can be no true sense of human solidarity. Now, it may be the case that Marxists and others who conceive of mankind as an integral part of Nature have to introduce surreptitiously into their thinking some notion of God and that their concept of human solidarity is as empty or impossible as the correlative notion of God.   But the pragmatists, who reject the idea of a bloc universe, are in a totally different position. Conflict between man and nature is a fundamental fact of life and it is quite sufficient to give humankind a vivid sense of solidarity—a sense of solidarity, moreover, which not only does not derive from any form of intra-human or divine-human conflict, but which actually tends to minimize or alleviate intra-human conflict.

It is significant that Anglo-American intellectuals who are religious by temperament but atheist by conviction generally adopt a perspective like that presented in Bertrand Russell's essay "A Free Man's Worship," where Man is pictured as pitted against Nature in a life-and-death struggle.   To be sure, as a concrete person tied to the here and now, one will be identified with particular groups or persons and define oneself in terms of these groups or persons.   At the same time it will be conceded that individuals or limited groups tend often to excite the imagination more powerfully than so large and indefinite a body as mankind in general.   Nevertheless, there is no logical limit to enlarging group consciousness to the point where mankind stands alone against the nonhuman, nor is there any a priori limit upon the powers of the human imagination making it impossible to adopt and to sustain a vision of mankind versus nature with intensity over a relatively long period of time.

The existentialist charge that humanism betrays an atrophy of the imaginative faculty could be turned against the existentialist. It may be that the existentialist has arbitrarily imposed limits upon the imagination. If we are trying to analyze human conflict and to understand its origins, metaphor and symbol are out of place. But if we are trying to sustain an essentially religious view of life and to enlarge the powers of the imagination, poetic metaphor is almost the only means we have. And the force of a metaphor has little to do with the size of that for which it stands. Poetic metaphors for mankind can in principle at least be quite as inspiring as poetic metaphors for a person, a family or a nation.

VII. Death

Death and the Intense Life

Death is a theme upon which all of the existentialists have written extensively. According to Jaspers, "philosophizing means learning to die." According to Camus in his most existentialist book, *The Myth of Sisyphus*, suicide is the only genuine philosophical issue. Unamuno seemed to be constitutionally incapable of writing a single page without mentioning the word "death" at least once. Not even those traditional philosophers such as St. Augustine and Pascal who are most akin to the existentialists gave this theme the prominence which it has assumed in existentialist literature.

The reason is immediately apparent once the traditional position with respect to death is contrasted with that of the existentialists. On this issue the mainstream of traditional thinking is best exemplified by the Stoics and Spinoza. For the Stoics death is nothing to us. Either, they argue, we are alive or dead; if alive, we need not fear death since life is still our treasured possession; if dead, we cannot fear death since fear is the manifestation of a living consciousness. The disingenuousness of this argument is not likely to escape detection in the twentieth century. But the attitude toward death which inspired the argument is by no means without its supporters. One still encounters approving quotations of Spinoza's famous dictum: "A free man thinks of nothing less than of death, and his wisdom is not a meditation upon death but upon life."

Plato had said in a well-known passage of which Jasper's quoted remark seems but a variation that the study of philosophy is a preparation for death. The apparent similarity of the two remarks is, however, wholly illusory. Despite the pathos and strange beauty of Socrates' death scene in the *Phaedo* it is clear that the attitude in the face of death which

Plato approved is that of Stoic calm, bordering on indifference. The lamentations of Socrates' wife Xantippe are represented as undignified and she is rudely expelled from the execution room that Socrates may use his last minutes to discuss philosophy. If he does not survive death, says Socrates, death will be a blessing since it means the end of pain.   If there is an afterlife, death will still be a blessing since he will then be able to expound his ideas without fear of exile or execution.

Even Christian attitudes toward death bear the impress of Stoic ideas. *The Consolation of Philosophy* by the Stoic Boethius has long been claimed as a Christian document and has influenced almost all unquestionably Christian literature of consolation, including the *Imitation of Christ*. Even St. Augustine, whom the existentialists fondly quote and who himself mercilessly ridiculed Stoic indifference to death, was so deeply influenced by the Stoics that he condemned as sinful his tears and grief upon the death of his mother.   That Augustine should ground his ideal of serenity and noble calm in the face of death upon faith in the mercifulness of God rather than, as the Stoics, upon a proud confidence in the resources of the individual human will is a difference too obvious to be ignored. But the similarity between his and the Stoic's ideal takes on a remarkable significance when one is reminded, as Christian existentialists never weary of reminding us, that Christ's death upon the cross was preceded by a lapse of faith and a tortured cry of despair: "My God, my God, why hast thou forsaken me?"   Most traditional Christians either ignored this text or explained it away with arguments which make the Stoic argument about death shine with an aura of sincerity.

In a certain sense the traditional philosopher's view about the proper attitude toward death is very similar to that of the ordinary man.   Both agree that a preoccupation with death smacks of morbidity.   Both agree that the wholesome man will divert his attention from the fact of death, especially in its uglier aspects, whenever this fact protrudes itself upon his consciousness.   Whereas, however, the ordinary man will attempt to divert himself from the thought of death by intensifying his pursuit of worldly goods such as pleasure, wealth, and prestige, the traditional philosopher recommends that the thought of death serve as a pretext for meditation upon other, presumably higher and spiritual, values.   For the Stoics death

is an occasion for glorying in a demonstration of man's
invincible will, suicide itself being an act of noble triumph over
adversity. For the traditional Christian philosopher, including Augustine and Pascal, the theme of death has value
only in so far as it draws our attention to God and reminds us
of our dependence upon his grace or renews our determination
to win his favor through obedient service. Spinoza and Hegel
would tame the fear of death by having us contemplate our
union with Nature or the Absolute Spirit; Plato and Aristotle,
by having us contemplate the eternal Ideas or the permanence
of the species; humanists and Marxists, by focusing our attention upon the ties which bind the individual to his race or to
his class.

Important as these differences between the ordinary man and
the traditional philosopher are, they pale into insignificance
when seen from the perspective of the existentialists. Man
neither can nor should, say the existentialists, shut out the
consciousness of death or refuse the anguish and despair which
the consciousness of death entails.

The *divertissement*, as Pascal called it, of the ordinary man
in the everyday activities and pleasures of the world is but a
desperate and inevitably unsuccessful effort to conceal from
himself the anguish which stirs in the depths of his being. But,
add the existentialists, the philosopher's attempt to immerse
himself in his "higher values" is of precisely the same character.
It is not necessary at this stage to elaborate upon this view in
so far as it pertains to the position of the atheistic existentialists.
The case of the Christian existentialists, however, would appear
at first sight to belie this generalization. Although the Christian
existentialists share with the atheistic existentialists an im-
patience with the other "comforting illusions" of traditional
philosophy, they have clearly not abandoned faith in an afterlife. It is necessary, however, to recall that the faith of the
Christian existentialist is a tortured faith in which the will to
believe is constantly undermined by doubt and disbelief.
Where what passes for a serene and confident faith is not a
mere habitual babbling of empty verbal formulae, it is the will
to believe, the energy of unremitting concern about one's
personal fate, mistakenly interpreted as steadfast adherence to
doctrine. What attracts the existentialists, be they atheist or

Christian, to Augustine and Pascal is the vitality of their religious concern, not their doctrinal orthodoxy.

"Faith is in its essence," says Unamuno, "simply a matter of will . . . , to believe is to wish to believe, and to believe in God is, before and above all, to wish that there may be a God."[1] Even the militant atheist who vigorously denies God fares better at the hands of the Christian existentialists than the "serene believer"; for the energy of his despair is more akin to faith than the calm of the man who recites a creed by rote, and he is more honest than the fanatic who has allowed the energy of his hope to blind him to the tragic contradictions of the human condition. In sum, the Christian existentialist does not regard faith in the afterlife as a comforting illusion born of bad faith, but he does regard as illusory and morally valueless a faith which is not perpetually sharpened and daily recreated in and through despair.

Whether one can or cannot in fact escape the consciousness of death is an issue which will be decided according to one's belief or disbelief in levels of consciousness and the reliability which one attributes to the methods by which the consciousness of death has allegedly been revealed as a permanent feature of some deeper level of consciousness. In the present discussion, however, this issue will be left in the background. The most important and interesting things which the existentialists say about death bear upon the moral claim that man ought deliberately to cultivate an intense and persistent surface consciousness of death. The ordinary man and the traditional philosopher interpret an injunction of this kind as a sign of morbidity. The existentialist retorts by interpreting the attitude of the ordinary man and the traditional philosopher as an instance of cowardly flight.

Behind this tiresome exchange of insulting epithets lies the existentialist conviction that the affirmation of life is impossible unless we hold steadfastly to the consciousness of death. Life has verve and meaning only for the person who lives in the shadow of death and resolutely faces the fact that each of us is condemned to die. Danger, conflict, moral decision, the act of faith—every form of human experience which arouses the individual to action and engages his energies—is heightened and rendered most acute when it carries with it the consciousness of death as a personal possibility. To shut out the consciousness of death is to rob life of its supreme value: in a word, intensity.

The obvious objection to the existentialist line of argument is that the fear of death, far from intensifying consciousness and releasing human energies, drugs and paralyzes. Common experiences referred to in ordinary English locutions such as "being petrified with fright" or "swooning from fright" tend to give weight to this objection. The answer of the existentialists is that the consciousness of death releases human energies only by revealing the insignificance of ordinary pursuits, thus breaking through the crust of convention, routine, and habit of which we are normally victims. If, therefore, the ordinary man reacts to the thought of death with numbing fright, it is not because the consciousness of death is intrinsically paralyzing, but because the ordinary man resists the consciousness of death, flees from it, in order to protect the mundane values which he has not the courage to abandon even though the consciousness of death has revealed their pettiness to him. The courageous man, on the contrary, will embrace the consciousness of death as an agent of liberation. He will not flee from it nor from the anguish which accompanies it, because he knows that it is absurd for a finite being to expect fulfillment and well-being as traditionally conceived and because he is aware of the values which the consciousness of death carries with it.

Up to this point the major existentialist thinkers are in complete agreement. Beyond this point they divide into two opposing camps, of which Heidegger and Sartre are fairly typical examples. Before attempting to elucidate the issues with respect to death on which the existentialists themselves part company, it should be pointed out that the existentialists are not alone among modern thinkers in their basic attitude toward death. William James paid his respects to the consciousness of death by saying that no man is truly educated unless he has toyed with the idea of suicide. Literary critics in their interpretation of tragedy have increasingly made use of themes similar to those of the existentialists. And a man as unlike the existentialists temperamentally as Freud has stated their central thesis with unmatched clarity and simplicity. Speaking of the days before World War I, he says:

. . . . we were of course prepared to maintain that death was the necessary outcome of life, that everyone owes nature a debt and must expect to pay the debt—in short, that death was natural, undeniable and unavoidable. In reality, however, we were accustomed to behave as if it were otherwise. We showed an unmistakable tendency to put death on one side, to eliminate it from life. We tried to hush it up. . . . But this attitude of ours toward death has a powerful effect on our lives. Life is impoverished, it loses in interest, when the highest stake in the game of living, life itself, may not be risked. It becomes as shallow and empty as, let us say, an American flirtation, in which it is understood from the first that nothing is to happen, as contrasted with a Continental love-affair in which both partners must constantly bear its serious consequences in mind.[2]

Heidegger on Death

The debate between Heidegger and Sartre revolves around two distinct theses propounded by Heidegger in *Being and Time*, although neither Heidegger nor Sartre clearly distinguished between them. One of these is to the effect that the consciousness of death not only vivifies the felt quality of experience but also acts as the crucial factor in producing individuality. Death, says Heidegger, is the one thing nobody can do for me; only the person who realizes that he must face death alone truly experiences the sense of his own individuality.

The importance which Heidegger attributes to this particular function of the consciousness of death is reflected obliquely in the stress he lays upon a particular technique of the inauthentic man to allay the fear of death. In fact, Heidegger stresses this technique to the exclusion of all others; and from a reading of Heidegger alone one would suppose that the inauthentic flight from death had no other manifestations. Essentially this technique consists in depersonalizing death by reducing it to an abstract and universal category for a purely biological or social phenomenon, refusing to recognize that it is a concrete experience of a spiritual order which all human beings and especially oneself must individually undergo. In the shorter but more specialized vocabulary of Heidegger it consists in saying to oneself, not "I shall die," but rather "One dies." For a literary representation of this technique Heidegger refers the reader to Tolstoy's story "The Death of Ivan Ilych." The lawyer and public prosecutor Ivan Ilych develops certain physical symptoms, which at first he ignores. Later, having begun to worry about these symptoms, he visits a doctor:

> To Ivan Ilych only one question was important: was his case serious or not? But the doctor ignored that inappropriate question. From his point of view it was not the one under consideration, the real question was to decide between a floating kidney, chronic catarrh, or appendicitis. It was not a question of Ivan Ilych's life or death, but one between a floating kidney and appendicitis. And that question the doctor solved brilliantly, as it seemed to Ivan Ilych, in favor of the appendix, with the reservation that should an examination of the urine give fresh indications the matter would be reconsidered. All this was just what Ivan Ilych had himself brilliantly accomplished a thousand times in dealing with men on trial. The doctor summed up just as brilliantly, looking over his spectacles triumphantly and even gaily at the accused. From the doctor's summing up Ivan Ilych concluded that things were bad, but that for the doctor, and perhaps for everybody else, it was a matter of indifference, though for him it was bad. And this conclusion struck him painfully, arousing in him a great feeling of pity for himself and of bitterness toward the doctor's indifference to a matter of such importance.
>
> He said nothing of this, but rose, placed the doctor's fee on the table, and remarked with a sigh: "We sick people probably often put inappropriate questions. But tell me, in general, is this complaint dangerous or not? . . ."
>
> The doctor looked at him sternly over his spectacles with one eye, as if to say: "Prisoner, if you will not keep to the questions put to you, I shall be obliged to have you removed from the court."
>
> "I have already told you what I consider necessary and proper. The analysis may show something more." And the doctor bowed.[3]

In all likelihood Tolstoy's primary intention in writing "The Death of Ivan Ilych" was to illustrate the ills of man's indifference to man. For Heidegger, however, the story has interest as an illustration of "the shattering and the collapse of the 'One dies.'" Prior to his illness Ivan Ilych's attitude toward death was no different from that of the doctor. He knew, of course, that he would die, but death to him was a biological or social category. He was neither more nor less mortal than a dog. He was someone who would die in the same way that he was a lawyer and a family man. The category of death, indeed, had even less significance for him than that of lawyer or married man. His illness changed all this. The insignificance of his social functions as lawyer, husband, and father was impressed upon him forcefully; and it may well have occurred to him for the first time that men alone among the animals know that they are going to die. The shopworn word "death," which had been previously no more than a coin used in the business of social intercourse, began to take on a unique meaning—a meaning for him as an individual human being. At last he was obliged to face the truth which he had for so long and with such art concealed from himself.

As Pascal puts it: "It pleases us to seek repose in the society of our fellowmen. But, since they are as miserable and as powerless as we are, they will not help us. We will die alone, and we ought therefore to act as if we were alone."

The second Heideggerian thesis which has become a bone of contention is even more distinctively Heideggerian than the first. The view that consciousness of death shatters the banality of everyday existence and liberates us from the petty mentality of the ordinary man is, as we have seen, common to all existentialists. The view which we have just presented according to which the consciousness of death heightens and intensifies individual self-awareness is one which Heidegger shares with many existentialists, especially the Christian existentialists Kierkegaard, Unamuno, and Shestov. The view which we are about to develop, however, is limited almost exclusively to Heidegger and his followers, although one aspect of it was clearly anticipated by Nietzsche.

In order adequately to understand this second thesis it will be necessary to bear in mind that for Heidegger, as for traditional philosophers and for most Christian existentialists, death is the prime expression of human finitude. Unlike traditional philosophers and Christian existentialists, however, Heidegger regards death as an ultimate and radical fact which cannot in any way be overcome. He refuses to tolerate even an anguished hope of personal survival. In part this refusal to entertain even the possibility of personal survival after death is based upon

a disdain for subterfuge and a belief that death is an ontological
necessity. There is, however, another reason which in all
probability weighed more heavily with Heidegger and which is
more pertinent in the present context.

According to the existentialists the pain and fright which
accompanies the consciousness of death is the price we must
pay for the values which consciousness of death brings with it.
Most of the existentialists nevertheless agree that the price may
be reduced, that is to say, that the uglier aspects of this complex
experience called the anguish of death may be mitigated. The
Christian existentialists' will to believe is obviously an effort to
reduce the price or to alleviate the pain. Heidegger, for his
part, believes that he has discovered a device which serves this
purpose even better. That device consists in going beyond
a mere recognition of human finitude and actually willing it.

Originally death appears to us as something which comes
from the outside and strikes us down, something over which we
have no control; and it is precisely this feature of our original
reaction to death which produces the greatest terror and drives
us most surely into an attitude of inauthenticity. If, however,
in a resolute decision we embrace our finitude and actively
assume our Being-for-Death (*Sein-zum-Tode*), we can allay this
terror far more effectively than by willing personal immortality.
This idea was clearly inspired by Nietzsche. In a chapter of
Thus Spake Zarathustra entitled "On Free Death" it is stated
unambiguously: "My death, I praise to you, the free death,
which comes to me because I want it. . . ." Also in *Twilight
of the Idols*: "Out of love for life we should want a different
death: free, conscious, without hazard, without ambush."

Heidegger, however, has wedded this theme to his own system
of ideas. For him the resolute decision to assume finitude
not only allays the original terror which the thought of death
inspires; it also serves to round off our life and to make of it
some kind of totality, thus modifying that deep rent in our
being caused by the ontological necessity of perpetual self-
transcendence. By assuming death we interiorize it as our
ultimate possibility, as the final term of all acts of self-transcendence. At death we are the totality we cannot be while
we are alive, but even while in life we can in a sense run ahead
of ourselves toward death and by thus assuming death adopt
a point of view upon ourselves as totalities. To gauge the

importance of this theme in Heidegger's analysis of death a glance at the title of the chapter in which the analysis occurs will suffice. It reads: "The possible Being-whole of *Dasein* and Being-toward-Death."

Sartre on Death

In *Being and Nothingness* Sartre informs us that for some time he was much attracted by Heidegger's views on death, especially what was called above Heidegger's second thesis. By humanizing and interiorizing death, man can apparently deprive death of its character as a restriction upon our freedom. The Heideggerian doctrine thus presented itself to Sartre as a way of safeguarding his theory of total freedom. "This apparent limit of our freedom," Sartre writes, "by being interiorized is recovered by freedom." Later, Sartre had second thoughts about this doctrine, which he also believed to be that of Rilke and Malraux. "Neither," he says, "the advantage of these views nor the undeniable portion of truth which they include should mislead us. It is necessary to take the question up from the beginning."[4]

In criticizing Heidegger's first thesis, viz., that the consciousness of death heightens self-awareness and confers upon us the status of individuality, Sartre concentrates upon Heidegger's statement that death is the only thing which nobody can do for me. It is, Sartre argues,

> perfectly gratuitous to say that "to die is the only thing which nobody can do for me." . . . If one considers death as the ultimate subjective possibility, the event which concerns only the for-itself, then it is evident that nobody can die for me. But then it also follows that none of my possibilities taken from this point of view . . . can be projected by anyone other than me. Nobody can love for me—if we mean by that to take vows which are my vows, to experience the emotions . . . which are my emotions. . . . On the other hand, if my acts in the world are considered from the point of view of their function, their efficacy, and their result, it is certain that the Other

can always do what I do.   If it is a question of making this woman happy, of safeguarding her life or her freedom, of giving her the means of finding her salvation, or simply of realizing a home with her, of "giving her" children, if that is what we call loving, then another will be able to love in my place, he will be able to love for me. . . . And so it is with all my conduct. . . . My death will also fall into this category.   If to die is to die in order to inspire, to bear witness, for the country, etc., then anybody at all can die in my place.[5]

Moreover, according to Sartre, Heidegger involves himself in a vicious circle in order to establish that death has the power of conferring individuality upon the human reality or *Dasein*.   It is only, says Sartre, because Heidegger had already insisted that the *Dasein* is always individual by ontological necessity that he can establish the claim that death is an individual phenomenon. By what right, then, can he assert that it is death which confers individuality upon the *Dasein*?   Has he not antecedently assumed the individuality of the *Dasein* in order to prove that death confers individuality?   "This incomparable individuality which he has conferred upon death in terms of the *Dasein*, he uses to individualize the *Dasein* itself. . . . But there is a circle here."[6]

As criticisms of Heidegger's statement "Death is the only thing nobody can do for me," Sartre's comments are unassailable.   It is clear, however, that this statement does not adequately characterize Heidegger's position.   No matter how badly Heidegger may have expressed himself, his intent was, not to assert that death as such individualizes, but rather that the consciousness of death individualizes.   And when Heidegger speaks of individuality in this connection it is not the individuality which belongs to all of us by virtue of ontological necessity but the individuality of the man who has through the consciousness of death wrenched himself away from everyday banality, escaped from the domain of *das Man* into the domain of self-consciousness and authenticity.

One must not conclude, however, that Sartre and Heidegger are separated on this point by a simple misunderstanding.   A more adequate understanding of Heidegger on Sartre's part would no doubt tend to diminish the distance between them, but it would also bring into clearer focus a very real issue on which they are genuinely divided.   For Heidegger the consciousness of death produces individuality directly by detaching

us from the banality of everyday life and by preparing us to
assume our *Sein-zum-Tode*. For Sartre, on the other hand,
the relationship between the consciousness of death and
individuality is more devious and indirect. According to
Sartre authentic moral choice or decision is the direct cause of
individuality; the consciousness of death heightens our individuality only in so far as it determines us to choose without
regard for inauthentic or conventional values. The syntax of
the following sentence, already quoted in another context, is
such as to accent Sartre's debt to Heidegger, but it none the
less illustrates the essential difference between the two authors:
"The choice that each of us made of his life was an authentic
choice because it was made face to face with death."

This crucial difference will emerge even more clearly at the
end of our analysis of Sartre's arguments against Heidegger's
second thesis, viz., that by running ahead of ourselves toward
death and willing our death we can restore a measure of totality
to our lives. Sartre will have none of this. For him death is
never a personal possibility, much less a personal possibility
which we can freely resolve to assume and which will give an
ultimate meaning to the series of acts which constitute our
individual lives. As Sartre sees it, death is merely an external
limit or a "wall" which we may encounter at any time in
pursuing our personal projects, but which we can never personally or freely project as an end to be pursued. More technically,
death is "an always possible nihilation of my possibles which is
outside my possibilities."[7]

The root of the difference turns on conflicting interpretations
of finitude, but it will be easier to grasp the import of these conflicting interpretations if Sartre's case against Heidegger's
doctrine of *Sein-zum-Tode* is first stated more or less informally.

Death may come to a man in any one of three ways. First,
there is the death of the suicide or martyr. Here, indeed, it
would seem that we are projecting ourselves toward death as an
ultimate possibility. Closer examination, however, reveals that
this is not so. What the hero or martyr is projecting as an
ultimate possibility is the cause for which he dies. It is the
triumph of Christianity or the triumph of Communism which is
willed. Death is only a means to an end. Similarly, the
woman who commits suicide because of disappointment in
love is not projecting her death; she is projecting revenge upon

her lover or merely liberation from her torment. There are also, of course, impulsive suicides, but by definition an impulsive suicide is one which has not been willed.

Second, there is the case in which death occurs at an appointed time: the death of a man who has been condemned by a tribunal, of a man who knows that he is dying of a fatal disease, or of a man who is reaching the natural term of his life. Can we in this case will our death and by so doing make of our lives meaningful totalities? Sartre's answer is "No." It is obvious, says Sartre, that "my death is not fixed by me; the sequences of the universe determine it."[8] How, then, can I claim to have willed it? Since death in these cases is determined by external circumstances, since it "does not appear on the foundation of our freedom," it cannot give meaning to our lives: "it can only remove all meaning from life."[9] If I know I shall die shortly, then the dimension of futurity is removed from my life and with it all possibility for the projection of possibles.

Sartre has illustrated this theme in the story *The Wall* and also in the play *The Victors*. In the latter work the heroine Lucy has been condemned to death for resistance activities. John, her ex-lover and fellow resistant, escapes her fate, but finds the means of visiting her in prison. This is a part of their dialogue:

> JOHN: Let me stay with you; I shall be silent, if you want, but I shall be here and you will not feel lonely.
> LUCY: Not lonely? With you? Oh, John, have you not understood yet? We no longer have anything in common.
> JOHN: Have you forgotten that I love you?
> LUCY: It was another woman that you loved. . . .
> JOHN: It is you.
> LUCY: I am another woman. I no longer recognize myself. . . . Well, you love me. And then? Our love is far behind us, why do you speak of it? It had really no importance.
> JOHN: You are lying! It was our life. . . .
> LUCY: Our life? Yes. Our future, I lived in expectation. I waited for the end of the war. I waited for the day when we could get married. . . . I waited for every evening. . . . Now, I no longer have a future, I expect nothing but my death, and I shall die alone.[10]

Finally, there is the case in which death comes suddenly and unpredictably. Sartre regards this type of death as most typical.

It has often been said that we are in the situation of a condemned man among other condemned men who is ignorant
of the date of his execution but who sees each day that his
fellow prisoners are being executed. This is not wholly exact.
We ought rather to compare ourselves to a man condemned
to death who is bravely preparing himself for the ultimate
penalty, who is doing everything possible to make a good showing on the scaffold, and who meanwhile is carried off by a
flu epidemic.[11]

Since it is Sartre's habit to think of death as fortuitous or
accidental, it is by examining his reflections on this type of
death that we come closest to the source of his disagreement
with Heidegger.

For Heidegger the whole series of our projects is suspended
from death. Death is the final term of our projects, and if we
could see ourselves from the standpoint of this final term the
meaning of each of our projects would become clear. If
Heidegger is right, says Sartre, by assuming our death

we should know once and for all whether a particular youthful experience had been fruitful or ill-starred, whether a particular crisis of puberty was a caprice or a real preformation
of my later engagements; the curve of our life would be fixed
forever. In short, the account would be closed. The
Reverend Father Boisselot in a private conversation with me
gave me to understand that the "Last Judgment" was precisely
this closing of the account which renders one unable any longer
to recover his stroke and which makes one finally be what one
has been—irremediably.[12]

But if, as both Heidegger and Sartre agree, man is always
free and if, as both men also agree, death is in the first instance
something which may strike us down from the outside at any
moment, then it will be impossible for us to view our lives from
the standpoint of the last term with sufficient fullness and concreteness to make of our lives a meaningful totality. Since we
are free, we may in the interval between now and our death
adopt projects the nature of which cannot now be foreseen
and which in any present effort to sum up our lives we will
necessarily fail to take into account. Moreover, even if we
now engaged ourselves not to undertake new projects, we could
still not take a point of view upon ourselves as a totality. The
reason is that the meaning even of our present projects depends
upon future developments. Suppose, says Sartre,

that Balzac had died before *Les Chouans*: he would remain the author of some execrable novels of intrigue. But suddenly the very expectation which this young man was, this expectation of being a great man, loses any kind of meaning; it is neither an obstinate and egotistical blindness nor the true sense of his own values since nothing will ever decide![13]

To put the whole matter in a different light. Suppose that it is possible for us now to review our lives from the standpoint of death and to close accounts. What then becomes of our freedom? Unless we ourselves choose the moment of death, our freedom is totally lost.

> There is an error here analogous to that which we pointed out earlier in connection with Leibniz although it is put at the other end of existence. For Leibniz we are free since our acts derive from our essence. Yet the single fact that our essence has not been chosen by us shows that all this freedom in particulars covers over a total slavery. God chose Adam's essence. Conversely, if it is the closing of the account which gives our life its meaning and its value, then it is of little importance that all the acts of which the web of our life is made have been free; the very meaning of them escapes us if we do not ourselves choose the moment at which the account will be closed.[14]

Sartre's illustration of this point is a story borrowed from Diderot:

> Two brothers appeared at the divine tribunal on the Day of Judgment. The first said to God, "Why did you make me die so young?" And God said, "In order to save you. If you had lived longer, you would have committed a crime as your brother did." Then the brother in turn asked, "Why did you make me die so old?"[15]

In sum, then, no matter what our situation with respect to death is, death is never one of our personal projects, and even less a personal project which might give meaning to our lives as totalities. If we choose death through suicide or martyrdom, death is merely an instrument which we use to realize our projects. It is not an ultimate possibility. If we are waiting for a death the moment of which has been determined from the outside, as in the case of the man condemned to death by a tribunal, death is not one of our projects in any sense, since we have not chosen it. And even if it had been chosen, it would not confer meaning on our lives; in fact, by depriving us of the dimension of the future it would deprive even our past and present of all meaning. If, finally, death comes upon us unawares, once again it is an external event rather than one of our projects, and since we do not know in advance when it will come we cannot run ahead of ourselves to assume it as a final term. "Death is never that which gives life its meaning; it is, on the contrary, that which on principle removes all meaning from life."[16]

Heidegger and Sartre Contrasted

Persuasive as all of Sartre's arguments are, they are not all equally pertinent or equally valid. He is at his best in pointing out that so long as we are unable to predict the moment of our death, so long as death comes upon us unawares, we cannot form a sufficiently full and concrete picture of our lives to give them meaning as totalities. He is less successful in dealing with the other two types of death. In fact, if it is true that the man who is waiting an imminent death at an appointed time no longer has a future and can no longer project plans, then there appears to be nothing which forbids him from taking a point of view with respect to his life as totality. His life is, so to speak, finished; there will be no free choices in the future which would have to be taken into account, and the meaning of his past projects will be wholly transparent. Face to face with death, he will know "whether a particular youthful experience had been fruitful or ill-starred, whether a particular crisis of puberty was a caprice or a real preformation of later engagements." Sartre has overlooked this only because he failed to distinguish between the meaning of an event for a passive spectator, i.e., its place as an element in a whole, and the meaning of an event for an actor, i.e., as a factor which has to be taken into account in order to realize a projected goal. Because face to face with death a man's past projects lack meaning for him in the second sense, they do not necessarily lack meaning for him in the first sense.

Moreover, Sartre is guilty of gross inconsistency when he argues that the knowledge of imminent death robs our life of future reference. Only the physical fact of death which puts an end to consciousness can do this. Of course, knowledge of imminent death will put an end to those projects whose realization depends upon a long life, such as Lucy's project of marriage to John. But it cannot put an end to the power of decision itself. Consciousness is in its essence that power or faculty, and so long as there is a breath of life in us we still possess it. Indeed, why did Sartre argue that voluntary death through suicide or martyrdom inevitably involves a project beyond death, if not because of his conviction that the human reality is in its essence and up to the very last minute a temporal *existence*, a projecting toward the future?

Finally, Sartre sometimes writes as if Heidegger were not aware that external circumstances determine in large measure both the nature and the moment of our death. In fact, however, it was an acute realization of this fact which inspired Heidegger to frame his own theory. The meaninglessness and absurdity of a death by accidental causes which strikes us down independently of our will was what he hoped to overcome. And in the first instance he hoped to overcome it not so much by denying its meaninglessness and absurdity as by willing death with its meaninglessness and absurdity. Heidegger's doctrine is quite clearly a variation on the Nietzschean theme of *amor fati*. Just as Nietzsche would have us affirm or say yes to a universe indifferent to human aspirations, so Heidegger would have us affirm or say yes to an absurd and meaningless death.

Much of the confusion here springs from the fact that neither Heidegger nor Sartre distinguished with sufficient clarity between the two aspects of the resolute decision to assume death. On the one hand, Heidegger designed his theory in order to mitigate the anguish of death. We project ourselves toward death by adopting an affirmative attitude toward it. This is the aspect of the doctrine which he owes to Nietzsche. On the other hand, Heidegger hoped that by assuming an affirmative attitude toward death one could overcome the rent in the *Dasein* caused by self-transcendence and make of one's life a totality. This aspect of the doctrine is original with him.

Now, when Sartre argues that face to face with death we can

form no projects at all because we have no future, he is striking at the first aspect of Heidegger's doctrine. And his argument is insufficient. He himself has repeatedly affirmed that no matter how adverse the circumstances of one's life may be, one can always project either revolt or acceptance. Sartre obviously prefers an attitude of revolt to an attitude of acceptance. But there is, according to his own principles, no ontological barrier to the adoption of either posture.

When, however, Sartre argues that in so far as death is accidental and unpredictable, our life cannot be for us a meaningful totality, he is striking at the second aspect of Heidegger's doctrine. And here he is on much firmer ground. The arguments summarized above fail to establish his point with respect to voluntary death through suicide or martyrdom and with respect to death in the near and foreseeable future. But they do have considerable weight in the other and most common instance: death the moment of which cannot be predicted.

Even here, however, Sartre's arguments are not altogether conclusive. It is undoubtedly true that the meaning of each project in that series of projects which constitutes our lives cannot be fully and finally established before death. So long as we are alive the meaning of each of our projects is more or less in suspense. We do not claim to know the full meaning of a particular battle until the war is over and we can see it in perspective. Similarly, we cannot claim to know the full meaning of our individual projects so long as life is in progress. But it does not follow from this that we cannot have some more or less adequate sense of our lives as a totality prior to death, any more than it follows that the actual participant in a war cannot have some more or less adequate picture of the war as a totality prior to its actual end. So long as we do not insist too much upon its concreteness or its accuracy, we can have a meaningful picture of our life as a totality prior to the moment of death. It is doubtful, however, that Heidegger would care to answer Sartre in this way. An unreliable and schematic picture of our life as a totality is too frail a thing to do the job which Heidegger wants done.

Curiously, the most persuasive argument against the second aspect of Heidegger's doctrine was never explicitly used by Sartre in this connection. Once again, according to Heidegger, the assumption of a point of view upon our life as a totality is

valuable as a means of overcoming the rent in our being produced by the perpetual act of self-transcendence.   But must not
the life-as-totality be an object for us as viewers in order that
this value may be realized?   And where in the totality could
we as viewers be placed?   In the story *The Wall* Sartre
makes this point most effectively.   A condemned man is
trying to contemplate his death.   "I tell myself: afterwards,
there will be nothing.   But I do not understand what this
means. . . . I see my corpse: that is not difficult, but it is *I* who
see it, with my *eyes*."[17]   Freud also made this point.   "It is
indeed impossible," he says, "to imagine our own death; and
whenever we attempt to do so we can perceive that we are in
fact still present as spectators."[18]   The rent in our being caused
by self-transcendence cannot be overcome in the manner suggested by Heidegger without denying that self-transcendence is
an ontological necessity.   The only possible object of human
regard is the in-itself; the complete human reality in its duality
as in-itself and for-itself can never be an object of regard.

This brings us to the very core of the difference between
Sartre and Heidegger.   For Sartre the most important feature
of the human reality is the fact of self-transcendence, the ontological necessity we are under to exist in and through choice.
All the anguish and tragedy of human existence can be traced
to this source.   And it is this feature of the human reality, this
feature alone, which constitutes our finitude.   For Heidegger,
on the other hand, death is the greatest source of anguish and
the prime symbol of human finitude.   He does not, of course,
deny self-transcendence.   Sartre's views on this subject were
drawn largely from him.   Neither does he ignore the anguish
involved in authentic decision making; nor does he deny anyone the right to regard this aspect of the *Dasein* as part of our
finitude.   None the less, death—not self-transcendence—holds
the centre of his interest.

Sartre writes:

> It will be well to separate radically the two usually combined
> ideas of death and finitude.   Ordinarily the belief seems to
> be that it is death which constitutes our finitude and which
> reveals it to us. . . . Heidegger in particular seems to have
> based his whole theory of *Sein-zum-Tode* on the strict identifica-
> tion of death and finitude.   In the same way Malraux, when he
> tells us that death reveals to us the uniqueness of life, seems

to hold that it is just because we die that we are powerless to recover our stroke and are therefore finite. But if we consider the matter a little more closely, we detect the error: death is a contingent fact which belongs to facticity; finitude is an ontological structure of the for-itself which determines freedom and exists only in and through the free project of the end which makes my being known to me. In other words human reality would remain finite even if it were immortal, because it makes itself finite by choosing itself as human. To be finite, in fact, is to choose oneself—that is, to make known to oneself what one is by projecting oneself toward one possible to the exclusion of others. The very act of freedom is therefore the assumption and creation of finitude. If I make myself, I make myself finite and hence my life is unique. Consequently even if I were immortal, it would be forbidden me to "recover my stroke"; it is the irreversibility of temporality which forbids me, and this irreversibility is nothing but the peculiar character of a freedom which temporalizes itself. . . . Death has nothing to do with this.[19]

The problem of distinguishing between so-called "ontological necessities" and universal though nonnecessary or contingent facts of human nature was discussed in an earlier chapter. For present purposes it is enough to point out that, whatever else may be involved, the elevation of a universal fact of human nature to the dignity of ontological necessity clearly reflects the cares and concerns of the philosopher. Sartre is more concerned about the problem of moral responsibility than about the problem of death; he is more afraid of making a choice which he will later regret than of no longer being present to the world. In Heidegger's case the reverse is probably true.

The remarkable fact is that Sartre's preoccupation with moral decision is at the root, not only of his disagreement with Heidegger's doctrine of *Sein-zum-Tode*, but also, as was seen earlier, of Heidegger's contention that the consciousness of death individualizes. For Heidegger, the "individual" in the honorific sense of that term is the man who has "the courage to allow the anguish of death to arise." For Sartre, the "individual" is the man who has the courage to make authentic decisions. The awareness of death has value only in so far as it obliges us or helps us to make authentic decisions.

Whereas, however, the awareness of death helps us, even if indirectly, to achieve authenticity, the attempt to view one's life as a totality is a barrier to authenticity. It necessarily involves a renunciation of the right to choose. It is, in fact, nothing

other than an impossible attempt to be for oneself the essence
or nature which one can only be for another.

> Death, in so far as it can be revealed to me, is not only the
> always possible nihilation of my possibles. . . . It is also the
> triumph of the point of view of the Other. . . . The unique
> characteristic of a dead life is that it is a life of which the
> Other makes himself the guardian. . . . To be dead is to be a
> prey for the living. This means therefore that the one who
> tries to grasp the meaning of his future death must discover
> himself as the future prey of others. We have here therefore
> a case of alienation.[20]

It remains at this point only to say a few words about
Heidegger's and Sartre's respective theories of salvation. Although Heidegger is trying to save us from the terror of death
and Sartre from the terror of perpetual division and self-
transcendence, the technique they recommend is essentially the
same. Sartre will have us will or freely assume perpetual self-
transcendence and division, whereas Heidegger will have us
will or freely assume death. Sartre says it is impossible for
us to escape the ambiguity of our being, but it is possible for us
to will that ambiguity. Heidegger says it is impossible for us to
escape death, but it is possible for us to will death. Neither
Heidegger nor Sartre is willing to blink the fact that man is
finite; but both hope somehow to conquer or master this
finitude by assuming it. Heidegger says that by contemplating
our death as our unique personal possibility we become a
totality—a finite totality, to be sure, but still a totality. Sartre
claims that by assuming our freedom we do finally coincide with
ourselves—but, of course, the self with which we coincide is
still the finite self.

Both theories are addressed to men who can no longer accept
traditional representations of the human situation and who have
lost faith in traditional answers to the perennial human problems. Both theories reveal a kind of honesty and courage on
the part of the authors which cannot but command respect.
The man whom contemporary life has reduced to despair will
appreciate their sublimity and will receive them as monuments
to the heroism of the human spirit. But may the hand of fate
spare us from a despair so deep that we cannot dispense with
them.

Notes

CHAPTER I

1. Karl Jaspers, *Man in the Modern Age*, rev. trans. Eden and Cedar Paul (London: Routledge & Kegan Paul, Ltd., 1951), pp. 70–71.
2. Fyodor Dostoyevsky, *Notes from Underground*, trans. Constance Garnett. Quoted from Dostoyevsky, *White Nights and Other Stories*, copyright 1925 by The Macmillan Company, London, pp. 65–69. Used by permission of the publishers.
3. Jean-Paul Sartre, *Being and Nothingness*, trans. Hazel E. Barnes (New York: Philosophical Library, 1956), p. 90.
4. Dostoyevsky, *op. cit.*, p. 76.
5. Miguel de Unamuno, *Tragic Sense of Life*, trans. J. E. Crawford Flitch (New York: Dover Publications, Inc., 1954), p. 43.
6. *Ibid.*, p. 207.
7. Nicholas Berdyaev, *Dialectique existentielle du divin et de l'humain* (Paris: J. B. Janin, 1947), pp. 96–97.
8. Albert Camus, *Caligula* (Paris: Gallimard, 1947), p. 209.
9. Jean-Paul Sartre, *Saint Genet* (Paris, Gallimard, 1952), pp. 151–52.

CHAPTER II

1. Quoted in Unamuno, *Tragic Sense of Life*, pp. 123–24.
2. *Ibid.*, p. 9.
3. Ludwig Wittgenstein, *Tractatus Logico-Philosophicus* (London: Routledge & Kegan Paul, Ltd., 1922), p. 187.
4. *Ibid.*, p. 187.
5. Jean-Paul Sartre, *La nausée* (Paris: Gallimard, 1938), p. 162.
6. Søren Kierkegaard, *Concluding Unscientific Postscript*, trans. David Swenson (Princeton: Princeton University Press, 1944), pp. 171–72.
7. Unamuno, *op. cit.*, p. 3.
8. Leo Tolstoy, "The Death of Ivan Ilych," trans. Aylmer Maude. Quoted from *Iván Ilých and Hadji Murád, and Other Stories* (London: Oxford University Press, 1957), pp. 44–45.
9. Sartre, *Being and Nothingness*, p. 453.

10. *Ibid.*, p. 435.
11. *Ibid.*, pp. 434–35.
12. *Ibid.*, p. 434.
13. *Ibid.*, p. 435.
14. *Ibid.*, pp. 435–36.
15. *Ibid.*, p. 437.
16. *Ibid.*, p. 485.
17. *Ibid.*, p. 38.
18. *Ibid.*, pp. 565–66.
19. *Ibid.*, p. 566.
20. *Ibid.*, p. 566.
21. *Ibid.*, p. 615.
22. *Ibid.*, p. 623.
23. *Ibid.*, p. 615.
24. *Ibid.*, p. 588.
25. *Ibid.*, p. 563.
26. *Ibid.*, p. 592.
27. Kierkegaard, *op. cit.*, p. 267.
28. Sartre, *Being and Nothingness*, p. 627.
29. Simone de Beauvoir, "Pour une morale de l'ambiguïté," *Les Temps Modernes* (November, 1946).

CHAPTER III

1. Søren Kierkegaard, *Journals*, trans. Alexander Dru (London: Oxford University Press, 1938), p. 41.
2. Jean-Paul Sartre, *Critique de la raison dialectique* (Paris: Gallimard, 1960), p. 22.
3. Alfred North Whitehead, *Science and the Modern World*, p. 27, copyright by The Macmillan Company, renewed 1953 by Evelyn Whiteside. Used by permission of The Macmillan Company.

CHAPTER IV

1. Sartre, *Being and Nothingness*, p. 87.
2. *Ibid.*, p. 495.
3. *Ibid.*, pp. 482–83.
4. *Ibid.*, p. 468.
5. Jean-Paul Sartre, *Situations III* (Paris: Gallimard, 1949), pp. 11–13.
6. Sartre, *Being and Nothingness*, pp. 450–51.
7. *Ibid.*, p. 52.
8. *Ibid.*, p. 52.
9. *Ibid.*, pp. 52-53.
10. *Ibid.*, pp. 573–74.
11. *Ibid.*, p. 574.

12. *Ibid.*, p. 441.
13. *Ibid.*, p. 447.
14. *Ibid.*, p. 557.
15. *Ibid.*, p. 444.
16. *Ibid.*, pp. 447–48.
17. *Ibid.*, p. 559.
18. *Ibid.*, p. 573.
19. *Ibid.*, p. 563.
20. *Ibid.*, p. 568.
21. *Ibid.*, p. 568.
22. *Ibid.*, p. 469.
23. *Ibid.*, p. 469.
24. *Ibid.*, pp. 461–62.
25. *Ibid.*, pp. 450–51.
26. *Ibid.*, pp. 471–75.
27. *Ibid.*, pp. 475–76.
28. Eliseo Vivas, *The Moral Life and the Ethical Life* (Chicago: University of Chicago Press, 1950), pp. 230–31. Copyright 1950 by the University of Chicago.
29. Sartre, *Being and Nothingness*, p. 464.
30. *Ibid.*, p. 553.
31. *Ibid.*, p. 464.
32. *Ibid.*, p. 403.
33. *Ibid.*, p. 470.
34. *Ibid.*, p. 470.
35. Sartre, *Critique de la raison dialectique*, p. 64.
36. Sartre, *Being and Nothingness*, p. 410.

CHAPTER V

1. Martin Heidegger, "The Way Back into the Ground of Metaphysics," trans. Walter Kaufmann. Published in Walter Kaufmann, ed., *Existentialism from Dostoyevsky to Sartre* (New York: Meridian Books, Inc., 1956), p. 215. Reprinted by permission of Meridian Books. Copyright © 1956 by Meridian Books.
2. *Ibid.*, p. 215.
3. Søren Kierkegaard, *The Sickness unto Death*, trans. Walter Lowrie (Princeton: Princeton University Press, 1951), p. 62.
4. *Ibid.*, pp. 54–55.
5. *Ibid.*, p. 55.
6. Sartre, *Being and Nothingness*, pp. 32–33.
7. *Ibid.*, p. 32.
8. *Ibid.*, pp. 63–65.
9. Jean-Paul Sartre, *The Reprieve*, trans. Eric Sutton (New York: Alfred A. Knopf, Inc., 1947), p. 135.

10. Sartre, *Being and Nothingness*, pp. 50–51.
11. *Ibid.*, pp. 51–52.
12. *Ibid.*, pp. 311–12.
13. John Dewey, *A Common Faith* (New Haven: Yale University Press, 1943), p. 51.

CHAPTER VI

1. D. H. Lawrence, *Studies in Classic American Literature* (New York: T. Seltzer, 1923), p. 155.
2. Georges Bernanos, *Présence de Bernanos* (Paris: Librairie Plon, 1947), pp. xviii–xxii.
3. Karl Jaspers, "On My Philosophy," trans. Felix Kaufmann. Published in Kaufmann, ed., *Existentialism from Dostoyevsky to Sartre*, p. 147.
4. William Faulkner, *Light in August* (New York: Modern Library, 1950), p. 407.
5. Sartre, *Being and Nothingness*, p. 251.
6. *Ibid.*, pp. 230–21.
7. *Ibid.*, p. 243.
8. *Ibid.*, p. 231.
9. *Ibid.*, pp. 259–60.
10. *Ibid.*, p. 261.
11. *Ibid.*, p. 527.
12. Sartre, *Saint Genet*, p. 55.
13. Sartre, *Being and Nothingness*, p. 302.
14. *Ibid.*, p. 263.
15. *Ibid.*, p. 410.
16. Sartre, *The Reprieve*, pp. 405–7.
17. Sartre, *Being and Nothingness*, p. 404.
18. *Ibid.*, p. 379.
19. *Ibid.*, p. 378.
20. *Ibid.*, pp. 367–69.
21. *Ibid.*, p. 377.
22. *Ibid.*, p. 409.
23. *Ibid.*, p. 429.
24. *Ibid.*, p. 427.
25. *Ibid.*, p. 423.

CHAPTER VII

1. Unamuno, *Tragic Sense of Life*, p. 114.
2. Sigmund Freud, "Thoughts for the Times on War and Death." Published in *Standard Edition of the Complete Psychological Works of Sigmund Freud*, Vol. XIV (London: Hogarth Press, Ltd., 1957), pp. 289–90.
3. Leo Tolstoy, " The Death of Ivan Ilych," pp. 32–33.

4. Sartre, *Being and Nothingness*, p. 533.

5. *Ibid.*, pp. 534–35.

6. *Ibid.*, p. 534.

7. *Ibid.*, p. 537.

8. *Ibid.*, p. 539.

9. *Ibid.*, p. 539.

10. Jean-Paul Sartre, *Morts sans sépultre* (Lausanne: Marguerat, 1946), pp. 147–48.

11. Sartre, *Being and Nothingness*, p. 533.

12. *Ibid.*, p. 538.

13. *Ibid.*, p. 539.

14. *Ibid.*, pp. 538.

15. *Ibid.*, p. 538.

16. *Ibid.*, p. 539.

17. Jean-Paul Sartre, *Le mur* (Paris: Gallimard, 1939), p. 22.

18. Freud, *op. cit.*, p. 289.

19. Sartre, *Being and Nothingness*, p. 546.

20. *Ibid.*, pp. 540–43.

Index

A CATALOG OF SELECTED

DOVER BOOKS

IN ALL FIELDS OF INTEREST

DOVER BOOKS

IN ALL FIELDS OF INTEREST

DRAWINGS OF REMBRANDT, edited by Seymour Slive. Updated Lippmann, Hofstede de Groot edition, with definitive scholarly apparatus. All portraits, biblical sketches, landscapes, nudes. Oriental figures, classical studies, together with selection of work by followers. 550 illustrations. Total of 630pp. 9⅛ × 12¼.
21485-0, 21486-9 Pa., Two-vol. set $29.90

GHOST AND HORROR STORIES OF AMBROSE BIERCE, Ambrose Bierce. 24 tales vividly imagined, strangely prophetic, and decades ahead of their time in technical skill: "The Damned Thing," "An Inhabitant of Carcosa," "The Eyes of the Panther," "Moxon's Master," and 20 more. 199pp. 5⅜ × 8½. 20767-6 Pa. $4.95

ETHICAL WRITINGS OF MAIMONIDES, Maimonides. Most significant ethical works of great medieval sage, newly translated for utmost precision, readability. Laws Concerning Character Traits, Eight Chapters, more. 192pp. 5⅜ × 8½.
24522-5 Pa. $5.95

THE EXPLORATION OF THE COLORADO RIVER AND ITS CANYONS, J. W. Powell. Full text of Powell's 1,000-mile expedition down the fabled Colorado in 1869. Superb account of terrain, geology, vegetation, Indians, famine, mutiny, treacherous rapids, mighty canyons, during exploration of last unknown part of continental U.S. 400pp. 5⅜ × 8½. 20094-9 Pa. $8.95

HISTORY OF PHILOSOPHY, Julián Marías. Clearest one-volume history on the market. Every major philosopher and dozens of others, to Existentialism and later. 505pp. 5⅜ × 8½. 21739-6 Pa. $9.95

ALL ABOUT LIGHTNING, Martin A. Uman. Highly readable nontechnical survey of nature and causes of lightning, thunderstorms, ball lightning, St. Elmo's Fire, much more. Illustrated. 192pp. 5⅜ × 8½. 25237-X Pa. $5.95

SAILING ALONE AROUND THE WORLD, Captain Joshua Slocum. First man to sail around the world, alone, in small boat. One of great feats of seamanship told in delightful manner. 67 illustrations. 294pp. 5⅜ × 8½. 20326-3 Pa. $4.95

LETTERS AND NOTES ON THE MANNERS, CUSTOMS AND CONDITIONS OF THE NORTH AMERICAN INDIANS, George Catlin. Classic account of life among Plains Indians: ceremonies, hunt, warfare, etc. 312 plates. 572pp. of text. 6⅛ × 9¼. 22118-0, 22119-9, Pa., Two-vol. set $17.90

THE SECRET LIFE OF SALVADOR DALÍ, Salvador Dalí. Outrageous but fascinating autobiography through Dalí's thirties with scores of drawings and sketches and 80 photographs. A must for lovers of 20th-century art. 432pp. 6½ × 9¼. (Available in U.S. only) 27454-3 Pa. $9.95

THE BOOK OF BEASTS: Being a Translation from a Latin Bestiary of the Twelfth Century, T. H. White. Wonderful catalog of real and fanciful beasts: manticore, griffin, phoenix, amphivius, jaculus, many more. White's witty erudite commentary on scientific, historical aspects enhances fascinating glimpse of medieval mind. Illustrated. 296pp. 5⅜ × 8¼. (Available in U.S. only)   24609-4 Pa. $7.95

FRANK LLOYD WRIGHT: Architecture and Nature with 160 Illustrations, Donald Hoffmann. Profusely illustrated study of influence of nature—especially prairie—on Wright's designs for Fallingwater, Robie House, Guggenheim Museum, other masterpieces. 96pp. 9¼ × 10¾.   25098-9 Pa. $8.95

LIMBERT ARTS AND CRAFTS FURNITURE: The Complete 1903 Catalog, Charles P. Limbert and Company. Rare catalog depicting 188 pieces of Mission-style furniture: fold-down tables and desks, bookcases, library and octagonal tables, chairs, more. Descriptive captions. 80pp. 9⅜ × 12¼.   27120-X Pa. $6.95

YEARS WITH FRANK LLOYD WRIGHT: Apprentice to Genius, Edgar Tafel. Insightful memoir by a former apprentice presents a revealing portrait of Wright the man, the inspired teacher, the greatest American architect. 372 black-and-white illustrations. Preface. Index. vi + 228pp. 8¼ × 11.   24801-1 Pa. $10.95

THE STORY OF KING ARTHUR AND HIS KNIGHTS, Howard Pyle. Enchanting version of King Arthur fable has delighted generations with imaginative narratives of exciting adventures and unforgettable illustrations by the author. 41 illustrations. xviii + 313pp. 6⅛ × 9¼.   21445-1 Pa. $6.95

THE GODS OF THE EGYPTIANS, E. A. Wallis Budge. Thorough coverage of numerous gods of ancient Egypt by foremost Egyptologist. Information on evolution of cults, rites and gods; the cult of Osiris; the Book of the Dead and its rites; the sacred animals and birds; Heaven and Hell; and more. 956pp. 6⅛ × 9¼.   22055-9, 22056-7 Pa., Two-vol. set $22.90

A THEOLOGICO-POLITICAL TREATISE, Benedict Spinoza. Also contains unfinished *Political Treatise*. Great classic on religious liberty, theory of government on common consent. R. Elwes translation. Total of 421pp. 5⅜ × 8½.   20249-6 Pa. $7.95

INCIDENTS OF TRAVEL IN CENTRAL AMERICA, CHIAPAS, AND YUCATAN, John L. Stephens. Almost single-handed discovery of Maya culture; exploration of ruined cities, monuments, temples; customs of Indians. 115 drawings. 892pp. 5⅜ × 8½.   22404-X, 22405-8 Pa., Two-vol. set $17.90

LOS CAPRICHOS, Francisco Goya. 80 plates of wild, grotesque monsters and caricatures. Prado manuscript included. 183pp. 6⅜ × 9⅜.   22384-1 Pa. $6.95

AUTOBIOGRAPHY: The Story of My Experiments with Truth, Mohandas K. Gandhi. Not hagiography, but Gandhi in his own words. Boyhood, legal studies, purification, the growth of the Satyagraha (nonviolent protest) movement. Critical, inspiring work of the man who freed India. 480pp. 5⅜ × 8½. (Available in U.S. only)   24593-4 Pa. $6.95

ILLUSTRATED DICTIONARY OF HISTORIC ARCHITECTURE, edited by Cyril M. Harris. Extraordinary compendium of clear, concise definitions for over 5,000 important architectural terms complemented by over 2,000 line drawings. Covers full spectrum of architecture from ancient ruins to 20th-century Modernism. Preface. 592pp. 7½ × 9⅝. 24444-X Pa. $15.95

THE NIGHT BEFORE CHRISTMAS, Clement C. Moore. Full text, and woodcuts from original 1848 book. Also critical, historical material. 19 illustrations. 40pp. 4⅝ × 6. 22797-9 Pa. $2.50

THE LESSON OF JAPANESE ARCHITECTURE: 165 Photographs, Jiro Harada. Memorable gallery of 165 photographs taken in the 1930s of exquisite Japanese homes of the well-to-do and historic buildings. 13 line diagrams. 192pp. 8⅜ × 11¼. 24778-3 Pa. $10.95

THE AUTOBIOGRAPHY OF CHARLES DARWIN AND SELECTED LETTERS, edited by Francis Darwin. The fascinating life of eccentric genius composed of an intimate memoir by Darwin (intended for his children); commentary by his son, Francis; hundreds of fragments from notebooks, journals, papers; and letters to and from Lyell, Hooker, Huxley, Wallace and Henslow. xi + 365pp. 5⅜ × 8. 20479-0 Pa. $6.95

WONDERS OF THE SKY: Observing Rainbows, Comets, Eclipses, the Stars and Other Phenomena, Fred Schaaf. Charming, easy-to-read poetic guide to all manner of celestial events visible to the naked eye. Mock suns, glories, Belt of Venus, more. Illustrated. 299pp. 5¼ × 8¼. 24402-4 Pa. $8.95

BURNHAM'S CELESTIAL HANDBOOK, Robert Burnham, Jr. Thorough guide to the stars beyond our solar system. Exhaustive treatment. Alphabetical by constellation: Andromeda to Cetus in Vol. 1; Chamaeleon to Orion in Vol. 2; and Pavo to Vulpecula in Vol. 3. Hundreds of illustrations. Index in Vol. 3. 2,000pp. 6⅛ × 9¼. 23567-X, 23568-8, 23673-0 Pa., Three-vol. set $41.85

STAR NAMES: Their Lore and Meaning, Richard Hinckley Allen. Fascinating history of names various cultures have given to constellations and literary and folkloristic uses that have been made of stars. Indexes to subjects. Arabic and Greek names. Biblical references. Bibliography. 563pp. 5⅜ × 8½. 21079-0 Pa. $9.95

THIRTY YEARS THAT SHOOK PHYSICS: The Story of Quantum Theory, George Gamow. Lucid, accessible introduction to influential theory of energy and matter. Careful explanations of Dirac's anti-particles, Bohr's model of the atom, much more. 12 plates. Numerous drawings. 240pp. 5⅜ × 8½. 24895-X Pa. $6.95

CHINESE DOMESTIC FURNITURE IN PHOTOGRAPHS AND MEASURED DRAWINGS, Gustav Ecke. A rare volume, now affordably priced for antique collectors, furniture buffs and art historians. Detailed review of styles ranging from early Shang to late Ming. Unabridged republication. 161 black-and-white drawings, photos. Total of 224pp. 8⅜ × 11¼. (Available in U.S. only) 25171-3 Pa. $14.95

VINCENT VAN GOGH: A Biography, Julius Meier-Graefe. Dynamic, penetrating study of artist's life, relationship with brother, Theo, painting techniques, travels, more. Readable, engrossing. 160pp. 5⅜ × 8½. (Available in U.S. only) 25253-1 Pa. $4.95

HOW TO WRITE, Gertrude Stein. Gertrude Stein claimed anyone could understand her unconventional writing—here are clues to help. Fascinating improvisations, language experiments, explanations illuminate Stein's craft and the art of writing. Total of 414pp. 4⅜ × 6⅜. 23144-5 Pa. $6.95

ADVENTURES AT SEA IN THE GREAT AGE OF SAIL: Five Firsthand Narratives, edited by Elliot Snow. Rare true accounts of exploration, whaling, shipwreck, fierce natives, trade, shipboard life, more. 33 illustrations. Introduction. 353pp. 5⅜ × 8½. 25177-2 Pa. $9.95

THE HERBAL OR GENERAL HISTORY OF PLANTS, John Gerard. Classic descriptions of about 2,850 plants—with over 2,700 illustrations—includes Latin and English names, physical descriptions, varieties, time and place of growth, more. 2,706 illustrations. xlv + 1,678pp. 8½ × 12¼. 23147-X Cloth. $89.95

DOROTHY AND THE WIZARD IN OZ, L. Frank Baum. Dorothy and the Wizard visit the center of the Earth, where people are vegetables, glass houses grow and Oz characters reappear. Classic sequel to *Wizard of Oz*. 256pp. 5⅜ × 8. 24714-7 Pa. $5.95

SONGS OF EXPERIENCE: Facsimile Reproduction with 26 Plates in Full Color, William Blake. This facsimile of Blake's original "Illuminated Book" reproduces 26 full-color plates from a rare 1826 edition. Includes "The Tyger," "London," "Holy Thursday," and other immortal poems. 26 color plates. Printed text of poems. 48pp. 5¼ × 7. 24636-1 Pa. $3.95

SONGS OF INNOCENCE, William Blake. The first and most popular of Blake's famous "Illuminated Books," in a facsimile edition reproducing all 31 brightly colored plates. Additional printed text of each poem. 64pp. 5¼ × 7. 22764-2 Pa. $3.95

PRECIOUS STONES, Max Bauer. Classic, thorough study of diamonds, rubies, emeralds, garnets, etc.: physical character, occurrence, properties, use, similar topics. 20 plates, 8 in color. 94 figures. 659pp. 6⅛ × 9¼. 21910-0, 21911-9 Pa., Two-vol. set $21.90

ENCYCLOPEDIA OF VICTORIAN NEEDLEWORK, S. F. A. Caulfeild and Blanche Saward. Full, precise descriptions of stitches, techniques for dozens of needlecrafts—most exhaustive reference of its kind. Over 800 figures. Total of 679pp. 8⅛ × 11. 22800-2, 22801-0 Pa., Two-vol. set $26.90

THE MARVELOUS LAND OF OZ, L. Frank Baum. Second Oz book, the Scarecrow and Tin Woodman are back with hero named Tip, Oz magic. 136 illustrations. 287pp. 5⅜ × 8½. 20692-0 Pa. $5.95

WILD FOWL DECOYS, Joel Barber. Basic book on the subject, by foremost authority and collector. Reveals history of decoy making and rigging, place in American culture, different kinds of decoys, how to make them, and how to use them. 140 plates. 156pp. 7⅞ × 10¾. 20011-6 Pa. $14.95

HISTORY OF LACE, Mrs. Bury Palliser. Definitive, profusely illustrated chronicle of lace from earliest times to late 19th century. Laces of Italy, Greece, England, France, Belgium, etc. Landmark of needlework scholarship. 266 illustrations. 672pp. 6⅛ × 9¼. 24742-2 Pa. $16.95

ILLUSTRATED GUIDE TO SHAKER FURNITURE, Robert Meader. All furniture and appurtenances, with much on unknown local styles. 235 photos. 146pp. 9 × 12. 22819-3 Pa. $9.95

WHALE SHIPS AND WHALING: A Pictorial Survey, George Francis Dow. Over 200 vintage engravings, drawings, photographs of barks, brigs, cutters, other vessels. Also harpoons, lances, whaling guns, many other artifacts. Comprehensive text by foremost authority. 207 black-and-white illustrations. 288pp. 6 × 9. 24808-9 Pa. $9.95

THE BERTRAMS, Anthony Trollope. Powerful portrayal of blind self-will and thwarted ambition includes one of Trollope's most heartrending love stories. 497pp. 5⅜ × 8½. 25119-5 Pa. $9.95

ADVENTURES WITH A HAND LENS, Richard Headstrom. Clearly written guide to observing and studying flowers and grasses, fish scales, moth and insect wings, egg cases, buds, feathers, seeds, leaf scars, moss, molds, ferns, common crystals, etc.—all with an ordinary, inexpensive magnifying glass. 209 exact line drawings aid in your discoveries. 220pp. 5⅜ × 8½. 23330-8 Pa. $5.95

RODIN ON ART AND ARTISTS, Auguste Rodin. Great sculptor's candid, wide-ranging comments on meaning of art; great artists; relation of sculpture to poetry, painting, music; philosophy of life, more. 76 superb black-and-white illustrations of Rodin's sculpture, drawings and prints. 119pp. 8⅜ × 11¼. 24487-3 Pa. $7.95

FIFTY CLASSIC FRENCH FILMS, 1912–1982: A Pictorial Record, Anthony Slide. Memorable stills from Grand Illusion, Beauty and the Beast, Hiroshima, Mon Amour, many more. Credits, plot synopses, reviews, etc. 160pp. 8¼ × 11. 25256-6 Pa. $11.95

THE PRINCIPLES OF PSYCHOLOGY, William James. Famous long course complete, unabridged. Stream of thought, time perception, memory, experimental methods; great work decades ahead of its time. 94 figures. 1,391pp. 5⅜ × 8½. 20381-6, 20382-4 Pa., Two-vol. set $25.90

BODIES IN A BOOKSHOP, R. T. Campbell. Challenging mystery of blackmail and murder with ingenious plot and superbly drawn characters. In the best tradition of British suspense fiction. 192pp. 5⅜ × 8½. 24720-1 Pa. $5.95

CALLAS: Portrait of a Prima Donna, George Jellinek. Renowned commentator on the musical scene chronicles incredible career and life of the most controversial, fascinating, influential operatic personality of our time. 64 black-and-white photographs. 416pp. 5⅜ × 8¼. 25047-4 Pa. $8.95

GEOMETRY, RELATIVITY AND THE FOURTH DIMENSION, Rudolph Rucker. Exposition of fourth dimension, concepts of relativity as Flatland characters continue adventures. Popular, easily followed yet accurate, profound. 141 illustrations. 133pp. 5⅜ × 8½. 23400-2 Pa. $4.95

HOUSEHOLD STORIES BY THE BROTHERS GRIMM, with pictures by Walter Crane. 53 classic stories—Rumpelstiltskin, Rapunzel, Hansel and Gretel, the Fisherman and his Wife, Snow White, Tom Thumb, Sleeping Beauty, Cinderella, and so much more—lavishly illustrated with original 19th-century drawings. 114 illustrations. x + 269pp. 5⅜ × 8½. 21080-4 Pa. $4.95

SUNDIALS, Albert Waugh. Far and away the best, most thorough coverage of ideas, mathematics concerned, types, construction, adjusting anywhere. Over 100 illustrations. 230pp. 5⅜ × 8½. 22947-5 Pa. $5.95

PICTURE HISTORY OF THE NORMANDIE: With 190 Illustrations, Frank O. Braynard. Full story of legendary French ocean liner: Art Deco interiors, design innovations, furnishings, celebrities, maiden voyage, tragic fire, much more. Extensive text. 144pp. 8⅞ × 11¾. 25257-4 Pa. $11.95

THE FIRST AMERICAN COOKBOOK: A Facsimile of "American Cookery," 1796, Amelia Simmons. Facsimile of the first American-written cookbook published in the United States contains authentic recipes for colonial favorites—pumpkin pudding, winter squash pudding, spruce beer, Indian slapjacks, and more. Introductory Essay and Glossary of colonial cooking terms. 80pp. 5⅜ × 8½. 24710-4 Pa. $3.50

101 PUZZLES IN THOUGHT AND LOGIC, C. R. Wylie, Jr. Solve murders and robberies, find out which fishermen are liars, how a blind man could possibly identify a color—purely by your own reasoning! 107pp. 5⅜ × 8½. 20367-0 Pa. $2.95

ANCIENT EGYPTIAN MYTHS AND LEGENDS, Lewis Spence. Examines animism, totemism, fetishism, creation myths, deities, alchemy, art and magic, other topics. Over 50 illustrations. 432pp. 5⅜ × 8½. 26525-0 Pa. $8.95

ANTHROPOLOGY AND MODERN LIFE, Franz Boas. Great anthropologist's classic treatise on race and culture. Introduction by Ruth Bunzel. Only inexpensive paperback edition. 255pp. 5⅜ × 8½. 25245-0 Pa. $7.95

THE TALE OF PETER RABBIT, Beatrix Potter. The inimitable Peter's terrifying adventure in Mr. McGregor's garden, with all 27 wonderful, full-color Potter illustrations. 55pp. 4¼ × 5½. 22827-4 Pa. $1.75

THREE PROPHETIC SCIENCE FICTION NOVELS, H. G. Wells. *When the Sleeper Wakes, A Story of the Days to Come* and *The Time Machine* (full version). 335pp. 5⅜ × 8½. (Available in U.S. only) 20605-X Pa. $8.95

APICIUS COOKERY AND DINING IN IMPERIAL ROME, edited and translated by Joseph Dommers Vehling. Oldest known cookbook in existence offers readers a clear picture of what foods Romans ate, how they prepared them, etc. 49 illustrations. 301pp. 6⅛ × 9¼. 23563-7 Pa. $8.95

SHAKESPEARE LEXICON AND QUOTATION DICTIONARY, Alexander Schmidt. Full definitions, locations, shades of meaning of every word in plays and poems. More than 50,000 exact quotations. 1,485pp. 6½ × 9¼.
22726-X, 22727-8 Pa., Two-vol. set $31.90

THE WORLD'S GREAT SPEECHES, edited by Lewis Copeland and Lawrence W. Lamm. Vast collection of 278 speeches from Greeks to 1970. Powerful and effective models; unique look at history. 842pp. 5⅜ × 8½. 20468-5 Pa. $12.95

CATALOG OF DOVER BOOKS

THE BLUE FAIRY BOOK, Andrew Lang. The first, most famous collection, with many familiar tales: Little Red Riding Hood, Aladdin and the Wonderful Lamp, Puss in Boots, Sleeping Beauty, Hansel and Gretel, Rumpelstiltskin; 37 in all. 138 illustrations. 390pp. 5⅜ × 8½. 21437-0 Pa. $6.95

THE STORY OF THE CHAMPIONS OF THE ROUND TABLE, Howard Pyle. Sir Launcelot, Sir Tristram and Sir Percival in spirited adventures of love and triumph retold in Pyle's inimitable style. 50 drawings, 31 full-page. xviii + 329pp. 6½ × 9¼. 21883-X Pa. $7.95

THE MYTHS OF THE NORTH AMERICAN INDIANS, Lewis Spence. Myths and legends of the Algonquins, Iroquois, Pawnees and Sioux with comprehensive historical and ethnological commentary. 36 illustrations. 5⅜ × 8½. 25967-6 Pa. $8.95

GREAT DINOSAUR HUNTERS AND THEIR DISCOVERIES, Edwin H. Colbert. Fascinating, lavishly illustrated chronicle of dinosaur research, 1820s to 1960. Achievements of Cope, Marsh, Brown, Buckland, Mantell, Huxley, many others. 384pp. 5¼ × 8¼. 24701-5 Pa. $8.95

THE TASTEMAKERS, Russell Lynes. Informal, illustrated social history of American taste 1850s–1950s. First popularized categories Highbrow, Lowbrow, Middlebrow. 129 illustrations. New (1979) afterword. 384pp. 6 × 9. 23993-4 Pa. $8.95

NORTH AMERICAN INDIAN LIFE: Customs and Traditions of 23 Tribes, Elsie Clews Parsons (ed.). 27 fictionalized essays by noted anthropologists examine religion, customs, government, additional facets of life among the Winnebago, Crow, Zuni, Eskimo, other tribes. 480pp. 6⅛ × 9¼. 27377-6 Pa. $10.95

AUTHENTIC VICTORIAN DECORATION AND ORNAMENTATION IN FULL COLOR: 46 Plates from "Studies in Design," Christopher Dresser. Superb full-color lithographs reproduced from rare original portfolio of a major Victorian designer. 48pp. 9¼ × 12¼. 25083-0 Pa. $7.95

PRIMITIVE ART, Franz Boas. Remains the best text ever prepared on subject, thoroughly discussing Indian, African, Asian, Australian, and, especially, Northern American primitive art. Over 950 illustrations show ceramics, masks, totem poles, weapons, textiles, paintings, much more. 376pp. 5⅜ × 8. 20025-6 Pa. $8.95

SIDELIGHTS ON RELATIVITY, Albert Einstein. Unabridged republication of two lectures delivered by the great physicist in 1920–21. *Ether and Relativity* and *Geometry and Experience*. Elegant ideas in nonmathematical form, accessible to intelligent layman. vi + 56pp. 5⅜ × 8½. 24511-X Pa. $3.95

THE WIT AND HUMOR OF OSCAR WILDE, edited by Alvin Redman. More than 1,000 ripostes, paradoxes, wisecracks: Work is the curse of the drinking classes, I can resist everything except temptation, etc. 258pp. 5⅜ × 8½. 20602-5 Pa. $4.95

ADVENTURES WITH A MICROSCOPE, Richard Headstrom. 59 adventures with clothing fibers, protozoa, ferns and lichens, roots and leaves, much more. 142 illustrations. 232pp. 5⅜ × 8½. 23471-1 Pa. $4.95

PLANTS OF THE BIBLE, Harold N. Moldenke and Alma L. Moldenke. Standard reference to all 230 plants mentioned in Scriptures. Latin name, biblical reference, uses, modern identity, much more. Unsurpassed encyclopedic resource for scholars, botanists, nature lovers, students of Bible. Bibliography. Indexes. 123 black-and-white illustrations. 384pp. 6 × 9. 25069-5 Pa. $9.95

FAMOUS AMERICAN WOMEN: A Biographical Dictionary from Colonial Times to the Present, Robert McHenry, ed. From Pocahontas to Rosa Parks, 1,035 distinguished American women documented in separate biographical entries. Accurate, up-to-date data, numerous categories, spans 400 years. Indices. 493pp. 6½ × 9¼. 24523-3 Pa. $11.95

THE FABULOUS INTERIORS OF THE GREAT OCEAN LINERS IN HISTORIC PHOTOGRAPHS, William H. Miller, Jr. Some 200 superb photographs capture exquisite interiors of world's great "floating palaces"—1890s to 1980s: *Titanic, Ile de France, Queen Elizabeth, United States, Europa,* more. Approx. 200 black-and-white photographs. Captions. Text. Introduction. 160pp. 8⅞ × 11¾. 24756-2 Pa. $10.95

THE GREAT LUXURY LINERS, 1927–1954: A Photographic Record, William H. Miller, Jr. Nostalgic tribute to heyday of ocean liners. 186 photos of *Ile de France, Normandie, Leviathan, Queen Elizabeth, United States,* many others. Interior and exterior views. Introduction. Captions. 160pp. 9 × 12. 24056-8 Pa. $12.95

A NATURAL HISTORY OF THE DUCKS, John Charles Phillips. Great landmark of ornithology offers complete detailed coverage of nearly 200 species and subspecies of ducks: gadwall, sheldrake, merganser, pintail, many more. 74 full-color plates, 102 black-and-white. Bibliography. Total of 1,920pp. 8⅜ × 11¼. 25141-1, 25142-X Cloth., Two-vol. set $100.00

THE COMPLETE "MASTERS OF THE POSTER": All 256 Color Plates from "Les Maîtres de l'Affiche", Stanley Appelbaum (ed.). The most famous compilation ever made of the art of the great age of the poster, featuring works by Chéret, Steinlen, Toulouse-Lautrec, nearly 100 other artists. One poster per page. 272pp. 9¼ × 12¼. 26309-6 Pa. $29.95

THE TEN BOOKS OF ARCHITECTURE: The 1755 Leoni Edition, Leon Battista Alberti. Rare classic helped introduce the glories of ancient architecture to the Renaissance. 68 black-and-white plates. 336pp. 8⅜ × 11¼. 25239-6 Pa. $14.95

MISS MACKENZIE, Anthony Trollope. Minor masterpieces by Victorian master unmasks many truths about life in 19th-century England. First inexpensive edition in years. 392pp. 5⅜ × 8½. 25201-9 Pa. $8.95

THE RIME OF THE ANCIENT MARINER, Gustave Doré, Samuel Taylor Coleridge. Dramatic engravings considered by many to be his greatest work. The terrifying space of the open sea, the storms and whirlpools of an unknown ocean, the ice of Antarctica, more—all rendered in a powerful, chilling manner. Full text. 38 plates. 77pp. 9¼ × 12. 22305-1 Pa. $4.95

THE EXPEDITIONS OF ZEBULON MONTGOMERY PIKE, Zebulon Montgomery Pike. Fascinating firsthand accounts (1805–6) of exploration of Mississippi River, Indian wars, capture by Spanish dragoons, much more. 1,088pp. 5⅜ × 8½. 25254-X, 25255-8 Pa., Two-vol. set $25.90

A CONCISE HISTORY OF PHOTOGRAPHY: Third Revised Edition, Helmut Gernsheim. Best one-volume history—camera obscura, photochemistry, daguerreotypes, evolution of cameras, film, more. Also artistic aspects—landscape, portraits, fine art, etc. 281 black-and-white photographs. 26 in color. 176pp. 8⅜×11¼.
25128-4 Pa. $14.95

THE DORÉ BIBLE ILLUSTRATIONS, Gustave Doré. 241 detailed plates from the Bible: the Creation scenes, Adam and Eve, Flood, Babylon, battle sequences, life of Jesus, etc. Each plate is accompanied by the verses from the King James version of the Bible. 241pp. 9 × 12. 23004-X Pa. $9.95

WANDERINGS IN WEST AFRICA, Richard F. Burton. Great Victorian scholar/ adventurer's invaluable descriptions of African tribal rituals, fetishism, culture, art, much more. Fascinating 19th-century account. 624pp. 5⅜ × 8½. 26890-X Pa. $12.95

HISTORIC HOMES OF THE AMERICAN PRESIDENTS, Second Revised Edition, Irvin Haas. Guide to homes occupied by every president from Washington to Bush. Visiting hours, travel routes, more. 175 photos. 160pp. 8¼ × 11.
26751-2 Pa. $9.95

THE HISTORY OF THE LEWIS AND CLARK EXPEDITION, Meriwether Lewis and William Clark, edited by Elliott Coues. Classic edition of Lewis and Clark's day-by-day journals that later became the basis for U.S. claims to Oregon and the West. Accurate and invaluable geographical, botanical, biological, meteorological and anthropological material. Total of 1,508pp. 5⅜ × 8½.
21268-8, 21269-6, 21270-X Pa., Three-vol. set $29.85

LANGUAGE, TRUTH AND LOGIC, Alfred J. Ayer. Famous, clear introduction to Vienna, Cambridge schools of Logical Positivism. Role of philosophy, elimination of metaphysics, nature of analysis, etc. 160pp. 5⅜ × 8½. (Available in U.S. and Canada only) 20010-8 Pa. $3.95

MATHEMATICS FOR THE NONMATHEMATICIAN, Morris Kline. Detailed, college-level treatment of mathematics in cultural and historical context, with numerous exercises. For liberal arts students. Preface. Recommended Reading Lists. Tables. Index. Numerous black-and-white figures. xvi + 641pp. 5⅜ × 8½.
24823-2 Pa. $11.95

HANDBOOK OF PICTORIAL SYMBOLS, Rudolph Modley. 3,250 signs and symbols, many systems in full; official or heavy commercial use. Arranged by subject. Most in Pictorial Archive series. 143pp. 8⅜ × 11. 23357-X Pa. $8.95

INCIDENTS OF TRAVEL IN YUCATAN, John L. Stephens. Classic (1843) exploration of jungles of Yucatan, looking for evidences of Maya civilization. Travel adventures, Mexican and Indian culture, etc. Total of 669pp. 5⅜ × 8½.
20926-1, 20927-X Pa., Two-vol. set $13.90

DEGAS: An Intimate Portrait, Ambroise Vollard. Charming, anecdotal memoir by famous art dealer of one of the greatest 19th-century French painters. 14 black-and-white illustrations. Introduction by Harold L. Van Doren. 96pp. 5⅜ × 8½.
25131-4 Pa. $4.95

PERSONAL NARRATIVE OF A PILGRIMAGE TO AL-MADINAH AND MECCAH, Richard F. Burton. Great travel classic by remarkably colorful personality. Burton, disguised as a Moroccan, visited sacred shrines of Islam, narrowly escaping death. 47 illustrations. 959pp. 5⅜ × 8½.
21217-3, 21218-1 Pa., Two-vol. set $19.90

PHRASE AND WORD ORIGINS, A. H. Holt. Entertaining, reliable, modern study of more than 1,200 colorful words, phrases, origins and histories. Much unexpected information. 254pp. 5⅜ × 8½.
20758-7 Pa. $5.95

THE RED THUMB MARK, R. Austin Freeman. In this first Dr. Thorndyke case, the great scientific detective draws fascinating conclusions from the nature of a single fingerprint. Exciting story, authentic science. 320pp. 5⅜ × 8½. (Available in U.S. only)
25210-8 Pa. $6.95

AN EGYPTIAN HIEROGLYPHIC DICTIONARY, E. A. Wallis Budge. Monumental work containing about 25,000 words or terms that occur in texts ranging from 3000 B.C. to 600 A.D. Each entry consists of a transliteration of the word, the word in hieroglyphs, and the meaning in English. 1,314pp. 6⅜ × 10.
23615-3, 23616-1 Pa., Two-vol. set $35.90

THE COMPLEAT STRATEGYST: Being a Primer on the Theory of Games of Strategy, J. D. Williams. Highly entertaining classic describes, with many illustrated examples, how to select best strategies in conflict situations. Prefaces. Appendices. xvi + 268pp. 5⅜ × 8½.
25101-2 Pa. $7.95

THE ROAD TO OZ, L. Frank Baum. Dorothy meets the Shaggy Man, little Button-Bright and the Rainbow's beautiful daughter in this delightful trip to the magical Land of Oz. 272pp. 5⅜ × 8.
25208-6 Pa. $5.95

POINT AND LINE TO PLANE, Wassily Kandinsky. Seminal exposition of role of point, line, other elements in nonobjective painting. Essential to understanding 20th-century art. 127 illustrations. 192pp. 6½ × 9¼.
23808-3 Pa. $5.95

LADY ANNA, Anthony Trollope. Moving chronicle of Countess Lovel's bitter struggle to win for herself and daughter Anna their rightful rank and fortune—perhaps at cost of sanity itself. 384pp. 5⅜ × 8½.
24669-8 Pa. $8.95

EGYPTIAN MAGIC, E. A. Wallis Budge. Sums up all that is known about magic in Ancient Egypt: the role of magic in controlling the gods, powerful amulets that warded off evil spirits, scarabs of immortality, use of wax images, formulas and spells, the secret name, much more. 253pp. 5⅜ × 8½.
22681-6 Pa. $4.95

THE DANCE OF SIVA, Ananda Coomaraswamy. Preeminent authority unfolds the vast metaphysic of India: the revelation of her art, conception of the universe, social organization, etc. 27 reproductions of art masterpieces. 192pp. 5⅜ × 8½.
24817-8 Pa. $6.95

CHRISTMAS CUSTOMS AND TRADITIONS, Clement A. Miles. Origin, evolution, significance of religious, secular practices. Caroling, gifts, yule logs, much more. Full, scholarly yet fascinating; non-sectarian. 400pp. 5⅜ × 8½.
23354-5 Pa. $7.95

THE HUMAN FIGURE IN MOTION, Eadweard Muybridge. More than 4,500 stopped-action photos, in action series, showing undraped men, women, children jumping, lying down, throwing, sitting, wrestling, carrying, etc. 390pp. 7⅞ × 10⅝.
20204-6 Cloth. $24.95

THE MAN WHO WAS THURSDAY, Gilbert Keith Chesterton. Witty, fast-paced novel about a club of anarchists in turn-of-the-century London. Brilliant social, religious, philosophical speculations. 128pp. 5⅜ × 8½. 25121-7 Pa. $3.95

A CÉZANNE SKETCHBOOK: Figures, Portraits, Landscapes and Still Lifes, Paul Cézanne. Great artist experiments with tonal effects, light, mass, other qualities in over 100 drawings. A revealing view of developing master painter, precursor of Cubism. 102 black-and-white illustrations. 144pp. 8¾ × 6⅜. 24790-2 Pa. $6.95

AN ENCYCLOPEDIA OF BATTLES: Accounts of Over 1,560 Battles from 1479 B.C. to the Present, David Eggenberger. Presents essential details of every major battle in recorded history, from the first battle of Megiddo in 1479 B.C. to Grenada in 1984. List of Battle Maps. New Appendix covering the years 1967–1984. Index. 99 illustrations. 544pp. 6½ × 9¼. 24913-1 Pa. $14.95

AN ETYMOLOGICAL DICTIONARY OF MODERN ENGLISH, Ernest Weekley. Richest, fullest work, by foremost British lexicographer. Detailed word histories. Inexhaustible. Total of 856pp. 6½ × 9¼.
21873-2, 21874-0 Pa., Two-vol. set $19.90

WEBSTER'S AMERICAN MILITARY BIOGRAPHIES, edited by Robert McHenry. Over 1,000 figures who shaped 3 centuries of American military history. Detailed biographies of Nathan Hale, Douglas MacArthur, Mary Hallaren, others. Chronologies of engagements, more. Introduction. Addenda. 1,033 entries in alphabetical order. xi + 548pp. 6½ × 9¼. (Available in U.S. only)
24758-9 Pa. $13.95

LIFE IN ANCIENT EGYPT, Adolf Erman. Detailed older account, with much not in more recent books: domestic life, religion, magic, medicine, commerce, and whatever else needed for complete picture. Many illustrations. 597pp. 5⅜ × 8½.
22632-8 Pa. $9.95

HISTORIC COSTUME IN PICTURES, Braun & Schneider. Over 1,450 costumed figures shown, covering a wide variety of peoples: kings, emperors, nobles, priests, servants, soldiers, scholars, townsfolk, peasants, merchants, courtiers, cavaliers, and more. 256pp. 8⅜ × 11¼. 23150-X Pa. $9.95

THE NOTEBOOKS OF LEONARDO DA VINCI, edited by J. P. Richter. Extracts from manuscripts reveal great genius; on painting, sculpture, anatomy, sciences, geography, etc. Both Italian and English. 186 ms. pages reproduced, plus 500 additional drawings, including studies for *Last Supper, Sforza* monument, etc. 860pp. 7⅞ × 10¾. 22572-0, 22573-9 Pa., Two-vol. set $35.90

THE ART NOUVEAU STYLE BOOK OF ALPHONSE MUCHA: All 72 Plates from "Documents Decoratifs" in Original Color, Alphonse Mucha. Rare copyright-free design portfolio by high priest of Art Nouveau. Jewelry, wallpaper, stained glass, furniture, figure studies, plant and animal motifs, etc. Only complete one-volume edition. 80pp. 9⅜ × 12¼.   24044-4 Pa. $10.95

ANIMALS: 1,419 Copyright-Free Illustrations of Mammals, Birds, Fish, Insects, Etc., edited by Jim Harter. Clear wood engravings present, in extremely lifelike poses, over 1,000 species of animals. One of the most extensive pictorial sourcebooks of its kind. Captions. Index. 284pp. 9 × 12.   23766-4 Pa. $10.95

OBELISTS FLY HIGH, C. Daly King. Masterpiece of American detective fiction, long out of print, involves murder on a 1935 transcontinental flight—"a very thrilling story"—*NY Times*. Unabridged and unaltered republication of the edition published by William Collins Sons & Co. Ltd., London, 1935. 288pp. 5⅜ × 8½. (Available in U.S. only)   25036-9 Pa. $5.95

VICTORIAN AND EDWARDIAN FASHION: A Photographic Survey, Alison Gernsheim. First fashion history completely illustrated by contemporary photographs. Full text plus 235 photos, 1840-1914, in which many celebrities appear. 240pp. 6½ × 9¼.   24205-6 Pa. $8.95

THE ART OF THE FRENCH ILLUSTRATED BOOK, 1700-1914, Gordon N. Ray. Over 630 superb book illustrations by Fragonard, Delacroix, Daumier, Doré, Grandville, Manet, Mucha, Steinlen, Toulouse-Lautrec and many others. Preface. Introduction. 633 halftones. Indices of artists, authors & titles, binders and provenances. Appendices. Bibliography. 608pp. 8⅜ × 11¼.   25086-5 Pa. $24.95

THE WONDERFUL WIZARD OF OZ, L. Frank Baum. Facsimile in full color of America's finest children's classic. 143 illustrations by W. W. Denslow. 267pp. 5⅜ × 8½.   20691-2 Pa. $7.95

FOLLOWING THE EQUATOR: A Journey Around the World, Mark Twain. Great writer's 1897 account of circumnavigating the globe by steamship. Ironic humor, keen observations, vivid and fascinating descriptions of exotic places. 197 illustrations. 720pp. 5⅜ × 8½.   26113-1 Pa. $15.95

THE FRIENDLY STARS, Martha Evans Martin & Donald Howard Menzel. Classic text marshalls the stars together in an engaging, nontechnical survey, presenting them as sources of beauty in night sky. 23 illustrations. Foreword. 2 star charts. Index. 147pp. 5⅜ × 8½.   21099-5 Pa. $3.95

FADS AND FALLACIES IN THE NAME OF SCIENCE, Martin Gardner. Fair, witty appraisal of cranks, quacks, and quackeries of science and pseudoscience: hollow earth, Velikovsky, orgone energy, Dianetics, flying saucers, Bridey Murphy, food and medical fads, etc. Revised, expanded In the Name of Science. "A very able and even-tempered presentation."—*The New Yorker*. 363pp. 5⅜ × 8.
                                                               20394-8 Pa. $6.95

ANCIENT EGYPT: Its Culture and History, J. E. Manchip White. From predynastics through Ptolemies: society, history, political structure, religion, daily life, literature, cultural heritage. 48 plates. 217pp. 5⅜ × 8½.   22548-8 Pa. $5.95

SIR HARRY HOTSPUR OF HUMBLETHWAITE, Anthony Trollope. Incisive, unconventional psychological study of a conflict between a wealthy baronet, his idealistic daughter, and their scapegrace cousin. The 1870 novel in its first inexpensive edition in years. 250pp. 5⅜ × 8½. 24953-0 Pa. $6.95

LASERS AND HOLOGRAPHY, Winston E. Kock. Sound introduction to burgeoning field, expanded (1981) for second edition. Wave patterns, coherence, lasers, diffraction, zone plates, properties of holograms, recent advances. 84 illustrations. 160pp. 5⅜ × 8¼. (Except in United Kingdom) 24041-X Pa. $4.95

INTRODUCTION TO ARTIFICIAL INTELLIGENCE: Second, Enlarged Edition, Philip C. Jackson, Jr. Comprehensive survey of artificial intelligence—the study of how machines (computers) can be made to act intelligently. Includes introductory and advanced material. Extensive notes updating the main text. 132 black-and-white illustrations. 512pp. 5⅜ × 8½. 24864-X Pa. $10.95

HISTORY OF INDIAN AND INDONESIAN ART, Ananda K. Coomaraswamy. Over 400 illustrations illuminate classic study of Indian art from earliest Harappa finds to early 20th century. Provides philosophical, religious and social insights. 304pp. 6⅜ × 9⅜. 25005-9 Pa. $11.95

THE GOLEM, Gustav Meyrink. Most famous supernatural novel in modern European literature, set in Ghetto of Old Prague around 1890. Compelling story of mystical experiences, strange transformations, profound terror. 13 black-and-white illustrations. 224pp. 5⅜ × 8½. 25025-3 Pa. $7.95

PICTORIAL ENCYCLOPEDIA OF HISTORIC ARCHITECTURAL PLANS, DETAILS AND ELEMENTS: With 1,880 Line Drawings of Arches, Domes, Doorways, Facades, Gables, Windows, etc., John Theodore Haneman. Sourcebook of inspiration for architects, designers, others. Bibliography. Captions. 141pp. 9 × 12. 24605-1 Pa. $8.95

BENCHLEY LOST AND FOUND, Robert Benchley. Finest humor from early 30s, about pet peeves, child psychologists, post office and others. Mostly unavailable elsewhere. 73 illustrations by Peter Arno and others. 183pp. 5⅜ × 8½. 22410-4 Pa. $4.95

ERTÉ GRAPHICS, Erté. Collection of striking color graphics: *Seasons, Alphabet, Numerals, Aces* and *Precious Stones.* 50 plates, including 4 on covers. 48pp. 9⅜ × 12¼. 23580-7 Pa. $7.95

THE JOURNAL OF HENRY D. THOREAU, edited by Bradford Torrey, F. H. Allen. Complete reprinting of 14 volumes, 1837–61, over two million words; the sourcebooks for *Walden,* etc. Definitive. All original sketches, plus 75 photographs. 1,804pp. 8½ × 12¼. 20312-3, 20313-1 Cloth., Two-vol. set $130.00

CASTLES: Their Construction and History, Sidney Toy. Traces castle development from ancient roots. Nearly 200 photographs and drawings illustrate moats, keeps, baileys, many other features. Caernarvon, Dover Castles, Hadrian's Wall, Tower of London, dozens more. 256pp. 5⅜ × 8¼. 24898-4 Pa. $7.95

AMERICAN CLIPPER SHIPS: 1833–1858, Octavius T. Howe & Frederick C. Matthews. Fully-illustrated, encyclopedic review of 352 clipper ships from the period of America's greatest maritime supremacy. Introduction. 109 halftones. 5 black-and-white line illustrations. Index. Total of 928pp. 5⅜ × 8½.
25115-2, 25116-0 Pa., Two-vol. set $21.90

TOWARDS A NEW ARCHITECTURE, Le Corbusier. Pioneering manifesto by great architect, near legendary founder of "International School." Technical and aesthetic theories, views on industry, economics, relation of form to function, "mass-production spirit," much more. Profusely illustrated. Unabridged translation of 13th French edition. Introduction by Frederick Etchells. 320pp. 6⅛ × 9¼. (Available in U.S. only)
25023-7 Pa. $8.95

THE BOOK OF KELLS, edited by Blanche Cirker. Inexpensive collection of 32 full-color, full-page plates from the greatest illuminated manuscript of the Middle Ages, painstakingly reproduced from rare facsimile edition. Publisher's Note. Captions. 32pp. 9⅜ × 12¼. (Available in U.S. only)
24345-1 Pa. $5.95

BEST SCIENCE FICTION STORIES OF H. G. WELLS, H. G. Wells. Full novel The Invisible Man, plus 17 short stories: "The Crystal Egg," "Aepyornis Island," "The Strange Orchid," etc. 303pp. 5⅜ × 8½. (Available in U.S. only)
21531-8 Pa. $6.95

AMERICAN SAILING SHIPS: Their Plans and History, Charles G. Davis. Photos, construction details of schooners, frigates, clippers, other sailcraft of 18th to early 20th centuries—plus entertaining discourse on design, rigging, nautical lore, much more. 137 black-and-white illustrations. 240pp. 6⅛ × 9¼.
24658-2 Pa. $6.95

ENTERTAINING MATHEMATICAL PUZZLES, Martin Gardner. Selection of author's favorite conundrums involving arithmetic, money, speed, etc., with lively commentary. Complete solutions. 112pp. 5⅜ × 8½.
25211-6 Pa. $3.95

THE WILL TO BELIEVE, HUMAN IMMORTALITY, William James. Two books bound together. Effect of irrational on logical, and arguments for human immortality. 402pp. 5⅜ × 8½.
20291-7 Pa. $8.95

THE HAUNTED MONASTERY and THE CHINESE MAZE MURDERS, Robert Van Gulik. 2 full novels by Van Gulik continue adventures of Judge Dee and his companions. An evil Taoist monastery, seemingly supernatural events; overgrown topiary maze that hides strange crimes. Set in 7th-century China. 27 illustrations. 328pp. 5⅜ × 8½.
23502-5 Pa. $6.95

CELEBRATED CASES OF JUDGE DEE (DEE GOONG AN), translated by Robert Van Gulik. Authentic 18th-century Chinese detective novel; Dee and associates solve three interlocked cases. Led to Van Gulik's own stories with same characters. Extensive introduction. 9 illustrations. 237pp. 5⅜ × 8½.
23337-5 Pa. $5.95

Prices subject to change without notice.

Available at your book dealer or write for free catalog to Dept. GI, Dover Publications, Inc., 31 East 2nd St., Mineola, N.Y. 11501. Dover publishes more than 400 books each year on science, elementary and advanced mathematics, biology, music, art, literary history, social sciences and other areas.